CHAINS OF LOVE

EMILY WEST

# Chains of Love

SLAVE COUPLES IN ANTEBELLUM

SOUTH CAROLINA

UNIVERSITY OF ILLINOIS PRESS

URBANA AND CHICAGO

Library of Congress Cataloging-in-Publication Data
West, Emily, 1971–
Chains of love : slave couples in antebellum South Carolina /
Emily West.
p.  cm.
Includes bibliographical references and index.
ISBN 0-252-02903-8 (cloth : alk. paper)
 1. Slaves—South Carolina—Social conditions—19th century.
2. Slaves—South Carolina—Family relationships—History—19th
century. 3. Couples—South Carolina—History—19th century.
4. Man-woman relationships—South Carolina—History—19th century.
5. Slaves—South Carolina—Biography. 6. Slavery—South
Carolina—History—19th century. 7. Plantation life—South
Carolina—History—19th century. 8. South Carolina—Race
relations. 9. South Carolina—History—1775–1865. I. Title.
E445.S7W47    2004
306.8′86′2509757—dc22    2003013736

*For Jamie*

# Contents

# *Acknowledgments*

---

Many people have provided me with help of one kind or another during this project, which began as a Ph.D. thesis at the University of Liverpool. First and foremost, I should like to express my gratitude to my dissertation supervisor, Mike Tadman. An excellent advisor and an historian of the utmost integrity, I only hope that he is pleased with my finished product. I should also like to thank other colleagues at the Universities of Liverpool, Newcastle, and Reading for their advice and encouragement, as well as the provision of cups of coffee when needed. Here I wish to single out Di Ascott, Sharon Messenger, and all the other "mad women of the attic," Brian Ward, George Lewis, Jon Bell, Anne Curry, Stuart Kidd, Anne Lawrence, David Laven, and Helen Parish. The friends and acquaintances I have met through British American Nineteenth-Century Historians (BrANCH), in particular Liese Perrin, have provided many insights on slave relationships, and I have always found it much easier to work on this project following the annual October conference.

The staff at the various libraries and archives I utilized during this project have been extremely helpful, especially in the United States, where I was made to feel particularly welcome by Tibby Steedly of the Institute of Southern Studies at the University of South Carolina and Brian Cuthrell of the South Caroliniana library. I shall also never forget the hospitality provided by Joe Sox, Jim Siti, and Susan Wolfe. Three awarding bodies made this project financially viable for me—the Economic and Social Research Council granted me a postgraduate award, which funded the first three years of my Ph.D. research; the British Academy awarded me a Small Research Grant, which enabled me to undertake my research into biracial Baptist churches; and last but by no means least, the Arts and Humanities Research Board provided me with a two-term sabbatical to complete the book, for which I am extremely grateful. Joan Catapano of the University of Illinois Press has proved helpful and patient, and I am also grateful to the two anonymous readers who commented on the first draft of this manuscript.

Finally, I have been fortunate to have a loving and supportive family who have offered help and encouragement at every step of the way. I could not have completed this book without the financial support of my paternal grandparents, Margaret and the late Aneurin West. My mother and father have offered much more than a polite interest in my work, and I am especially grateful to them for encouraging my initial interest in American history. My husband, Jamie, to whom this book is dedicated, has proven more than a diligent proofreader. I do not believe this book would have reached publication without his help, and for this I cannot possibly thank him enough. Lastly, my son, Conor, was kind enough to take to nursery like a duck to water, thus providing me with the hours I needed to write the final manuscript. I look forward to the day when he is old enough to read it.

---

Some of the arguments espoused in this book originally appeared in article form. See "Surviving Separation: Cross-Plantation Marriages and the Slave Trade in Antebellum South Carolina," *Journal of Family History* 24:2 (1999): 212–31 (© 1999 by Sage Publications; used by permission of Sage Publications; "The Debate on the Strength of Slave Families: South Carolina and the Importance of Cross-Plantation Marriages," *Journal of American Studies* 33:2 (1999): 221–41 (© 1999 by Cambridge University Press; used by permission of Cambridge University Press); and "Masters and Marriages, Profits and Paternalism: Slave Owners' Perspectives on Cross-Plantation Unions in Antebellum South Carolina," *Slavery and Abolition* 21:1 (2000): 56–72 (© 2000 by Frank Cass & Co.; used by permission of Frank Cass & Co.).

CHAINS OF LOVE

# Introduction

This book explores intimate areas of the slave experience—relationships between men and women, love and affection between spouses, the abuse of female slaves by whites, the consequences of forced separations, and the overall sense of family among communities held in bondage. These are difficult areas to explore, partly because the typicality of intimate sentiments is always hard to establish. Historical evidence also poses a problem: southern white sources tend to rationalize white exploitation of blacks, but those left by slaves are few, and their reliability has often been challenged. This work relies heavily on the careful use of certain exceptionally rich slave testimonies, complemented by a critical analysis of white documents and perspectives. It combines some quantitative analysis of broad patterns that have emerged in the evidence from slave sources with a more textual, qualitative approach, thus allowing the overall themes of spousal and gender cooperation, flexible family networks, and resilience and resistance to be established.

The significance of slave bonding *across* gender lines is highlighted here. While those of the same sex did maintain close ties—especially, for example, when a slave had an "abroad" spouse and spent the greater part of the working week on their own, or when a partner had been sold away—relationships between married men and women were generally more important to slaves than were same-gender networks. Also highlighted is resistance to the oppression of bondage. This was achieved primarily through the existence of "social space" between the lives of slaves and owners. Moreover, the affection between enslaved men and women facilitated the creation and maintenance of this distance.[1] Indeed, bonding between spouses provided slaves with their primary means of surviving and ultimately resisting the brutal institution under which they lived.

American slavery has attracted immense scholarly interest, and this work draws upon four major historiographical strands. The first revolves around the concept of gender, which has traditionally been neglected as a conceptual tool for historical analysis. Previously, female slaves have either been ignored or characterized as "Jezebels" and "Mammies"—stereotypes recently dismantled by Deborah G. White and Elizabeth Fox-Genovese.[2] A second and closely related historiographical trend has seen a shift toward examining the perspectives of slaves rather than their masters. Stanley L. Engerman has noted how attention has shifted to the study of the enslaved "and to their actions and reactions within the slave system. This is referred to as regarding the 'slave as actor.'"[3] The move toward the writing of "history from below" thus enabled the development of "women's history from below" and, in turn, a similar approach to black women's history. As Anne Firor Scott noted in 1983: "The recent developments in women's history have been paralleled by a new wave of slavery studies. As the history of slavery comes to be written with more attention to the slave's point of view we might expect women to emerge as historical actors in their own right."[4]

This second trend came to the fore in the 1970s, when a number of texts focusing upon the cultural life of slave communities were published.[5] These works also argued that cultural autonomy provided slaves with the opportunity to distance themselves psychologically from their owners. This led to the third major historiographical strand, encompassing what Engerman has referred to as "the positive accomplishments of slaves under slavery." Historians investigating the life and culture of those held in bondage have focused upon their desires and demands and emphasized the importance of their families, religion, community life, and economic behavior.[6] Some writers and historians have begun to react against this, however. Peter Kolchin, for one, believes that the emphasis on resiliency and autonomy has been overstated and will be modified on the basis of future evidence.[7]

Fourthly, scholars have witnessed the emergence of smaller, more detailed case studies of American slavery. Charles Joyner has noted how "historians describe *the* slave community without having probed in depth any *particular* slave community."[8] Concentrating on one particular area can allow historians to add depth and texture to their work, primarily through the utilization of numerous source materials.[9] This work therefore fits into and extends these trends in the historiography of American slavery. A small-scale study of life under bondage in antebellum South Carolina, it focuses on the lives of those enslaved rather than upon the institution of slavery, though exploring the former undoubtedly reveals much about the latter. It also emphasizes the positive accomplishments of slaves while living under an oppressive regime. Gender has been utilized as a conceptual tool in that the interaction, similarities, and differences in the lives of men and women are investigated. Moreover, it is argued that the previous emphasis upon the bonding between enslaved females has led historians to neglect the primary importance of spousal support as a means of facing oppression.[10] This study also employs a broad definition of slave resistance—incorporating many actions that did not directly threaten the system of slavery.[11] This is especially relevant when investigating the lives of slave women, since they were more likely than men to engage in indirect resistance.[12]

Therefore, although Kolchin has argued that the case for autonomy has been overstated, he fails to recognize that emphasizing resilience and the desire for independence does not necessarily mean that exploitation by owners (for example, through sale, separation, or sexual abuse) was not significant.[13] Rather, the fact that slaves *strove* for independence under adversity is of immense importance, since it highlights the desire for freedom *within the context* of the restraints imposed by slaveholders. The relationships between spouses facilitated the desire for and the development of a social space between the lives of slaves and owners and a means of resistance against oppression.

The nature of the relationships *between* married slaves has been somewhat neglected. Hence, this study stresses the fundamentally important role of meeting a member of the opposite sex and of marrying. Bonding occurred between enslaved spouses despite the influence of owners and the existence of considerable gender differences in the lives of men and women. These were especially pronounced in the realm of work, where males and females (in laboring for their masters and for their families) were often employed at gender-specific tasks. The work lives of slave men and women were therefore not characterized by equality but by different, complementary roles.[14]

Owners caused considerable disruption to family life by sexually harassing or abusing slave women and by forcibly separating families through sale, gift, or the division of estates. Slaves, however, tried to withstand these exploitations by drawing on the strength of their spousal relationships and the system of cross-plantation family networks. Such mechanisms of support meant that the impact of local forced separations might not have been severe, and it was long-distance rather than local sales that members of slave communities feared. Considering the oppression of bondage and the consequent strains that were imposed upon spouses, slaves' desire to live out shared experiences through supportive roles is all the more remarkable. Through an investigation into the lives of enslaved males and females and by focusing on their perspectives, the essentially loving and supportive nature of these vital relationships becomes apparent. Despite gender differences in their lives, slave men and women forged relationships characterized by strength and solidarity that enabled them to find psychological distance from their owners.

## Methodology

Various primary source materials are utilized quantitatively and qualitatively to explore the slave's perspective in antebellum South Carolina. These techniques illuminate the nature of slave families and communities and the roles of men and women within them. Two major types of slave source materials are used: the South Carolina Works Progress Administration (WPA hereafter) slave narratives, compiled by George P. Rawick, who collated the transcriptions of 2,358 interviews that WPA workers had conducted with ex-slaves in the American South in the 1930s. From a total of 344, 334 of the interviews conducted in South Carolina are included here.[15] In addition, eleven volume-length slave autobiographies have been consulted, adding extra dimensions to the analysis of slavery obtained by using the WPA testimony. A variety of manuscript source materials are also examined, facilitating an assessment of the nature of the relationships between slaves and their owners. However, the primary emphasis will be on male and female slaves and their relationships with each other rather than white perceptions of slaves.

Antebellum South Carolina is focused upon for various reasons. Firstly, particularly rich primary source collections exist for the state, allowing for the consultation of a wide variety of materials.[16] Secondly, a thorough and systematic investigation into available primary evidence can be undertaken by examining a single state. Thirdly, South Carolina at this time was home to two major crops associated with slave labor—rice and cotton. This work will therefore reveal some of the similarities and differences in the lives of slaves laboring under these respective regimes.[17] Fourthly, with 45.8 percent of white families owning slaves, South Carolina had the highest percentage of slaveholders in the United States. It also had a high concentration of slaves, some of the South's largest plantations, and the low-country area, where rice and sea-island cotton dominated, was home to some of the South's largest concentrations of blacks.[18] In 1850, slaves comprised 57.7 percent of the total population of South Carolina, but in the Georgetown District of the low country they constituted between 85 and 89 percent of the population from 1810 to 1860.[19] Spatial variation in the experience of slaves is also significant, since life for those enslaved on large, low-country rice plantations would have been quite different from life on small, up-country slaveholdings. However, it has been found that regardless of size or location of unit, the attitudes and aspirations of slaves remained broadly the same. Slaves strove to meet and to marry someone of their own choosing, despite the pressures of the regime.

## THE WPA NARRATIVES

The interviews conducted with ex-slaves are of vital importance in moving beyond the stereotypical conceptions of those held in bondage that are found in white manuscript materials. WPA evidence allows for an investigation of bondage from the perspective of the enslaved and, significantly, offers more representative insights into the lives of ordinary "rank-and-file" slaves. The narratives are used quantitatively to assess trends relating to the lives of the enslaved and to investigate gender differences, while, in a qualitative sense, they permit the documentation of significant or memorable experiences. It is from these often vivid and graphic recollections that exploitation and slaves' resilience in the face of oppression can be understood. C. Vann Woodward summed up well some of the problems associated with the use of WPA testimony when he wrote: "Confusing and contradictory as they [the WPA narratives] are, they represent the voices of the normally voiceless, the inarticulate masses whose silence historians are forever lamenting."[20] It also remains true that WPA evidence is of particular value when investigating the lives of rank-and-file female slaves, for whom testimony is scarce.[21]

Attempting to quantify WPA testimony can be problematic because it is immensely difficult to "measure" the comments of the informants.[22] However, in this work, a small database that included evidence from 334 of the South Carolina respondents was constructed, of whom 190 were male and 144 were female. Furthermore, all who testified about their residence lived in South Carolina for the duration of their enslavement, with the exception of eleven individuals.[23] Information that the ex-slaves related on their own lives, those of their parents, and on their communities at large was then entered into the database.[24] Since their average age was less than ten years in 1865, the majority held only childhood memories of bondage. Therefore, their testimony on their parents was extremely important to this study.[25] Slave children had a lot to say about the lives of their mothers and fathers, especially with regard to issues such as cross-plantation marriages, work patterns, and sales and separations.

Teenage slaves also had much to say about courtship rituals. For more sensitive areas, including affection and antagonisms between spouses and sexual abuse, other source materials have proven more valuable, although again, the WPA evidence has yielded a surprising amount of information.

A systematic analysis of the WPA narratives thus constitutes a vital part of this work, providing a quantitative context from which other primary source materials can be examined. Furthermore, by cross-referencing the different comments of individual respondents, a detailed picture of the trends in the lives of individual slaves can be established.[26] Notwithstanding the clearly informative nature of quantitative data, such evidence is more productive when used in conjunction with other, more textual information. A large amount of quantitative information at the aggregate level does not fully capture the feelings expressed by the WPA informants about life under slavery. The claim made by Robert W. Fogel and Stanley L. Engerman that slaves in the American South received, on average, "0.7 whippings per year" has been widely used in highlighting the problems associated with quantification, as it fails to relate anything about the severity of whippings and offers no insights into the slaves' fear of the lash.[27] Combining quantitative data with information gleaned from a textual reading of the narratives and other source materials thus allows for a richer, fuller picture of slave life.

Many criticisms have been directed at the use of the WPA testimony, including the cautionary claim that the ex-slaves might have been reserved when speaking to white interviewers.[28] Another argument is that because over two-thirds of respondents were more than eighty years old when they were interviewed, they might have had dimmed memories or only childhood recollections of bondage. Because the interviews were conducted during the Depression of the 1930s—a period of racial segregation—some ex-slaves, it has been argued, might have looked back favorably on the slavery period in comparison with the harshness of their current lives. Some also hoped that their interviewers would help them to get old-age pensions and therefore desired to please. The fact that some of the informants knew their white interviewers, which might have encouraged reticence, is a further claim against the reliability of WPA evidence, especially since some of the interviewers were descendants of the ex-slaves' owners.[29] A final methodological problem with the WPA narratives is their pronounced bias toward house servants or skilled slaves, with the majority of those who described their own work patterns or those of their parents stating that they performed such labor. This issue is considered more fully in chapter 3, where it was found that despite an overrepresentation of house servants within the WPA testimony and the fact that such ex-slaves may have been more likely to relate fond anecdotes of their white owners, significant mental and emotional distance between masters and slaves was the norm.[30]

It is possible to overcome some of the methodological problems associated with WPA testimony through careful use of the evidence. Take, for example, the claim that the respondents might have been reticent when talking to white interviewers (whether because of their race, because they had known them as slaves, or because they contrasted the Depression of the 1930s with their childhood experiences of bondage). Evidence contradicts the notion that the ex-slaves were reluctant to discuss certain issues with their interviewers, and they did not merely say what they thought their interviewers wanted to hear. If they were reluctant to discuss anything, it was sensitive issues such as sexual abuse or other personal and sexual matters, especially when men interviewed women and a "fear factor" may have been apparent.[31] South Carolina WPA testimony, however, contains information on a range of sensitive issues, including those of a sexual nature. This evidence, though not necessarily totally candid, reveals much about slave experiences that would otherwise be almost completely hidden from view.

In order to construct data on critical, sexual issues, where evidence has proven patchy, a wide sample of WPA narratives, encompassing all of the southern states, was occasionally used. In chapters 2 and 4, when investigating sexual abuse that was black on black or inflicted upon female slaves by white men, the entire collection of WPA narratives (including some supplementary volumes) was examined.[32] Including evidence from outside South Carolina, such as the published autobiographies of women, has sometimes proven necessary to build a more comprehensive picture of slaves' lives.[33] Adopting a broader context can add detail and texture without distracting from the focus upon slavery in South Carolina.

With regard to the claim that because the respondents were very old they had dimmed memories of bondage, it is true that since most of them were youngsters during slavery, they remembered it from a child's perspective.[34] In the South Carolina database the average age of the informants in 1865 (when slavery was abolished) was only ten years. Thus the majority were eighty-two years old when interviewed. Certainly their memories may have dimmed with age, but they did remember a great deal about life under the peculiar institution.[35] Moreover, faded memories notwithstanding, the narratives constitute such a unique source and contain such a rich amount of evidence that, even with imperfect recall, they hold immense historical value. It is also true that for this study, a deep significance is attached to the comments made on the lives of the respondents' parents. For example, while few informants entered wedlock during slavery, many made interesting and revealing observations on their parents' marriages. Similarly, many who were too young to work during bondage mentioned the types of labor performed by their mothers and fathers. Such references make it possible to construct a detailed picture of the lives of adult slaves.

## FULL-LENGTH SLAVE AUTOBIOGRAPHIES

Using various types of source materials is likely to be most beneficial in any study of slave experiences, since no one type of evidence can adequately explain what their lives were like. A sample of full-length slave autobiographies is therefore used here in conjunction with the WPA testimony. The use of autobiographical narratives adds depth to the image of bondage obtained from the WPA evidence alone. Various texts written by enslaved men have substantial South Carolina content, several of which have been used here.[36] However, due to the paucity of female slave autobiographies from the state, a selection of full-length narratives written by enslaved women from elsewhere in the South are used here to give voice to otherwise voiceless women.[37] While it is true that these women were not South Carolinian slaves, their testimony has proven vital in understanding certain aspects of female slavery, especially on issues such as sexual abuse. In particular, Harriet Jacobs, who wrote under the pseudonym Linda Brent, reveals in her autobiography much about the ways in which sexual exploitation impinged upon entire families.[38]

While these autobiographies undoubtedly contain a great deal more personal detail than can be found in the WPA testimony, their representativeness has been questioned precisely because of their uniqueness. They tend to display even more of a bias toward house, skilled, or gifted slaves than do the WPA narratives.[39] However, although it is true that published autobiographies were mostly written by individuals whose circumstances might not have been typical, the authors tended to see themselves as writing for and about the sentiments of all slaves. In particular, the autobiography of Charles Ball contains much information upon the everyday routines of rank-and-file field workers, despite the fact that Ball himself only labored in the cotton fields for a short time. These volumes also contain many references to the lives of those whose experiences may have been more "typical" than those of the narrators. Another common criticism of published autobiographies has revolved around the question of their authenticity. Illiteracy often forced slaves or ex-slaves to rely upon amanuenses, many of whom came from the ranks of the abolitionist movement.

The extent to which their writings have been "doctored" by persons other than the slave has caused concern among some scholars.[40] Again, though, it is possible to overcome this methodological problem, since most of the autobiographies depict plantation activities and other daily routines that "are striking in the consistency of themes that appear among individuals who lived on widely separated plantations, in different states, and in different decades."[41]

The style in which published autobiographies were written has also led some to question their authenticity. It had been commonly assumed that Lydia Maria Child, Harriet Jacobs's editor, had written *Incidents*, "for how could a slave woman have written in the flowery style of middle-class domestic fiction?"[42] Jacobs's surviving correspondence, collated by Jean Fagan Yellin, however, has proven the critics wrong.[43] Indeed, the style of her prose may have been self-motivated, in that she wanted to reach a large, white, northern, middle-class, and potentially abolitionist audience. Elizabeth Fox-Genovese suggests that by highlighting the violation of her virtue in the style of a piece of domestic fiction, Jacobs "stood a much better chance of appealing to northern sensibilities than a pronunciamento for woman's individual rights, if only because it reaffirmed woman's essentially domestic nature."[44] Male autobiographers also adopted this tactic: "Frederick Douglass . . . assumed that the most effective way to reach his readers was to remind them that he was a man like themselves."[45]

MANUSCRIPT SOURCE MATERIALS

Manuscript source materials are used here in conjunction with slave sources to gain a fuller picture of life under oppression. While slave evidence is vital in any assessment of bondage as witnessed by its victims, manuscript materials are necessary to provide a window for viewing slavery through the eyes of owners. Furthermore, comparing these two vastly different perspectives shows how the opposing worldviews of slaves and owners led to the emergence of psychological distance between them. The principal set of manuscript materials used here includes the letters, diaries, and plantation journals of antebellum South Carolina men; the letters, diaries, and plantation journals of antebellum South Carolina mistresses and female owners; a small number of antebellum petitions to the South Carolina State Assembly relating to issues of sexual contact between blacks and whites; and a collection of South Carolina biracial Baptist church records that, through their disciplinary committees, provide a unique insight into the relationships of slaves and the issues that caused spousal antagonisms.

The testimony of slaveholders is of immense value in explaining their attitudes toward slaves and the ideological framework within which the institution of bondage operated. It does, however, pose a set of methodological problems. While offering unique insights into the minds of individuals, especially in the case of personal diaries, some significant evidence would have been destroyed shortly after it had been written or by descendants, especially that containing information of an intimate nature. Historians are left only with surviving records. However, through careful reading of a selection of owners' materials, some extremely valuable information relating to masters and slaves emerges. Most slaveholders defined a minority of their slaves as "key slaves" and singled them out for benevolent treatment.[46] It is these "special" individuals who crop up most frequently in owners' letters and diaries, offering insights into how they rationalized bondage. Given that the majority of references to slaves tend to focus on the putative "close relationship" between master and slave, using black sources in conjunction with white records allows for the construction of a fuller, rounder picture of life under the peculiar institution, one that includes the perspectives of rank-and-file "non-key" individuals who were ignored in their owners' testimony. In reality, ties of affection between the enslaved and their masters existed only for a minority, and the notion that such attachments were enjoyed by all was a product of owners' inaccurate worldview.

## Chapter Outlines

Chapters 1 and 2 explore relationships between slave couples and slave family life. Chapter 1 examines courtship and marriage rituals, their temporal evolution, and how they were influenced by African and white American cultural patterns. Significantly, these are hitherto underexplored areas of slave life. Courtship also reveals some of the gender differences that operated within enslaved communities, exemplified by the fact that, as with white society at this time, males were expected to take the lead in affairs of the heart. Courtship and marriage will also be examined from the profoundly different perspectives of the enslaved and their masters. While slaveholders' sources reveal something of whites' rationalization and selective vision of bondage, a combination of black and white testimony points to the existence of antithetical worldviews among slaves and owners. Despite a prevailing climate whereby slaveholders frequently belittled the concept of slave romantic love, and despite their marriages not being recognized by American law, the relationships between most enslaved spouses were characterized by great affection. This allowed them to develop a degree of social space between their lives and those of their masters, striving to live according to their own cultural norms.

Chapter 2, which considers family life and the residential arrangements of spouses, furthers the claim that a strong sense of family was the norm among the enslaved. Emphasized here is the importance and the extent of cross-plantation marriages (where husband and wife lived on different holdings). The use of slave source materials, especially the WPA testimony, allows the numerical importance of these marriages to be estimated, and it is argued that those concerned usually vigorously supported cross-plantation (or abroad) unions, as they did same-residence partnerships. This points to the prevailing resilience of spousal relationships. While some lived in abroad marriages because of practical necessity (for example, because they lived on small slaveholdings with no suitable partners), the very existence of cross-plantation unions among slaves who lived on larger holdings suggests a widespread desire for autonomy from owners in these affairs. Abroad marriages also highlight gender differences in the lives of enslaved men and women, exemplified by the fact that it was mostly men who visited spouses. Male slaves frequently risked the wrath of their owners and the patrollers, suggesting the existence of strong relationships and a male identification with the role of initiator, protector, and provider. This chapter also investigates the reasons for antagonisms between men and women and the sexual and physical abuse of slave women at the hands of black men. It is argued that instances of black-on-black abuse within slave communities were rare, with slave testimony emphasizing positive attachments and a great deal of affection between spouses.

Chapter 3 focuses more on the interaction between slaves and owners in the realm of labor. Gender distinctions in the tasks completed for masters and for families are examined, and the implications of these differences for relationships between enslaved men and women are assessed. Owners tended to separate males and females in the workplace, thus restricting opportunities for courtship in this realm. This meant such opportunities within the cultural life of slave communities, as detailed in chapter 1, were extremely valuable. With regard to work performed for their own families, slave women carried the heaviest load in bearing and rearing children in addition to carrying out tasks for owners and their families. This disproportionate allocation of familial chores did not, however, preclude the existence of a profound sense of solidarity between enslaved partners: both men and women labored hard to provide for their own and to create a supportive atmosphere for themselves and for their children.

This chapter also examines the social structure of slave communities and the ways in which work completed for owners and families related to social standing. The ways in which owners assigned status reveals much about their rationalizations of slavery. In contrast, slaves regarded highly those who performed important roles within their communities and tended to be relatively egalitarian in their treatment of women when it came to ascribing status: like men, they could gain considerable prestige with age and experience. However, the burden of laboring for owners and their families in addition to childbearing and rearing affected their work and therefore negatively influenced women's status.

The exploitation inflicted on slaves by their owners is examined in chapters 4 and 5. Sexual abuse and enforced separations are considered here, both of which had the potential to affect spousal relationships severely. While exploitation per se was a universal characteristic of slavery, the precise nature of that inflicted upon slaves was often gender-specific, affecting males and females in different ways. Chapter 4 explores issues of sexual contact and abuse between black men and white women and between white men and slave women. While sexual liaisons of the former type appear to be exceptional, those of the latter were much more widespread. Indeed, the sexual harassment and abuse of female slaves by white men constituted one of the major differences in the lives of enslaved men and women. It was owners rather than overseers who were the main abusers of female slaves, thus necessitating an exploration of its implications upon owners' wives and their relationships with their slave women. Finally, the question of whether sexual contact was a significant route to freedom for enslaved females is addressed here; it is argued that they strove to survive their oppression through gaining the love and support of a spouse rather than by seeking intimate contact with masters.

Chapter 5 examines the forced separations of slaves, including long-distance and local sales, the transfer of family members as gifts, and the (nonsale) divisions of slaveholdings between the heirs of an estate. A crucial finding here is that because of the system of abroad marriages and family networks, local sales and separations did not inevitably lead to severe family disruption, especially in comparison with the impact of long-distance (interstate) sales. Through cross-plantation family ties, slaves managed to resist many of the potential threats to family and to marriage viability. This chapter also analyzes the impact of gender upon the patterns of sales. Finally, at a broader level, the impact of separation would have again contributed to the psychological distance between the lives of slaveholders and slaves. All those held in bondage had to live under the threat, if not the reality, of being torn apart from their loved ones, making the strength and resilience of the relationships between spouses all the more impressive.

Overall, this study highlights the intrinsic fight for autonomy within enslaved communities and the distance between the lives of slaves and owners that provided the former with an opportunity to resist oppression. The chains of love that bound enslaved couples—strong and meaningful relationships that were sought by the majority—provided a vital opportunity to foster cultural autonomy and mutual support in the face of adversity. Despite the existence of significant gender differences in their lives, male and female slaves would go to great lengths in their desire to love, support, and protect their spouses, their families, and their communities.

## Notes

1. On the concept of social space between the lives of slaves and slave owners, see Hudson, "'All That Cash.'" On resistance, see Engerman, "Concluding Reflections"; and Kolchin, *American Slavery*, 137.

2. See White, *Ar'n't I a Woman?* chap. 1; and Fox-Genovese, *Within the Plantation Household*, 291–92, for a fuller discussion of the stereotypes of female slaves.

3. Engerman, "Concluding Reflections," 235.

4. Scott, "Historians Construct the Southern Woman," 104–5.

5. See, for example, Gutman, *Black Family in Slavery and Freedom*; Blassingame, *Slave Community*; and Levine, *Black Culture and Black Consciousness*.

6. Engerman, "Concluding Reflections," 235.

7. Kolchin, *American Slavery*, 137–38. William Dusinberre has also warned against romanticizing views that claim slavery left slaves spiritually unscathed in *Them Dark Days*, 430. See also the thoughts of the sociologist Orlando Patterson in *Rituals of Blood*, 25–44. For more on the historiography of American slavery, see Parish, *Slavery*; and Smith, *Debating Slavery*.

8. See Joyner, *Down by the Riverside*, xvi.

9. Orville Vernon Burton, for example, in his study of family and community in Edgefield District and County, South Carolina, refers to the concept of uncovering the "total history" of the area; see *In My Father's House*. Similarly, Charles Joyner attempted to reconstruct the life of one slave community in All Saints Parish, Georgetown District, in the low country; see *Down by the Riverside*. William Dusinberre has recently conducted an investigation into slavery in the rice swamps of the South Carolina and Georgia low country in *Them Dark Days*. Brenda E. Stevenson's *Life in Black and White* focuses on the residents of Loudoun County, Virginia. At the South Carolina level, two works that explore gender issues are Leslie A. Schwalm, *A Hard Fight for We*, and Marli F. Weiner, *Mistresses and Slaves*. Finally, Walter Edgar has recently published the first comprehensive history of South Carolina for nearly fifty years; see *South Carolina*.

10. The work of Deborah G. White, for example, has shown that female networks of support were very important to slave women. I do not dispute this claim, but I believe that the neglect of spousal relationships by historians has meant that the love and support that united most enslaved husbands and wives has been relatively ignored.

11. Stanley L. Engerman has also noted that many historians have widened the defi-

nition of slave resistance to include actions that did not directly threaten the system of slavery. See "Concluding Reflections," 239.

12. David Barry Gaspar and Darlene Clark Hine have shown how slave women were less likely to engage in direct resistance because of their childbearing and rearing responsibilities. See the preface to Gaspar and Hine, eds., *More Than Chattel*, ix–x. See also Wood, "Some Aspects of Female Resistance"; and Fox-Genovese, "Strategies and Forms of Resistance."

13. Kolchin, *American Slavery*, 137–38.

14. In stating that slave spouses acted out complementary roles, this book supports the propositions made by Deborah G. White in *Ar'n't I a Woman?* 158.

15. Rawick, *American Slave*, vols. 2 and 3, and Supplement Series 1, vol. 11, contain the South Carolina narratives that were used here. Belinda Hurmence has also collated South Carolina WPA testimony in *Before Freedom*. There were 344 interviews conducted with South Carolina ex-slaves, representing 14.6 percent of the total number of WPA interviews. However, ten respondents included in Rawick's collection were excluded from this study. Six of these appeared to be white, a fact exposed by the context in which they mentioned "slaves," "negroes," or "darkies." Furthermore, their interviews were not recorded in dialect. Interviewers usually were compelled to mention if an ex-slave was recorded as not having a dialect. These included Caroline Bevis (Rawick, *American Slave*, vol. 2, pt. 1, 55–56); John Boyd (ibid., 70–73); Charlie Jeff Harvey (ibid., vol. 2, pt. 2, 247–51); Mary Ann Lipscomb (ibid., vol. 3, pt. 1, 103–4); William P. Houseal (ibid., vol. 11, 205–7); and Henry Gray Klugh (ibid., 233). Four other respondents were excluded because they did not relate anything about slavery times. These were Will Bees, who only related a postslavery anecdote (ibid., 61–62); Lillie Knox, a friend of the informant Hagar Brown, who was only thirty-five years old and did not contribute anything that would prove significant to the sample (ibid., 234–36); George Washington Murray, who was not actually a respondent but had an unfinished story written about him because he reached the U.S. House of Representatives (ibid., 258–60); and John Widgeon, who did not testify but had an obituary written about him because of his connections with the Maryland Academy of Sciences (ibid., 312–13).

16. See Edgar, *South Carolina*, 681.

17. An 1853–54 survey of rice production in the United States lists 559 planters who produced more than twenty thousand pounds of rice annually. Of these, 446 (79.8 percent) were from South Carolina. In 1821 South Carolina had been the leading cotton producer in the nation, but by 1850, despite the fact that the cotton crop was three times larger than it had been in 1820, South Carolina ranked fourth behind Alabama, Georgia, and Mississippi (ibid., 269, 275).

18. While around 12 percent of southern slaveholders owned twenty or more slaves (placing them in the planter class), in South Carolina 20 percent fell into this category. Georgetown District (the low-country parishes of All Saints Waccamaw and Prince George Winyah) led the United States in terms of rice production. In 1850, South Carolina produced 74.6 percent of the nation's rice, and Georgetown District produced 44.6 percent of South Carolina's total and 33.3 percent of the nation's (ibid., 269, 311).

19. See Jones, *Born a Child of Freedom*, 6. For more on the evolution of slavery in South Carolina, see Wood, *Black Majority*; Berlin, *Many Thousands Gone*, chap. 6; and Morgan, *Slave Counterpoint*.

20. Woodward, "History from Slave Sources," 52.

21. Martia Graham Goodson has said that the WPA interviews "are ideally suited for attempts to fill the void of Afro-American women's history because they contain some of the most illuminating testimony available concerning the lives of slave women." See "Slave Narrative Collection," 488.

22. Eugene Genovese admitted that he simply used sources qualitatively and bypassed the problem of quantifying evidence. He tried to weigh different kinds of testimony against each other to assess the representativeness of the experiences related by the WPA respondents. See *Roll, Jordan, Roll*, 675–76.

23. Gracie Gibson was born in Palakta, Florida, but moved with her owner to Richland County (Rawick, *American Slave*, vol. 2, pt. 2, 113). John Graves was similarly brought from Kentucky to Charleston by his master (ibid., 188). Anson Harp was born in Mississippi but sold to James Henry Hammond (ibid., 237). Jimmie Johnson was sold from his home in Virginia to Spartanburg (ibid., vol. 3, pt. 3, 53). The owner of Sallie Layton Keenan, Matt Wallace, moved all his slaves to Mississippi in an attempt to set up a new home in Arkansas, but various problems meant that they all returned home to Union County (ibid., 74–77). Richard Mack was sold from his home in Virginia to Orangeburg (ibid., 151). Virginia was also where Reuben Rosborough was born before he was sold to South Carolina (ibid., vol. 3, pt. 4, 45). Eliza Scantling went with her "young missus" from their home in South Carolina to Screven, Georgia, although she returned after freedom (ibid., 78–79). North Carolina had been the home of Nina Scott under slavery, although she did not indicate when she moved to the Palmetto State (ibid., 88). Ransom Simmons was born in Mississippi but brought to South Carolina by his master, Wade Hampton (ibid., 91). Isaac Suits was born in the Hickory Mountains of North Carolina before moving South after emancipation (ibid., vol. 11, 302–4).

24. See appendix 1 for a description of the database criteria.

25. Writings on the advantages and disadvantages of the WPA narratives from a methodological perspective are extensive. See, for example, Blassingame, *Slave Testimony*; Brownmiller, *Against Our Will*; Cade, "Out of the Mouths of Ex-Slaves"; Crawford, "Quantified Memory" and "Slave Family"; Davidson and Lytle, *After the Fact*, chap. 7; Davis and Gates, *Slave's Narrative*; Escott, *Slavery Remembered*; and Spindel, "Assessing Memory."

26. Two other works have used the WPA narratives in a quantitative fashion. Paul D. Escott has argued that the slave narratives provide a window onto the thoughts and feelings of slaves. He also maintains that, despite slavery, slaves "did not lose their mental independence." See *Slavery Remembered*, 179–80. Stephen Crawford argues that only through quantification can "the isolation of the real tendencies in the slave narrative sample" be established. He suggests that interaction between slaves and masters was founded on the provision of incentives and disincentives, which contrasts with Escott's conclusion that masters and slaves lived in separate, antagonistic worlds. See Crawford, "Quantified Memory," 241–44, and "Slave Family." It is argued here, in a similar way to Escott, that masters and slaves existed in distinctly different environments, each characterized by separate and conflicting desires, which allowed the enslaved a degree of space for resistance.

27. See Fogel and Engerman, *Time on the Cross*, 145.

28. All the WPA interviewers for the South Carolina volumes appear to have been white, with the exception of Augustus Ladson, who interviewed Thomas Goodwater, Elijah Green, Susan Hamlin, and Prince Smith. Susan Hamlin, of Charleston, was the only South Carolina informant interviewed by a black man (Augustus Ladson) and a white woman (Jessie Butler). See chap. 5 for how her testimony on slave sales was influenced by her interviewer's race.

29. See Blassingame, "Using the Testimony of Ex-Slaves," 85. Ben Leitner provides an example of this when he said to his interviewer, W. W. Dixon: "Well, I's knowed you since you was knee-high and Marse Thomas say maybe you help me to get a pension. If you can't, nobody can." See Rawick, *American Slave*, vol. 3, pt. 3, 100.

30. For a discussion of this distance between slaves and slave owners, see Escott, *Slavery Remembered*, 27; and Hudson, "'All That Cash,'" 94.

31. Susan Brownmiller has written: "When the female ex-slave was asked to tell of her experiences, not surprisingly, she did not dwell on sex . . . and a combination of propriety, modesty and acute shame on the part of narrator and recorder must have conspired to close the door on any specific revelations." See *Against Our Will*, 160.

32. For this sample, I relied upon Donald Jacobs's *Index to "The American Slave."*

33. Gloria Shepherd has noted that full-length personal narratives are more revealing than those of the WPA for the study of rape under slavery. See "Rape of Black Women during Slavery," 5.

34. Wilma King's *Stolen Childhood* shows that this in itself can be worthy of historical investigation. See also Schwartz, *Born in Bondage*, where she follows the life cycle of slave children from birth to young adulthood.

35. Donna J. Spindel, in an article that appears skeptical toward the use of WPA testimony, suggests that "the general thrust of the literature in psychology is that long-term memory is suspect." See "Assessing Memory," 259. Alternatively, Paul D. Escott has suggested that "the brain records and preserves the events of an individual's life and . . . older people often dwell more in memory than the young. Recent studies have shown that aging does not impair the recollection of the elderly, despite society's common assumption that it does." See *Slavery Remembered*, 6–7.

36. Sam Aleckson was a Charleston slave who wrote *Before the War and after the Union*. Charles Ball was born in Maryland but was sold to South Carolina and Georgia; see *Fifty Years in Chains*. Tom Jones was enslaved in North Carolina, whereas "Wild Tom" was held in bondage in South Carolina; see *Experience and Personal Narrative*. Rev. I. E. Lowery, a slave in Sumter County, wrote *Life on the Old Plantation*. Moses Roper was born in North Carolina and sold to Georgia and South Carolina; he wrote *A Narrative of the Adventures and Escape of Moses Roper*. Finally, Jacob Stroyer was a plantation slave who lived near Columbia, South Carolina; see *My Life in the South*.

37. Female slave autobiographies used here include that of the North Carolinian slave Harriet Jacobs, author of *Incidents in the Life of a Slave Girl*; Annie L. Burton of Alabama, who wrote *Memories of Childhood's Slavery Days*; Lucy A. Delany of Missouri, the author of *From the Darkness Cometh the Light*; Kate Drumgoold of Virginia, who wrote *A Slave Girl's Story*; and Mattie J. Jackson of Missouri, author of *The Story of Mattie J. Jackson*. The last four are reprinted in William L. Andrews, ed., *Six Women's Slave Narratives*.

38. See Fleischner, *Mastering Slavery*, 7. It is significant that Jacobs chose to write under a pseudonym, and it has been suggested that she seems to have been motivated by a desire to appeal to a white audience. Linda Brent was a character she hoped white women would recognize and sympathize with. Elizabeth Fox-Genovese has argued that Jacobs used the character of Linda Brent as a mask to conceal her identity. Importantly, this allowed her certain freedoms when writing her autobiography, not least in her claim that Brent managed to resist the sexual advances of her owner, Dr. Flint. Fox-Genovese writes that while this "stretches the limits of all credulity . . . the point of the narrative lies not in her 'virtue,' which was fabricated for the benefit of her Northern readers, but in her resistance of domination, which the preservation of virtue imperfectly captures." See *Within the Plantation Household*, 392, 394. P. Gabrielle Foreman has argued persuasively that Dr. Flint (James Norcom) did rape Linda Brent (Harriet Jacobs) in "Manifest in Signs," 82–83. Throughout this study the name Linda Brent will be used when referring to Jacobs's writings.

39. Osofsky, "Significance of Slave Narratives," 10.

40. Ibid., 12.

41. Ibid., 14.

42. Fox-Genovese, *Within the Plantation Household*, 374.

43. See ibid., 374; Fleischner, *Mastering Slavery*, 18; Yellin, "Texts and Contexts;" and Carby, *Reconstructing Womanhood*, chap. 3.

44. Fox-Genovese, *Within the Plantation Household*, 375.

45. Ibid.

46. On the concept of key slaves, see the introduction to Tadman, *Speculators and Slaves*; and Tadman, "Persistent Myth of Paternalism." Also see chap. 3.

# 1  Courtship and Marriage

> It seems to me that no one can have such fondness of
> love, and such intensity of desire for *home* and home af-
> fections, as the poor slave. Despised and trampled upon
> by a cruel race of unfeeling men, the bondman must die
> in the prime of his wretched life, if he finds no refuge in
> a dear home, where love and sympathy shall meet him
> from hearts made sacred to him by his own irrepressible
> affection and tenderness for them.
>
> —Tom Jones, *Experience and Personal Narrative*

What were the courtship and marriage rituals of antebellum
South Carolina slaves, and from where did they originate? What was the
nature of slave marital life? Little is known about these aspects of the lives
of slaves, since traditional accounts of their social lives (largely written
by white owners) tended to misinterpret the nature and significance of the
customs associated with such personal issues. The fact that the law did
not recognize slave marriages has also meant that they have traditionally
been belittled as insignificant. However, in examining courtship, marriage,
and family from the perspectives of the enslaved, the extent of the love and
affection holding spouses together and how this affection enabled members of slave communities to survive and even resist the oppression of the
regime becomes apparent.

This chapter utilizes evidence from slaves found in published autobiographies and the South Carolina WPA narratives. These experiences offer
us a glimpse into their lives "after sundown"—an aspect of bondage that
has received only limited attention in the source materials left by owners.[1]
Overwhelmingly, in these records, slaves are found to have treasured family and familial memories. Had relationships within marriage been tainted

by bitterness and distrust, some reflection of this would have been expected; it is therefore significant that negative comments were rare and that in the majority of cases spouses were recalled with deep affection. Indeed, a common theme throughout the slave testimony was the love between husbands and wives—and also within slave families as a whole—achieved despite hardships such as sales, separations, and sexual abuse, or suffering the anguish of running away. Slave narratives clearly illustrate the existence of romantic love in their society. Further, their ties of affection served as a means of resistance against oppression and illustrate how slaves of all generations were not demoralized by bondage. The tone of the evidence suggests that entering wedlock and married life was an anchor and a positive reference point for the enslaved, ultimately enabling them to survive the regime. Moreover, this was the case for all individuals, regardless of their status within slave society or as defined by whites.[2] To a certain extent, slaves were able to live according to the norms and values set by their own communities, despite the constraints imposed by owners.

The origins of courtship and marriage customs and the concept of slave romantic love are considered first, especially with regard to how these rituals compared with those of precolonial West Africa and white society. Changes in courtship and marriage over time will also be taken into account. Second, perceptions of these rituals from the profoundly different perspectives of slaves and their owners are examined. White sources reveal something of their rationalization and selective vision of slavery, and a combination of black and white testimony points to the antithetical worldviews of slaves and owners and to the vast social space dividing these two worlds.[3] Slave sources, especially detailed life histories in the full-length autobiographies, are used to explore love between spouses and male and female roles in courtship and marriage. Finally, the wider implications of these findings for gender relations under oppression are addressed.

## The Origins of Slave Courtship and Marriage Rituals

Historians have long disagreed over the relative influences of white and black cultural patterns upon the enslaved. During the 1950s, the conventional view, most notably espoused by Kenneth M. Stampp, claimed that they were "caught between two cultures"—losing their African heritage yet unable to adopt white cultural patterns.[4] An alternative, more "Pan-African" view held that African influences upon the lives of slaves were more extensive than had previously been thought. Melville J. Herskovits believed that their culture was basically African in outlook, and

Nathan I. Huggins and Sterling Stuckey later developed this view.[5] Somewhat differently, Lawrence W. Levine highlighted the "fusion" of white European and black African cultures in the creation of a new "Afro-American" (later "African American") culture.[6] More recently, Charles Joyner has argued that when considering the creation of a "southern culture," the influence of black cultural patterns upon the white South deserves to be recognized. For Joyner, too much emphasis has been placed upon what blacks absorbed rather than what they gave, on blacks as passive receivers rather than active agents.[7]

Of course, the dynamics by which culture was transmitted and mutated by blacks and whites were complicated and reciprocal, with cultural patterns passing from one group to another and vice-versa. Cultural traits could also be changed to suit one group's particular needs and aspirations. Change over time is also important here. African patterns in slave culture would obviously have been stronger when slaves were being imported from Africa. Once the abolition of the international slave trade in 1808 prevented all but a minority of slaves from entering the United States, African influences tended to diminish, and white cultural traits assumed a greater importance within the lives of the enslaved.

In assessing the extent to which African and white American influences played a role in slave relationship customs, it is therefore useful to examine courtship and marriage in precolonial West Africa as well as in white European and American societies. Most of those enslaved in America tended to come from Africa's west coast, which was known as "Guinea" by traders. This area can be divided into three geographic zones, each of which possessed shared cultural and linguistic patterns: Upper Guinea, Lower Guinea, and the area that accounted for around 40 percent of all slaves brought to South Carolina, Congo/Angola.[8] However, it is also important not to generalize about West Africa as one cultural entity; this was a large, geographically, culturally, and politically diverse area. There was also considerable diversity within African family life, where norms about household structure and marriage customs varied. For example, some Africans lived in clans and lineages, while others did not. Some traced their descent from men, others from women.[9] While some important research has been carried out into the nature of marriage and the structure of the family in these areas, the scarcity of source materials has rendered some level of generalization inevitable. Some significant evidence also derives from anthropological studies of contemporary African life.[10] Rarity of evidence has also meant that most testimony relating to family patterns in precolonial West Africa has, unsurprisingly, come from the elite. Little is known about common African families in the seventeenth century.[11]

The problems of available evidence notwithstanding, most historians agree that the predominant family form in precolonial West Africa was the lineage family—extended clans tracing their ancestry in common. These clans shared certain characteristics and traditions. Elders, who arranged and legitimized marriages, were male in most cases. Marriage often involved the exchange of goods and services such as labor between lineages over a period of time. Overall, though, blood relationships took priority over conjugal ties, rendering the celebration of birth and death more important than that of marriage.[12] As in other societies, there was a concern to build up populations and colonize land. Since land was plentiful, monogamous marriage assumed a secondary significance when compared with the need for wives and children to cultivate it. This resulted in considerable competition for women and an obsession with matters relating to potency and fertility—both were considered more important than fidelity. There were several types of marriage, ranging from abduction at one end of the spectrum to formal payment of bridewealth at the other. Under this arrangement, families of new husbands would compensate the fathers of brides for the loss of their daughters. Polygamy was therefore more common among the wealthy. This type of system also meant that women were more likely to marry young, while men tended to marry late.[13] John Iliffe has written that the competition for wives in polygamous societies "made conflict between male generations one of the most dynamic and enduring forces in African history. . . . Young men might cultivate a distinct subculture stressing beauty, dress, ornament, virility, insolence, and aggression."[14] Similarities can therefore be seen with the courtship practices of young male slaves in antebellum South Carolina. They also played the dominant role in competing with each other to win the affections of women.

Olaudah Equiano makes some fascinating observations about West African marriage ceremonies in his *Interesting Narrative,* a rare example of an autobiographical account of life in West Africa, first published in 1789. He reinforces the significance of polygamy but also suggests that both males and females married when young. His description of marital celebrations following a feast is worth quoting at length:

> The bride and bridegroom stand up in the midst of all their friends, who are assembled for the purpose, while he declares that she is thenceforth to be looked upon as his wife, and that no other person is to pay any address to her. This is also immediately proclaimed in the vicinity, on which the bride retires from the assembly. Some time after, she is brought home to her husband, and then another feast is made, to which the relations of both parties are invited: her parents then deliver her to the bridegroom, accom-

panied with a number of blessings, and at the same time they tie round her waist a cotton string on the thickness of a goose-quill, which none but married women are permitted to wear: she is now considered completely his wife; and at this time the dowry is given to the new married pair, which generally consists of portions of land, slaves, and cattle, household goods, and implements of husbandry. These are offered by the friends of both parties; besides which the parents of the bridegroom present gifts to those of the bride, whose property she is looked upon before marriage; but after it she is esteemed the sole property of her husband. The ceremony now being ended, the festival begins, which is celebrated with bonfires, and loud acclamations of joy, accompanied with music and dancing.[15]

He also describes the importance of dance in African society: "Every great event, such as a triumphant return from battle, or other cause of great rejoicing, is celebrated in public dances, which are accompanied with songs and music suited to the occasion. The assembly is separated into four divisions. . . . The first contains the married men, who in their dances frequently exhibit feats of arms, and the representation of a battle. To these succeed the married women, who dance in the second division. The young men occupy the third; and the maidens the fourth."[16]

Music and dance were significant components at marital celebrations among different tribes and across regions in West Africa. Anthropological studies have shown how Umbanda women would sing songs welcoming new brides to their village. Similarly, the Wolof has a category of songs known as *cheit* songs, which are sung for brides whose husbands are already married. "The words of one *cheit* song are: 'Bride, there will be sweet food where you sleep / And the drums will play until dawn.'"[17] It is easy to draw parallels between these celebrations and those of other societies across time and space, including antebellum slave society, where music and dance were important elements of courtship and marriage rituals.

The pervasive influence of other African traditions is evident at various slave social gatherings. Harvest festivals known as corn-shuckings (where corn was husked) were occasions not only for courtship but also for passing on African cultural traits related to music and dance from one generation to the next.[18] Dance ceremonies, such as the popular counterclockwise "ring shout," originated in Africa, and the circle of dancers, among the Mende and Temne, constitutes the "chief symbol of ceremony that leads to marriage and the renewal of the life process with the birth of children."[19] Conjurers and sacred charms also introduced an African element into slave courtship and marriage rituals. Young men sometimes used the conjurer to help them "woo" a desirable female. Similarly, as will be shown, trickster stories such as those of Brer Rabbit often revolved around competition over women. African customs are therefore evident in certain realms of life for antebellum South Carolina slaves: namely music, dancing, and the courtship ritual of men initiating relationships. Obviously, though, there were exceptions and variations. For example, in the large sea-island rice plantations of the low country, the concentration of blacks meant that African survivals as a whole were more pronounced, most likely resulting in a greater degree of African influences in courtship and marriage patterns.

However, slave music, dance, and courtship initiation procedures may also have been influenced by white norms. Roger D. Abrahams has linked corn-shuckings to harvest ceremonies in England, which were also important community events.[20] He makes the point that slaves observed and imitated white culture, especially that displayed at their balls and dances.[21] Courtship was, for the most part, as pleasurable for whites as it was for blacks. Young southern women had considerable freedoms in choosing their marriage partners, and many reveled in their years spent attending dances, balls, and parties as Southern Belles.[22] Among young white men, the "language of honor" and the significance of competition (including vying for the affections of women) bear many similarities to the contests between enslaved men for prized or beautiful females.[23] The parents of white youngsters also played a role in courtship matters, as did the parents of slaves, who often urged caution in affairs of the heart.[24]

Slave courtship and marriage rituals therefore share many of the characteristics of white American as well as black African cultural patterns. However, among men in precolonial West Africa, the *motives* for winning the affections of women were different; while antebellum slaves (and, to a lesser extent, white southern men) desired a spouse for companionship,[25] men in precolonial West Africa gained wealth and status through acquiring a number of wives. As such, they may have been more limited in their choice of partner. Niara Sudarkasa writes: "Marriage in Africa was a contractual union which often involved long-lasting companionate relationships, but it was not expected to be the all-encompassing, exclusive relationship of the Euro-American ideal type."[26] Moreover, in Africa, "marriage was not normally arranged by partners but by lineage elders to meet socioeconomic and political needs, often in consultation with the prospective groom; sometimes prospective brides exercised influence over choice of spouse and sometimes not."[27] The role of love and affection between spouses was less pronounced in West African marriages, emphasizing a marked contrast to marriages in the modern western world.

A. R. Radcliffe-Brown and Daryll Forde have argued that the "most important factor in the development of the modern English (and American) conception of marriage was the idea of romantic love, a theme that was elaborated in the nineteenth century in novel and drama."[28] Precolonial West African marriage, by contrast, was very much an economic partnership and bore more similarities to spousal unions in preindustrial Europe and America, where matrimony bound families together. With the emergence of the concept of romantic love, the nature of marriage in the West began to alter. John D'Emilio and Estelle B. Freedman, in their pioneering survey of sexuality in America, claim that by the nineteenth century, love and intimacy had become increasingly important in preparing for marriage: "courting couples in all English colonies began to employ the language of romantic love, expressing passion in their correspondence and exploring intimate emotions, rather than mere property arrangements."[29]

There were various reasons for this change. At a broad level, they encompass the economic and social changes that upset traditional community life and morality, forcing Americans to rely more heavily on the family as a source of social stability. Individual choice became more important, often at the expense of parental or state control. Religious revivals also encouraged people to take responsibility for their own actions. Other significant factors include the development of European Enlightenment ideas about the relationship of the individual to society and the decline of the traditional patriarchal family: "Enlightenment writers . . . elevated all that was related to nature, including sexuality, as good and desirable. . . . At the same time, new scientific accounts of the functioning of the reproductive system reconceptualized sexuality as something distinct from procreation."[30] The increasing control over fertility also loosened the link between reproduction and sexuality, resulting in the latter becoming more closely associated with love: "By the late eighteenth century the ideal of affective relationships within the family had become widespread. Most couples now recognized that the mutual rights and obligations of spouses included emotional and sexual pleasure."[31]

While slave courtship rituals were similar to those of precolonial Africa and of white America, their marital patterns were rather different from those in precolonial Africa. Here, white influences were much more pronounced, exemplified by the decline in polygamy. Allan Kulikoff, in his study of the Chesapeake colonies, writes that some Africans would have brought the practice of polygamy to the United States. However, far too few African women (in relation to the number of men) immigrated to make polygamous marriage common. By the antebellum period, this practice had mostly died out. Similarly, Philip D. Morgan has noted that, along with many other African cultural traits, polygamy was more common among low-country slaves than elsewhere in British North America, despite the admonition of owners and religious ministers.[32]

So what were the motivational forces driving slaves to marry? Some historians, for example Claire Robertson, have regarded matrimony as the continuation of an African practice in the New World, where economic factors were paramount.[33] Slaves may have sought partners to complement their practical needs under the work and garden system with romantic affection being a secondary (though still important) consideration.[34] Evidence obtained from slave sources, however, suggests that by the antebellum period this was not the case. Slaves married for love. Furthermore, the transformation from African to "modern" marriage was an adaptive process. It would have been impractical if not impossible to continue African patterns of marriage when the concept of "economic partnership" had no real relevance under a system of bondage. Modern marriages had a great deal to offer, with the combined benefits of love, support, and affection offering a bulwark against oppression. Slaves followed the white norm of romantic love because it was of immense value to them.

## Slave Courtship and Marriage: White Rationalization and Black Experience

Slaveholders viewed slave courtship and marriage patterns very differently than did slaves, an antithesis that suggests that the meaning and significance of such rituals have largely been misinterpreted. Only through an investigation into the respective worldviews of owners and slaves can the vast differences between their systems of values be comprehended. How owners and those they enslaved carved out compromises over the extent of slaves' autonomous community activities can therefore be seen through an exploration of slave courtship and marriage rituals. Such negotiations often involved role-playing by slaves in order to preserve the paternalist self-image of their masters.

Owners could influence their slaves' courtship and marriage patterns through a variety of ways, and their attempts to do so unwittingly reveal how they frequently belittled the concept of romantic love among slaves.[35] Slaves and slaveholders were engaged in a battle over the extent of autonomy in these realms of life. Slaves strove to meet and marry a partner of their own choosing, while owners sought to impose their own restrictions upon courtship and matrimonial decisions. Methods employed included preventing their slaves from socializing by limiting the amount of free time they enjoyed, imposing constraints upon their geographical mobility (for example, by limiting the amount of time that they could spend off their place of residence), and implementing systems of rewards and punishments to influence their slaves' marital choices.[36]

The control of courtship and marriage patterns should be seen as part of the process by which owners developed and maintained a benevolent self-image. They believed they knew best when it came to their slaves' affairs of the heart. However, slave testimony suggests that owners believed their sway over courtship and marriage patterns to be greater than it actually was. Slaves may have engaged in a certain amount of role-playing in this realm. Acting according to their owners' expectations allowed them to carve out compromises with their masters over the extent of autonomy permitted. Reaching such agreements meant that owners could maintain a benevolent paternalistic worldview, while slaves would gain the social space necessary to undertake various activities in their own communities.[37]

The meanings that slaves and owners ascribed to courtship and marriage rituals are of immense significance. Take, for example, the fact that men were often allowed to leave their own plantations and holdings to visit women. This gave them an opportunity to develop autonomous cultural patterns as well as to marry outside of their place of residence. However, the fact that they were able to do this was largely conditional on their individual owners, who made decisions that facilitated the maintenance of control while also reinforcing their self-image as benevolent masters. Comments made by the South Carolina WPA respondents reveal much about these compromises. For example, George Fleming, a slave in Laurens County, noted that sometimes on a Saturday night, "frolics" (dances) took place on other plantations. He explained how the rules set by whites were different for frolics than for events where whites attended too, such as corn-shuckings. Fleming stated: "Didn't need no passes when a bunch of slaves went to other plantations to dem big gatherings. 'Rangements was already made so de patrollers wouldn't bother nobody. Dat policy didn't hold fer de frolics, though. Sho had to have a pass frum de marse if you went."[38]

When there was a corn-shucking, Fleming's owner (Sam Fleming) would allow his slaves to leave their plantation without a pass, thereby reinforcing his self-image as a caring master. However, in the case of the more autonomous frolics, he imposed tighter constraints, which often resulted in frolics taking place in secrecy. The WPA respondent Madison Griffin illustrates this point: "De niggers went to de cornshuckings and was give pumpkin custards to eat and liquor. Wasn't allowed to dance, but sometimes we had secret dances, shut up in de house so de master culdn't hear us."[39] By means of a contrast, slaves in urban environments often had more opportunities than their plantation counterparts to partake in courtship activities. Between September 1836 and September 1837, 573 slaves were convicted for being on the streets of Charleston without a pass after the evening curfew. It is likely that many of these were either visiting loved ones or attending illicit social events where attracting a member of the opposite sex was high on the agenda. Charlestonian slaves embraced a diverse social life that involved "grog shops," where they could drink and gamble, and horse racing, as well as the more conventional parties and dances.[40]

A comparison of white and black source materials also illustrates the different level of significance they ascribe to social events. A pair of white brothers, John and Charles Marshall, received a letter from their grandmother, Mrs. R. H. Marshall, in which she described the corn-shucking festivities of plantation slaves near Laurens. She described how overseers would often invite slaves from neighboring plantations to corn-shuckings and that they would march over burning torches of pine and singing. She wrote: "Their captain mounts the heap of corn, and all sing a call song for the others to come, which is immediately answered from the other plantations, in a song that 'they are coming,' you can hear them distinctly more than a mile, they sing as they march all the way, and when they arrive at the spot, they all join in one grand chorus—and make the forest sing with their music, they then appoint captains to succeed each other from the different companies—who mount the heap in turn and play their monkey pranks while they take the lead in singing as those around them shuck and toss their corn into the air—seemingly the happiest beings that live." Mrs. Marshall not only found all of this activity highly amusing; in emphasizing the "happiness" of the slaves involved she also reflected white notions of planter benevolence. She perceived the slaves to be so contented that she found herself questioning the harshness of the plantation regime. "White folks" of the North who worked for a living had a much harder time, she believed. Mrs. Marshall also suggested that any abolitionist traveling to the southern states would soon find that their sympathy resided with masters rather than slaves. Slaves were happy with their lot—caring for them was the difficult task.[41]

Owners believed that the methods of control that they imposed on the social lives of those they held in bondage, including their courtship rituals, were borne out of a desire to act in their slaves' best interests. Maria Bryan Harford described how her slave, Jenny, caused her and her husband a considerable amount of frustration by having a "great many suitors" who nearly "turned her head with flatteries." Jenny began courting a man belonging to a neighbor, but Mrs. Harford resented the amount of time he spent in their kitchen with Jenny. The situation worsened when he refused to go home one night and then had the audacity to run into Jenny's bedroom. Mr. Harford consequently banned him from the premises. However, Jenny's suitor was resilient—Maria Harford described how, despite the ban, he was still sending Jenny messages and presents.[42] Mr. and Mrs. Harford had no doubts that they were the ones best qualified to make decisions regarding Jenny's courtship affairs, although the persistence of Jenny's suitor suggests that owners' interference was not always accepted. Despite their belief that they were acting in the interests of those they enslaved, owners' actions exposed their lack of regard for romantic love among slaves.

Ultimately, owners possessed the authority to break up courting slaves as well as married couples, a power displayed most trenchantly through sales or separations.[43] However, other methods of control—namely, systems of rewards and punishments—were also utilized by owners in their battle with slaves over courtship and matrimonial affairs. A slave named Mary-Ann was sent from the home of Mordecai Cohen in Charleston to the plantation of Michael Lazarus in Barnwell, despite Cohen's description of her as "the most valuable wench I have, being an excellent seamstress, house servant. In fact I never owned one more so." Cohen wanted to make an example of Mary-Ann, who was to be punished by wearing "a suit of coarse white plains, which I beg you to make her wear and keep her at as hard labor as you possibly can." Mary-Ann's crime was to have begun courting a slave of whom her owner disapproved, with Cohen describing him as a "rascally fellow." Further, she had continued to meet with her suitor despite being forbidden to do so. Cohen believed that a stint of hard field labor would "cure" Mary-Ann of her infatuation, and rather ironically he emphasized the great hardship inflicted upon himself and his wife in having to cope without a slave whose "fine disposition and the many good qualities united together, rendered [her] the most valuable servant we ever had."[44]

Physical violence could also be used to prevent slaves from courting. H. H. Townes of Greenville wrote of the problems caused by his slave, Squire, who was "as fat as an old bear. All the trouble I have with him, is to keep him from having a wife. I expect to have to whip him severely yet about his love affairs."[45] Slaveholders developed their own rules and regulations concerning courtship and marriage, and if their slaves refused to subscribe to them the consequences could be severe. Linda Brent fell in love with a free black man, but her master, Dr. Flint, forbade her from marrying him. Dr. Flint's motivations were likely complex. He was harassing Brent sexually and was also affronted that she was courting a free man rather than one held in bondage. Brent describes how Dr. Flint told her, "'I'll soon convince you whether I am your master, or the nigger fellow you honor so highly. If you *must* have a husband, you may take up with one of my slaves.'" She retorted, "'Don't you suppose, sir, that a slave can have some preference about marrying? Do you suppose that all men are alike to her?'" She then told Dr. Flint that she was in love with her suitor. Greatly angered, he prevented Brent from marrying the man she loved.[46]

Sometimes owners used physical violence to prevent slaves from visiting their loved ones, as will be seen in chapter 2. Ironically, while such measures allowed them to reaffirm their paternalistic notions that they were acting in the interests of their slaves, slaveholders' actions would have naturally caused resentment within enslaved communities, through the knowledge that their masters did not truly respect the notion of slave romantic love. Such reactions would have increased the psychological distance or "social space" between the lives of slaves and owners, with both parties negotiating over the extent of independence within slaves' social lives and their associated courtship affairs. The same may also be said of marriage rituals. Owners frequently demanded that their slaves ask permission before marrying, and they often attended their weddings themselves. These acts affirmed owners' view of themselves as guardians yet also imposed an element of control over the autonomy of those they held in bondage.

The South Carolina WPA respondent Andy Marion eloquently illustrated the frustrations felt by the enslaved in their struggle to court and marry within the confines imposed by owners. Despite living on a plantation of seventy-two slaves, he said, "A nigger had a hell of a time gittin' a wife durin' slavery. If you didn't see one on de place to suit you and chances was you didn't suit them, why what could you do? Couldn't spring up, grab a mule and ride to de next plantation widout a written pass. S'pose you gits your marster's consent to go? Look here, de gal's marster got to consent, de gal got to consent, de gal's daddy got to consent, de gal's mammy got to consent. It was a hell of a way."[47] However, the fact that slaves did enter matrimony and did choose to live in cross-plantation marriages illustrates the strength of their romantic love and, more broadly, the resilience of their communities.

Many of the WPA respondents emphasized the fact that permission was needed from masters before slaves could get married. Exercising control over wedding ceremonies was yet another part of the process by which owners maintained their desired image. For example, Sam Mitchell, enslaved on Ladies Island, stated: "If Maussa say, 'No, you can't marry dat girl,' den dat settle it, you can't marry um." He also said that most were married in the master's house by a white preacher.[48] Washington Dozier, a Florence County slave, said: "Aw colored peoples hadder do to marry den was to go to dey massa en ge' uh permit en consider demselves man en wife."[49] Other ex-slaves highlighted the control that owners tried to enforce over wedding ceremonies, whether through the use of a white preacher or by locating the service within the master's house.[50] George Fleming testified that on his plantation near Laurens slaves were married by a white preacher in their master's backyard.[51] Similarly, Lucinda Miller told her interviewer that slaves had to be married by white preachers on her plantation.[52] Albert Means, married during slavery, emphasized the fact that his master provided all the food and gifts at his wedding.[53] Susan Hamlin of Charleston told her black interviewer, Augustus Ladson, that most slave weddings took place in the living room of the Big House with the master and mistress as witnesses. She poignantly described how no minister ever said "let no man put asunder" at these ceremonies, because "a couple would be married tonight an' tomorrow one would be taken away en be sold."[54]

Even when slaves were permitted to wed an individual of their own choosing, the patronizing attitudes of owners toward their marriages reflect deeply held stereotypes. For slaves, spousal love and support was of vital importance in the fight for cultural autonomy. While married life could be fun, matrimony was also an immensely significant and serious institution. Owners, however, who could not afford to take too seriously the concept of slave romantic love, often belittled their courtship and marriages. Typical were the sentiments of Thomas B. Chaplin, the owner of the Tombee plantation on St. Helena Island. He felt that most slaves only "played" at being married. Their innate selfishness, he believed, prevented them from intimacy. He lamented the involvement of his wife, who put on a "grand supper" at slave wedding ceremonies, and often stayed away himself. At the marriage of his maids Eliza and Nelly, he peevishly wrote: "I do not wish to be here to see the tomfoolery that was going on about it, as if they were ladies of quality."[55]

The following description of a slave wedding by Anne Simons Deas, a white woman, exemplifies how owners and slaves interpreted wedding rituals in different ways and reveals much about the paternalistic worldview of slaveholders. It will be seen later in this chapter how the South Carolina WPA respondents frequently mentioned the community parties that were held at slave weddings *after* the departure of whites. However, owners assumed that it was their own participation in the betrothal ceremony that was of significance. Moreover, through the clever use of role-playing, slaves conned their owners into feeling a sense of importance. Deas wrote:

> The bride was Tena, the assistant washerwoman, and as she is the niece of Maum Myra's deceased husband, Maum Myra took possession of the wedding festivities. She spent the whole day making and icing a cake, the materials being furnished by cousin Rachel. The wedding dress was an old party dress of Kathleen's, which Maum Myra "did-up" beautifully for the occasion. The ceremony was performed at Maum Myra's house, and all the juniors of the family were invited. . . . As soon as we had arrived, the bride and her four bridesmaids, all in white and looking very bashful, came out of the bedroom and were stationed by Maum Myra in a straight line across the floor, facing us. Across half the floor I should have said, for the bridegroom—Mauney—and his groomsmen came in from outside, and completed the line, the bride and groom standing side by side in the middle, and the others on each hand. Then the minister, who proved to be Sambo, popped up from somewhere, and took his station in front of the couple. . . . He produced a prayer book, and read the Episcopal marriage service. He read correctly, but literally, giving us rubrics and all—"Then the minister shall say" etc. etc. But first he lined out a hymn, and everyone in the room sang vigorously. When the service was over, he duly congratulated the bride, and we, perceiving from Maum Myra's fidgetiness that it was our turn, stepped forth and expressed our good wishes. Then we retired gracefully, leaving them to partake of the wedding supper.[56]

Deas's description exposes some of the limitations of using white source materials for the study of slave life. It is likely that the slaves involved would have perceived the wedding described as a significant, serious, yet fun community event. However, the tone adopted by Deas is rather mocking, and she can reveal nothing of the wedding supper that took place after her departure.

Slaveholders typically dwelled on the weddings of slaves that took place in the Big House.[57] It seems likely that these celebrations would have been those of key slaves, a privileged few referred to frequently in their owners' manuscript materials.[58] For the mass of field slaves, weddings would most likely have been very different affairs, with more involvement from the black community, a private wedding supper, and less involvement on the part of owners. I. E. Lowery, an ex-slave who can hardly be described as a militant critic of the system of bondage, states in his narrative that, for most slaves, there was neither a religious wedding ceremony nor a feast. However, "there were a few isolated cases where the slaves were allowed to marry in due form and were given a wedding supper. These were the more prominent or favorite slaves, such as butlers, coachmen, nurses, chambermaids or cooks."[59] As a "favored" slave himself, though, it is likely that Lowery was sheltered from the weddings of the rank and file and their associated community events. Also, it is probable that, in writing his conservative narrative, he included only what he thought whites would want to hear.[60]

Shane White and Graham White, in their innovative analysis of African American expressive culture, have noted how slaves could assert their independence from their owners at wedding ceremonies through the clothes that they wore. While slave weddings did tend to be modeled on those of their owners, especially the brides' dresses, "their dress still manifested the small but significant differences that generally characterized African American clothing." Brightly colored sashes, stockings, and scarves were especially important.[61] White and White conclude that "clothing was a vital and integral part of a culture that, fashioned out of adversity, made the lives of African Americans during their time of enslavement bearable."[62]

Evidence relating to rank-and-file slaves has to be examined to fully understand the nature of slave weddings. Some of the WPA respondents, for example, mentioned that they were married by colored preachers rather than by their master or by a white minister.[63] Many couples took part in the symbolic ritual of jumping over a broom, although it has been argued the WPA ex-slaves inflated the importance of this custom. As children during slavery, they most likely remembered the broom but not the actual ceremony.[64] Overall, it is unlikely that these more "ordinary" slave weddings would be mentioned in the manuscript materials of owners, since they would instead be concerned with the betrothals of their favored slaves. It is important, however, to acknowledge the significance of the community affairs of the rank and file in their struggle to forge an autonomous cultural life. The WPA respondents frequently mentioned the festivities they took part in *after* a more formal wedding ceremony, events that would be nearly impossible to trace from white testimony. For example, Gus Feaster said that although slaves did not "dress up" for marriages, there were big feasts after the wedding.[65] Similarly, Morgan Scurry of Newberry County said that whites attended weddings, but afterward slaves had their own feasts.[66] Margaret Hughes, enslaved near Columbia, testified: "We had a big time when any of de slaves got married. Massa and missus let them get married in de big house, then we had a big dance at one of de slave house. De white folks furnish all kinds of good things to eat, and de colored peoples furnish de music for de dance."[67] Owners convinced themselves that they made an important contribution to the weddings of their slaves, thus reinforcing their paternalistic worldview. This was at odds with the slaves' clear attempts to maintain an autonomous culture through the independent celebrations that occurred after the departure of whites. Owners' attitudes were also selective. They stressed their caring self-image through benevolence to key individuals, while their belittling of slave romantic love was part of the rationalization of white dominance.

## Affection between Spouses

Men and women held in bondage acted out their courtship and matrimonial rituals through their community activities, striving to betroth someone of their own choosing before settling down to life in a stable nuclear family unit. Their marriages also tended to be characterized by great affection: if an individual fell in love with someone who belonged to another master or someone of whom their owners disapproved, the desire for autonomy within slave communities, coupled with the social space that existed between the lives of masters and slaves, meant that the enslaved fought to marry whom *they* chose regardless of the circumstances. Some of the most eloquent expressions of spousal affection can be found within full-length slave autobiographies because many of the authors were forcibly separated from their spouses and families. A common theme is, therefore, the love that existed between men and women despite adversity.[68] Furthermore, this romantic affection was the defining characteristic of spousal relationships for all phases of the antebellum period. This is significant because it suggests a persistent pattern of commitment between spouses and considerable intergenerational morale within enslaved communities.

Charles Ball was sold to a slave trader and taken from his home in Maryland to South Carolina and Georgia. The anguish he felt at being parted from his wife and children caused him many a sleepless night, and when he did sleep, he had nightmares in which his wife and children were "weeping and lamenting my calamity; and beseeching and imploring my master on their knees, not to carry me away from them. My little boy came and begged me not to go and leave him, and endeavored, as I thought, with his little hands to break the fetters that bound me." Ball's immense emotional agony left him so depressed that he was unable to pray. "I felt as if there was no mercy in heaven, nor compassion on earth, for a man who was born a slave."[69] Happily, Ball was eventually reunited with his family, though in keeping with the genre of his autobiography, his description of their reunion concentrates on his wife's emotional responses at seeing him.[70] She thrust their three children into Ball's lap while laughing, clapping, and crying at the same time. He also notes how "in her ecstasy [she] forgot to give me any supper until I at length told her I was hungry."[71]

Despite the forcible separation from his family, Ball never lost his love for them; indeed, it was the desire to see them again that enticed him to run away. The urge for spousal companionship, therefore, should not be underestimated. Tom Jones is even more explicit about his desire for gaining the love of a wife as a means of resistance to oppression: "I wanted a friend to whom I could tell my story of sorrows, of unsatisfied longing, of new and fondly cherished plans . . . of whom I might think when toiling for a selfish, unfeeling master; who should dwell fondly on my memory when we were separated during the severe labors of the day, and with whom I might enjoy the blessed happiness of social endearments after the work of each day was over." The yearning for a life partner who would provide a bulwark against adversity existed simultaneously with the human urges simply to love and be loved. Tom Jones "wanted a companion with whom I could love with all my warm affections, who should love me in return with a true and fervent heart." However, there were risks involved in allowing oneself emotionally to become involved while living under an institution where physical abuse and enforced separations were very real possibilities. Slaves responded to this dilemma in different ways. Typically, Tom Jones chose love, describing passionately how "[m]y heart yearned to have a home, if it was only the wretched home of the unprotected slave. . . . I sought to love . . . with a full knowledge of the desperate agony that the slave husband and father is exposed to. . . . I saw it in every public auction, where men and women and children were brought upon the block, examined, and bought. I saw it on such occasions, in the hopeless agony depicted on the countenance of husband and wife, there separated to meet no more in this cruel world. . . . And yet I sought to become a husband and father, because I felt that I could live no longer unloved and unloving."[72]

For Jones, the desire for the love of a wife as a means of gaining companionship and meaning in life—being able to survive and ultimately to resist the oppression of slavery—easily outweighed the risk of heartache that any slave marriage might face. Further, the fact that most slaves did marry illustrates the vital importance of giving and receiving love under adversity. Jones was therefore devastated when, having married another slave, his wife's mistress moved from North Carolina to Alabama, taking his wife with her. Jones eloquently describes their separation: "Our sobs and tears were our only adieu. Our hearts were too full of anguish for any other expression of our hopeless woe. I have never seen that dear family since, nor have I heard from them since I parted from them there. God only knows the bitterness of my agony, experienced in the separation of my wife and children from me."[73]

Love and affection between slaves of the opposite sex is also an important theme in the full-length autobiographies of female slaves, although a noteworthy exception can be found in the story of Linda Brent. Sexually harassed from an early age by her master, Dr. Flint, she writes in rather pessimistic tones about falling in love. Brent had become romantically involved with a free black man but was banned from seeing him by Dr. Flint. Possibly as a result of the cruelty inflicted upon her by her master, she states, somewhat cynically: "Why does the slave ever love? Why allow the tendrils of the heart to twine around objects which may at any moment be wrenched away by the hand of violence?"[74] Brent's sentiments, however, appear to be atypical. Evidence gleaned from the WPA and other full-length narratives suggests that the majority of slaves saw marriage and settling into a stable nuclear partnership as the norm. John Collins was a WPA respondent enslaved in Chester County. He recalled the matrimonial joy of his parents, remembering that "Daddy used to play wid mammy just lak she was a child. He'd ketch her under de armpits and jump her up mighty high to de rafters in de little house us lived in."[75] Similarly, a Newberry slave, Isabella Dorroh, recalled: "Marse didn't make slave women marry if dey didn't want to. Befo' my mammy and daddy married, somebody give a note to take to Mrs. Fair, her mistress. Mistress wouldn't tell what was in it, but daddy run every step of de way, he was so glad dey would let 'em marry."[76] Slaves strove for the love of a spouse despite all the problems and heartache that this could bring. It is true that for most, there were numerous perils associated with falling in love: namely, being separated through enforced separations, sales, or death. Male slaves also had sometimes to witness the physical or sexual abuse of their womenfolk by white owners. However, the fact that the majority of slaves still desired to fall in love and to overcome the hardships of bondage with the support of a partner must be recognized as one of their most positive accomplishments under a brutal and repressive institution.[77]

Significant gender differences existed in the courtship and marriage patterns of slaves. Males played a dominant role by trying to win the affections of females and appeared to enjoy their courting days.[78] When Frank Adamson of Newberry was asked if he did any courting under slavery, he replied: "Did me ever do any courtin? You knows I did. Every he thing from a he king down to a bunty rooster gits 'cited 'bout she things. I's lay wake many nights 'bout sich things. It's de nature of a he, to take after de she."[79]

It was also most often slave men who traveled to visit wives, girlfriends, and children, as will be shown in the next chapter. Men therefore faced the considerable risk of being caught and whipped by patrollers for being off their quarters. Even so, female slaves, although generally not at risk of punishment by patrollers, still worried about their husbands, boyfriends, and fathers who were doing the visiting. Julia Woodberry, enslaved in Marion County, claimed: "Cose dey [slave men and women] wouldn' live together cause dey wives would be here, dere en yonder. . . . White folks had dese guard, call patroller, all bout de country to catch en whip dem niggers dat been prowl bout widout dat strip [paper] from dey Massa."[80]

Male WPA respondents appear to have been more willing to talk to their interviewers about courtship than the females. A theme that frequently cropped up was that of impressing women and girls at social events.[81] This desire for pleasure and enjoyment illustrates that slaves possessed the capability of autonomy. For example, George Fleming recalled the fun had by slaves at frolics where music was made by fiddles and by quills made from cane. Fleming was a quill blower, and he reminisced how "gals wouldn't look at nobody else when I start blowing de quills." He also highlighted the importance of large corn-shuckings, where slaves from numerous plantations would gather to shuck and sing. These were happy occasions, especially when, according to Fleming, there was a jug of liquor at the bottom of the corn-shucking pile: "Everybody try to be first to get to de liquor." The involvement of whites at such events did not pose a problem for Fleming; indeed, often the "white folks have big supper ready; liquor, brandy, and everything."[82]

Gable Lockier illustrated the significance of corn-shuckings to courtship: "De first one shuck red corn had to tell who his best girl was en all dem things."[83] Moreover, since corn-shuckings often involved slaves from different plantations, they also widened the pool of potential marriage partners. Young men tried to impress girls in other ways: Gus Feaster emphasized what he described as "vulgar songs," where the young men sang to the girls, "I'll give you half-dollar if you come out tonight; I'll give you half-dollar if you come out tonight." The girls responded by picking honeysuckle and rose petals, which they then hid in their breasts.[84] Other courtship games played by young slaves included "please and displease" and "hack-back." During the former, the girls asked boys what it would take to please them, and the boys responded by stating, "a kiss frum dat purty gal over dar." The latter was a dance where young men and women faced each other and danced back and forth.[85]

Attitudes toward premarital sex are notoriously difficult to uncover, since the WPA respondents, unsurprisingly, were not forthcoming in this area.[86] Records of illegitimate births show that some premarital sex did occur, possibly from the mid-teens onward.[87] However, premarital sex mostly served as a prelude to marriage, and Steven E. Brown has shown how slave attitudes toward premarital sex were clear manifestations of a developed set of community values.[88] Herbert G. Gutman pointed to the African influences upon the premarital sex of slaves, while John W. Blassingame highlighted the African influences upon slave courtship rituals as a whole, especially the use of metaphor, indirection, storytelling, poems, songs, riddles, and symbolic language. These combined with the American traditions of corn-shucking, frolics, and other dances and celebrations to create a unique set of courtship practices that tested the wits of those involved though riddles, boasting, innuendos, and circumlocution.[89]

In his study of African American folk thought, Lawrence W. Levine describes the ways in which slave folk tales dealt with everyday human relationships through their allegories, including courtship, matrimony, and the relationships between men and women. Frequently in courtship tales, women were regarded as possessions to be fought over. One particular Brer Rabbit story relates how Rabbit and Wolf compete for the affections of a woman. Rabbit feigns surprise that the woman could be interested in Wolf because, after all, he is only Rabbit's horse. This insult angers Wolf, and he confronts Rabbit, who unsurprisingly denies ever making such a claim. Rabbit promises to go to the woman and counter the slander but informs Wolf that he is too ill to go at present. Wolf is anxious for amends to be made with the woman, so he offers to carry Rabbit on his back to the woman's home. Rabbit agrees, so long as Wolf wears a saddle and bridle for support. When they arrive, Rabbit immediately tightens the reins and shouts out: " 'Look here, girl! What I told you? Didn't I say I had Brother Wolf for my riding-horse?' "[90] Within these folk tales, Levine argues, mastery for the slave is achieved through possessing the two paramount symbols of power: food and women.[91] He also notes how slave stories often referred to the "moral inconsistency and overweening pride of women," while fathers normally emerged as "the chief protector and avenger of children."[92] This reveals much about the nature of gender relations under the peculiar institution and runs counter to the assertion that males were emasculated by the experience of bondage.

It is clear that black sources, whether folk tales or slave narratives, open up a social world that is invisible in most white evidence. Slave testimony consistently emphasizes the importance of marriage and family, and it is rare to find ex-slaves denigrating family life. Folk tales might hint at "macho" adventures, but the slave evidence suggests that more settled family attitudes were the norm in the long term. An examination of courtship and marriage rituals is therefore immensely illuminating in any investigation into the lives of the enslaved. Comparing black and white source materials reveals much about the patterns of courtship and marriage and, at a broader level, the nature of slavery itself. While owners saw themselves as benevolent and paternalistic (a self-image they sought to reinforce through their intervention in the courtship and matrimonial lives of those they held in bondage), the mass of slaves viewed their masters very differently. They strove to act out their affairs of the heart despite the constant interference of their owners, whose various rules, regulations, incentives, and punishments inhibited their autonomous community lives. A gulf therefore existed between the worldview of owners and their actual treatment of their slaves.[93] While white sources emphasized slave "promiscuity" and took slave marriage and family less than seriously, slave testimony tells a very different story. The overwhelming tone of this evidence is positive: slaves sought autonomous family lives, and the mutual support and affection of husband and wife was the norm. They took matrimony and family life very seriously and strove for social space in these realms. Furthermore, their quest for autonomy drove slaves to act upon their desire to live in stable, nuclear partnerships.

## Notes

1. For a discussion of the use of the WPA narratives in studying the lives of slaves after sundown, see Rawick, *From Sundown to Sunup.*

2. See chap. 3 for a more detailed discussion of the differences in slave and owner perceptions of social status.

3. On the concept of social space between masters and slaves, see Hudson, "'All That Cash,'" 77–94.

4. See Stampp, *Peculiar Institution,* chap. 8.

5. See Herskovits, *Myth of the Negro Past;* Huggins, *Black Odyssey;* and Stuckey, *Slave Culture.*

6. Levine, *Black Culture and Black Consciousness,* esp. pts. 1 and 2.

7. See Joyner, *Down by the Riverside* and *Shared Traditions,* intro. and chaps. 1–4.

8. Kolchin, *American Slavery,* 19. See also Higgins, "Geographical Origins of Negro Slaves."

9. See Kulikoff, "Beginnings of the Afro-American Family in Maryland" and *Tobacco and Slaves,* chaps. 8 and 9.

10. See, for example, Miers and Kopytoff, eds., *Slavery in Africa.*

11. See Thornton, *Africa and Africans,* 207.

12. See Robertson, "Africa into the Americas?" 18.

13. Iliffe, *Africans,* 93–94.

14. Ibid., 95–96.

15. Equiano, *Interesting Narrative,* 33–34.

16. Ibid., 34.

17. Jackson, "Black Women and Music," 385–86.

18. Stuckey, *Slave Culture,* 64–65. Corn-shuckings took place at harvest time and were, for most of America, a community effort. See Abrahams, *Singing the Master,* xxi.

19. Stuckey, *Slave Culture,* 12–15.

20. See Abrahams, *Singing the Master,* 26. He acknowledges that corn-shuckings also had African origins (58).

21. Ibid., 34.

22. Fox-Genovese, *Within the Plantation Household,* 207–10. Undoubtedly, though, this freedom was inhibited by financial calculation among the wealthy planters. See Collins, *White Society in the Antebellum South,* 136. See also Clinton, *Plantation Mistress,* 61–66.

23. See, for example, Greenberg, *Honor and Slavery.*

24. See Wyatt-Brown, *Southern Honor,* chap. 8.

25. On the importance of making a "good" marriage, see ibid., 199–207.

26. Sudarkasa, "Interpreting the African Heritage," 34.

27. Robertson, "Africa into the Americas?" 17–18.

28. Radcliffe-Brown and Forde, eds., *African Systems of Kinship and Marriage,* 45.

29. D'Emilio and Freedman, *Intimate Matters,* 42.

30. Ibid., 40–41.

31. Ibid., 40–41 and 56–57. See also Seidman, *Romantic Longings,* pt. 1; and Lystra, *Searching the Heart,* chap. 2. The latter two works largely ignore the notion of slave romantic love in nineteenth-century America.

32. Kulikoff, "Beginnings of the Afro-American Family in Maryland," 173; Morgan, *Slave Counterpoint,* 553–54. Drew Gilpin Faust claims that there may have been a couple of polygamous marriages upon James Henry Hammond's Silver Bluff plantation. See *James Henry Hammond and the Old South,* 84.

33. Robertson writes: "It is clear, then, that the economic conditions of slavery reinforced the utility of certain African practices . . . [such as] marriage as a predominantly economic arrangement." See "Africa into the Americas?" 18.

34. See Hudson, *To Have and to Hold,* 158. See also D'Emilio and Freedman, *Intimate Matters,* 98.

35. Owners also revealed their lack of regard for the concept of slave romantic love by forcibly separating spouses from one another and through their sexual abuse of female slaves. These issues will be dealt with in later chapters.

36. On the systems of punishments and rewards designed to influence the marital decisions of slaves, see Fogel and Engerman, *Time on the Cross,* 86–85.

37. For a discussion of the meanings and compromises reached between masters and slaves, see Genovese, *Roll, Jordan, Roll,* 5–7. He accepts the ideology of paternalism but believes that "the slaves found an opportunity to translate paternalism itself into a doctrine different from that understood by their masters and to forge it into a weapon of resistance to assertions that slavery was a natural condition for blacks" (7).

38. Rawick, *American Slave,* vol. 11, 129.

39. Ibid., vol. 2, pt. 2, 213. On illicit dances, see also Schwartz, *Born in Bondage,* 179.

40. See Powers, *Black Charlestonians,* 22–24. The historiography of urban slavery and its opportunities for increased freedoms are discussed in Parish, *Slavery,* 98–101.

41. Letter to John and Charles Marshall from their grandmother, 19 April 1852, Marshall Family Papers, William R. Perkins Library (hereafter WRPL).

42. Letter to Julia A. B. Cumming from Maria Bryan Harford, ca. 20 March 1833, Hammond-Bryan-Cumming Family Papers, South Caroliniana Library (hereafter SCL).

43. See chap. 5 for a fuller discussion of sales and separations.

44. See Letters to Michael Lazarus from Mordecai Cohen, 2 October 1809 and 10 November 1809, Lewis Malone Ayer Papers, SCL.

45. Letter to Mrs. Rachael Townes from H. H. Townes [son], 19 December 1833, Townes Family Papers, SCL.

46. Jacobs, *Incidents*, 61.

47. Rawick, *American Slave*, vol. 3, pt. 3, 167–68. See also Schwalm, *A Hard Fight for We*, 52–53.

48. Rawick, *American Slave*, vol. 3, pt. 3, 201.

49. Ibid., vol. 2, pt. 1, 331.

50. See King, *Stolen Childhood*, 63–64.

51. Rawick, *American Slave*, vol. 11, 136.

52. Ibid., vol. 3, pt. 3, 192.

53. Ibid., 183–84.

54. Ibid., vol. 2, pt. 2, 234. When interviewed by Jessie A. Butler, a white woman, Hamlin did not mention slave weddings.

55. See Rosengarten, *Tombee*, 154.

56. Deas, "Two Years of Plantation Life," 85–87, SCL. This is a fictionalized account, written in the 1890s, of life on Cedar Grove plantation. Her cousin Alston Deas, in an introduction to the volume, states that Cedar Grove probably represented the Comingtee plantation of her uncle, Mr. Keating Ball.

57. On slave weddings, see Sides, "Slave Weddings and Religion," 85–86; Genovese, *Roll, Jordan, Roll*, 479; and King, *Stolen Childhood*, 63–64.

58. For a definition and discussion on the concept of key slaves, see the introduction to Tadman, *Speculators and Slaves* and "Persistent Myth of Paternalism," 7–23.

59. Lowery, *Life on the Old Plantation*, 61.

60. Ibid., 15. Lowery was a domestic slave who lived in the Big House with his master and mistress.

61. White and White, *Stylin'*, 33; see also "Slave Clothing and African-American Culture." For a similar argument on the significance of slave hairstyles, see White and White, "Slave Hair and African American Culture."

62. White and White, *Stylin'*, 36.

63. George Wood, a York County slave, said that a "jack-legged" colored preacher married slaves. See Rawick, *American Slave*, vol. 3, pt. 4, 250. A colored preacher also married Gordon Bluford, a female slave from Laurens County who was married before emancipation (ibid., vol. 2, pt. 1, 63).

64. King, *Stolen Childhood*, 64. White and White also argue that the importance of "jumping the broom" has been overemphasized by historians. See *Stylin'*, 32. Brenda Stevenson claims it was a relic of pre-Christian western Europe in *Life in Black and White*, 228–29. A more dated analysis of jumping the broom can be found in Taylor, "'Jumping the Broomstick.'"

65. Rawick, *American Slave*, vol. 2, pt. 2, 47.

66. Ibid., vol. 3, pt. 4, 90.

67. Ibid., vol. 3, pt. 2, 329.

68. John W. Blassingame has noted how "affection was apparently the most important factor which kept partners together. This emerges most clearly in the lamentations and resentments which pervade the autobiographies over the separation of family members" (*Slave Community*, 171).

69. Ball, *Fifty Years in Chains*, 31–32.

70. In their quest to reach a broad audience, female autobiographers frequently mentioned their alleged domesticity, while the men wanted to remind readers of their assertive masculinity. See Fox-Genovese, *Within the Plantation Household*, 375.

71. Ball, *Fifty Years in Chains*, 387.

72. Jones, *Experience and Personal Narrative*, 22–23.

73. Ibid., 24.

74. Jacobs, *Incidents*, 58.

75. Rawick, *American Slave*, vol. 2, pt. 1, 224–25.

76. Ibid., 326.

77. Historians have recently stressed the positive accomplishments of slave life and culture. This signals a move away from the previous emphasis upon the negative impacts upon the slaves of the master's behavior. For further analysis of this concept, see Engerman, "Concluding Reflections," 233–41, esp. 235. Deborah G. White has also made this point: Despite the fact that slave men had a lot to lose from romantic liaisons, they also had a lot to gain and thus still strove to find a wife. See *Ar'n't I a Woman?* 145–46.

78. Several other historians have pointed to the pattern of males initiating courtship. See, for example, Blassingame, *Slave Community*, 159–60; Levine, *Black Culture and Black Consciousness*, 95–111; Jones, *Labor of Love*, 33; White, *Ar'n't I a Woman?* 143–45; Genovese, *Roll, Jordan, Roll*, 468–71; and King, *Stolen Childhood*, 61.

79. Rawick *American Slave*, vol. 2, pt. 1, 16.

80. Ibid., vol. 3, pt. 4, 238.

81. See also King, *Stolen Childhood*, 60–61; and Brown, "Sexuality and the Slave Community."

82. Rawick, *American Slave*, vol. 11, 128. Fleming's testimony also shows how owners set limits to the autonomy of their slaves' social events through their own involvement (in the above case, by preparing the supper). This allowed owners to reaffirm their belief in their own benevolent paternalism, as has been seen earlier in this chapter.

83. Rawick, *American Slave*, vol. 3, pt. 3, 115.

84. Ibid., vol. 2, pt. 2, 51–52. See also King, *Stolen Childhood*, 61.

85. George Fleming in Rawick, *American Slave*, vol. 11, 127–28.

86. Dan Smith, enslaved in Richland County, hints, however, at premarital sex in postbellum times in his testimony. See Rawick, *American Slave*, vol. 3, pt. 4, 97–98.

87. For the debate over the age of slave women at first birth and its links to premarital sex, see Fogel and Engerman, *Time on the Cross*, 137–39; Gutman and Sutch, "Victorians All?" 138–44; Gutman, *Black Family in Slavery and Freedom*, 62–83; Steckel, "Slave Marriage and the Family"; and Diedrich, "'My Love Is Black as Yours Is Fair.'"

88. Brown, "Sexuality and the Slave Community," 6–7.

89. Gutman, *Black Family in Slavery and Freedom*, 64–67; Blassingame, *Slave Community*, 157–58.

90. Levine, *Black Culture*, 111.

91. Ibid.

92. Ibid., 95–97.

93. On the gulf between the worldview of slave owners and their treatment of their slaves, see Tadman, *Speculators and Slaves*, xxi–xxii, and "Persistent Myth of Paternalism."

# 2 Family Life

> My husband was a slave of de Sloans and didn't get
> to see me as often as he wanted to; and of course, as
> de housemaid then, dere was times I couldn't meet him,
> clandestine like he want me. Us had some grief over dat,
> but he got a pass twice a week from his marster, Marse
> Tommie Sloan, to come to see me. . . . Sam was a field
> hand and drive de wagon way to Charleston once a year
> wid cotton, and always bring back something pretty
> for me.
> —Louisa Davis, an ex-slave

In order to take further the argument that, despite owners, a
strong sense of family was the norm among South Carolina slaves, the
structure and nature of their families will now be examined. This chapter
is concerned with the extent to which two-parent families were common
among slaves, and particular attention will be paid to cross-plantation marriages (where husband and wife lived on different slaveholdings). The family lives as well as the family structures of slaves are explored, focusing
particularly on issues relating to antagonisms between couples. The main
causes of marital disharmony for the enslaved are notoriously difficult to
uncover, since their testimony reveals little about hostilities between husbands and wives, although owners did sometimes mention slave marital
problems in their personal letters and diaries. Two sets of historical materials have proven particularly fruitful in uncovering the more negative sentiments between married couples under bondage. The records of antebellum biracial Baptist churches, through their disciplinary committees, offer
a unique insight into slaves' relationships and the issues that divided couples.[1] The records of the Freedmen's Bureau, although dealing with the

postbellum era, also illustrate some of the "troubles" between black husbands and wives that had begun under slavery. However, despite the considerable pressures facing slaves, instances of black-on-black antagonisms were rare. Moreover, slave evidence (unlike white sources) emphasizes not promiscuity and lack of sensitivity but positive relations between spouses.

Historians have found it difficult to assess the extent and nature of cross-plantation or "abroad" marriages, largely because white sources give no basis for estimating their scale or character. Estate papers and business records often list slaves belonging to a particular owner, but they generally give no indication of spouses and other relatives of those slaves who might belong to neighbors. Similarly, except for scattered comments on visiting privileges given to certain individuals or references to the possible advantages and inconveniences of allowing slaves to marry off the plantation, owners took little interest in the vigor of such unions. The WPA narratives, along with other black evidence, are probably the only sources from which we can reconstruct the numerical importance of cross-plantation marriages and from which a substantial sample can be gathered to investigate their character. In the South Carolina WPA testimony, cross-plantation unions accounted for nearly 34 percent of slave households, and they were far from weak and nominal relationships; indeed, slaves supported these marriages in the same way that they did same-residence unions. Cross-plantation marriages therefore point to the resilience of enslaved communities.

Although historians have not closely researched them, many have assumed that cross-plantation marriages were weak and unstable. Speculative interpretations on the nature of these unions have been developed by historians from a combination of their overall view of slavery and the use of scattered quotations. Kenneth M. Stampp, in *The Peculiar Institution*, emphasized the impact of absent fathers and the weakness of slave marriages, and this tradition passed on into the Moynihan Report of 1965.[2] Later, in seeking to reinstate the husband-oriented nuclear slave family, Herbert G. Gutman focused mainly on consolidated residence households, although he did emphasize that when freedom came, ex-slaves made great efforts to reunite families that had been split between different locations.[3] Some writers have commented on the possible benefits for *owners* of cross-plantation marriages. Eugene Genovese claims that slaveholders "knew that a man who fell in love with a woman off the place would be a poor and sullen worker, and probably soon a runaway, if deprived of his choice."[4] Similarly, Richard H. Steckel has argued that masters benefited from slave wedlock, including cross-plantation unions, since "slaves were probably better workers when connected to a desirable home life and [for the owner of the wife] the marriages also yielded offspring."[5]

Paul D. Escott's investigation of the WPA testimony touches briefly and impressionistically on cross-plantation marriages and suggests that such unions were viable.[6] Stephen Crawford's study of WPA narratives, however, is much more detailed than Escott's and includes some analysis of the statistical importance and viability of cross-plantation unions.[7] His overall conclusion is that "an overwhelming majority of those mentioning anything about visiting [to maintain cross-plantation unions] claimed that their fathers visited regularly."[8] However, more ambitious claims about the importance of abroad marriages within enslaved communities are made here.

Some lived in cross-plantation unions because of practical necessity. For example, they might have lived on small holdings with no suitable marriage partners. Slaves might also choose a "home" marriage if they felt that their material conditions were satisfactory. There were considerable disadvantages associated with residing in cross-plantation unions, including the risks involved with visiting.[9] But the very existence of abroad marriages among slaves who lived on larger units suggests a desire on their part for autonomy from their owners, a need to make their own marital decisions. Moreover, these marriages are also suggestive of the gender patterns that operated within the world of the slaves. The fact that men frequently risked the wrath of their owners and the patrollers in visiting their wives and girlfriends illustrates not only the extent of male-female bonding but also notions of masculinity. It was men, not women, who saw it as their duty to undertake visits, and this role-adoption suggests wider conclusions—that male slaves, despite living under oppression, saw themselves as initiators, protectors, and providers.

## The Extent of Cross-Plantation Marriages: Methodology and Results

The South Carolina WPA narratives can be used to estimate the numerical importance of cross-plantation unions before the vigor of such relationships is explored. In concluding that an abroad marriage was sustained (rather than there being simply a broken family), certain criteria had to be met. These conditions related primarily to the marriages of the parents of the WPA respondents, since few were of an age to enter wedlock during slavery. Cross-plantation unions were assumed in cases where a respondent specifically stated that his or her father belonged to another master and spoke of being in touch with him during slavery. Similarly, instances where an informant commented on his or her father visiting, without necessarily stating his residence, were included. Again, examples were included where a respondent gave the name of his or her father's owner and (despite the fact that this name was different from the name of the owner of the respondent and their mother) expressed a familiarity with their father's owner. These results produced significantly higher percentages of cross-plantation households than most other studies.[10]

It was possible to calculate family structure for 158 of the 334 South Carolina informants (47.3 percent of all respondents). The figures were derived from those who discussed the residential arrangements of their parents and also from five ex-slaves who were married before the Civil War.[11] In total, seventy-one stated that their parents lived together, and two married during slavery resided with their spouses. Thus the sample contains seventy-three reported marriages that were nuclear (46.2 percent of the 158). A further fifty-three reported marriages met the required criteria for cross-plantation unions (33.5 percent of the 158). This fifty-three comprised fifty who said that their parents resided with different masters and three who lived in cross-plantation unions themselves. Another twenty respondents recalled that they resided with their mother and (sometimes) their siblings, with no father being mentioned. Thus 12.7 percent of the 158 families were defined as female-headed, compared with ten who testified that they lived within families in which there was a stepparent (6.3 percent of the 158). Finally, two ex-slaves said that their parents belonged to the same owner but resided in different houses (1.3 percent of the 158).[12] The overall results from the evidence given by the South Carolina ex-slaves therefore suggest a big majority living in viable families.[13]

Despite the fact that this sample of 158 individuals represents a little less than half of the total number of respondents, it would seem likely that those who testified about the structure of their families were representative of the South Carolina experience as a whole. This is because, firstly, they were not prompted to answer questions about their family structures, indicating that their comments were made in the natural flow of conversation. Secondly, a reticence to discuss details of basic family structure with white interviewers would have been less likely than with sensitive issues such as sexual abuse or physical punishments.

Several other points should be noted about the nature of the sample: it was not possible to undertake extensive quantitative work on the relationship between size of unit and incidences of cross-plantation marriages, since only twenty-six ex-slaves mentioned both the size of their holding and the residential arrangements of their parents under slavery. It was found, however, that those on smaller holdings were more likely to have parents who lived apart, while those on larger quarters were more likely to have parents who resided together. Practical considerations were obviously important here. For example, Nancy Washington, an ex-slave from Marion County who had an abroad marriage, would have been forced to look for a spouse away from her quarters, since her master only owned her, her siblings, and her mother.[14] The geographical contexts of these findings are also important. Those residing in the South Carolina low country were more likely to live on large holdings with many other slaves because of the preponderance of large rice and sea-island cotton plantations in this region.[15] The sample did not, however, show any skew toward same-residence marriage in this area, despite the fact that a greater opportunity to marry on-plantation prevailed. Of the twenty-five respondents who stated that they lived in the South Carolina low country as slaves, thirteen had parents in cross-plantation unions, and twelve lived in nuclear families.

It will later be shown that Stephen Crawford's technique for classifying family structure appears to have led to a consistent undercount of cross-plantation unions. Nevertheless, his study is important, and several results from his large WPA sample should be noted. He found, as did this smaller sample, that size of slaveholding was important. Crawford noted that on units of fewer than sixteen slaves, two-thirds of unions were cross-plantation, whereas on units of sixteen to forty-nine slaves (or higher), only about 14 to 20 percent were cross-plantation. He found, too, that in the slave-exporting states (such as South Carolina), the proportion of cross-plantation marriages was higher (at 14.7 percent) than in the slave-importing states (where the proportion was only 5.2 percent). Finally, Crawford discovered that, in overall patterns, occupation made no difference to the ratio of same-residence and cross-plantation marriages: "Quite clearly there was no difference between the family structure of houseservants and field-hands. It is possible that the family relationship differed in other ways, but there was no significant difference in the proportion of two-parent and one-parent families."[16] However, it was found here that those whose parents were house servants or skilled slaves were slightly more likely to live in nuclear households with a higher proportion of field hands, when compared to domestics, residing in cross-plantation families.[17] Perhaps owners may have indulged their favored house slaves by buying their chosen partners, an issue that will be considered later.

## Cross-Plantation Marriages:
## A Comparison with Other Studies

Few studies have explored cross-plantation marriages seriously. Comparisons can, however, be made with Stephen Crawford and Paul D. Escott's WPA-based studies; with Anne Patton Malone's analysis of Louisiana plantation records; with Brenda E. Stevenson's investigation into the slaves belonging to George Washington in 1799; and with Carole E. Merritt's case study of two small groups of slaves held on Georgia plantations. The results of the various studies differ greatly. This is partly because of the source bases used and partly due to differing criteria for defining abroad unions. Escott found that 72.5 percent of WPA slaves lived in nuclear residences, while 27.5 percent lived in cross-plantation families. He suggested that slave marriages were of only two types: "One was marrying at home and the other was called marrying abroad [cross-plantation]."[18] Differences between Escott's results and the findings here arise to a great extent because he considered only reported *marriages* and did not include family structures such as female-headed households. Furthermore, he does not give any indication of the criteria he used for classifying testimony on marriage types.

Crawford's work is more directly comparable to the findings stated here. He found that 51.1 percent of WPA slave families consisted of two parents living together in nuclear households, a figure slightly higher than the 46.2 percent for the South Carolina sample. However, Crawford found only 12.4 percent of slaves living in cross-plantation families, compared to 33.5 percent in the South Carolina sample. In addition, 33.2 percent of Crawford's respondents lived in female-headed families, compared with 12.7 percent of South Carolina slaves.[19] It is difficult to know how Crawford reached these figures, as he provides no clues as to his technique. He does state that roughly 20 percent of female-headed families might actually have been of the cross-plantation type, but 20 percent of 33.2 is only 6.6 percent, leaving the maximum number of cross-plantation marriages that Crawford could have at only 19 percent of the total.[20] It appears that the differences are due to variations in criteria for identifying cross-plantation unions. It is possible that Crawford defined a family as female-headed when, for example, a respondent mentioned his mother but not his father, although his father could have actually resided elsewhere. In this study, female-headed families were defined as those households where an ex-slave specifically mentioned that they lived only with their mother and did not comment on their father visiting. It seems likely, then, that Crawford's technique systematically underrepresented cross-plantation marriages.

Anne Patton Malone has also offered a classification of the structure of slave families in her study of rural Louisiana, based upon evidence from plantation and parish records.[21] The nature of Malone's sources is highly significant, since these records—essentially lists of slaves belonging to a particular owner or plantation—almost never include reference to abroad unions, because the missing spouses from within such marriages belonged to other owners. Generally, it is only when the records left by slaves themselves are examined that quantitative estimations of the extent of abroad partnerships can be made. Malone's work, therefore, almost completely ignores cross-plantation households. She found that nearly three-quarters of the slaves in her sample lived in "simple families." Such households included married couples, with and without children, and single persons with children. Within this type, "standard nuclear families" (fathers, mothers, and children) made up 49 percent of the sample. This is a similar proportion to the 46.2 percent of South Carolina WPA slaves who lived in same-residence unions. Within her sample, Malone also found that single-parent households, predominantly women and children, made up around 14.5 percent.[22] Again, this mirrors the 12.7 percent found among the South Carolina respondents. Malone argues that "slightly fewer than half of the sampled Louisiana slaves . . . were members of two-parent nuclear families."[23] This is important, since she goes on to emphasize the stability of the female-headed family unit within their society.

However, Malone does not investigate cross-plantation marriages, apart from claiming that there is little evidence that such unions were common in Louisiana, except on small holdings, "where marriage choices were so limited as to convince owners that the merits outweighed the risks."[24] This omission constitutes a major limitation of her work. Instead, Malone stresses the significance of female-headed families, arguing that they were a consistent feature in the nineteenth century and also an accepted family form. She states: "Although this percentage [14.5] by no means constitutes a matriarchal structure, in slave society single parenthood was viewed as a viable option for slave women to a greater degree than was true of contemporary white society."[25] By not considering abroad unions, Malone details a far from complete picture of slave household structure. Furthermore, her claims on the stability of female-headed families are not borne out by an exploration into the WPA evidence.

In a similar vein, Stevenson claims that matrifocality (mother-centeredness) was prominent in slave domestic life. She downplays the role of slave fathers: "Slave owners' preferential treatment of slave mothers made it difficult for slave men to have equal influence in the day-to-day activities of their families, particularly since many of them did not live with their children. . . . [M]atrifocality was a fundamental characteristic of most slave families even when fathers lived locally."[26] George Washington owned five farms in Loudoun County, Virginia, and according to Stevenson, as many as 72 percent of his slaves had abroad spouses.[27] In a similar way to Malone, though, Stevenson regards cross-plantation fam-

ilies as inferior to those that were nuclear in type. She also believes that
they had a negative impact on the status of slave fathers: "Most slave
children in Virginia did not grow up in two-parent homes [and] the slave
man's roles as father and husband were much diminished."[28] Evidence
presented here, however, contradicts the notion that abroad marriages
in any way emasculated slave fathers. If anything, the opposite is true,
with fathers going to great lengths in their desire to visit, protect, and
cherish their wives and children.

Problems encountered in defining family types also become apparent
when Merritt's work is examined. Merritt undertook a case study of the
families of slaves belonging to Lindsey Durham of Piedmont, Georgia, finding that by 1860, Durham had a workforce of seventy-five slaves residing
on two plantations.[29] She states: "Although the Durham slave plantations
were relatively large slave ownership units, they were too small to incor-
porate within the plantation's boundaries most nuclear and extended family relationships."[30] This meant that cross-plantation marriages were common among the Durham slaves. Merritt claims that they accounted for
76.4 percent of the total number of adult slaves whose marital status could
be established, compared with only 19.2 percent of slaves who lived in two-
parent families.[31] Rather than using the fact that many slaves lived in
cross-plantation marriages as evidence of the strength of the relationship
between spouses, though, Merritt seems to assume that women in such
unions saw themselves as lone parents. She writes: "Single-parent families represented one of the constraints within which slave families func-
tioned. The slave man's residence apart from his wife and children restricted family interaction."[32] The WPA evidence, as will be seen, suggests
instead that cross-plantation unions were usually highly resilient institu-
tions.

## Owners' Perspectives on Cross-Plantation Marriages

Few owners left their slaves to their own devices when it came to
matters of the heart. As has been shown in chapter 1, many slaves had to
conduct their courtship affairs within the confines imposed by their masters. This was also the case when it came to relationships between married couples. The Louisiana slave owner Bennet Barrow suggested that
slaves in cross-plantation marriages "'are liable to be separated from each
other, as well as their children, either by the caprice of either of the parties [owners], or when there is a sale of property.'"[33] Indeed, owners often
gave the impression that they simply did not regard off-plantation unions
as seriously as they did same-residence marriages. Some were openly hos-

tile to such unions; one South Carolina owner wrote that abroad marriage "'creates [in slaves] a feeling of independence from being, of right, out of the control of their master for a time.'"[34]

Unsurprisingly, when they did comment on cross-plantation unions, owners almost always did so from their perspective rather than from that of their slaves. Frequently we hear of the problems caused by such marriages. Elizabeth Franklin Perry, a mistress in Greenville, did not sympathize with her slave, Eliza, who appeared to have greatly missed Powel, her off-plantation husband. Perry wrote to her husband, Benjamin: "I would be thankful if I could get rid of Eliza, she calls for Powel her husband, says she has been living with him five years, sends her children on messages to him, abuses me, won't let her children work for us, and is an abominable creature, a pollution to any yard."[35] Thomas B. Chaplin, the owner of Tombee plantation on St. Helena Island, reluctantly realized that social custom and the desire to have his workforce reproduce meant that he should permit abroad marriages. However, he resented the fact that cross-plantation unions would undoubtedly lead to more movement among—and, perhaps, a greater degree of independence for—his slaves. "Don't like it at all," he wrote in his diary.[36] An abroad marriage caused a legal wrangle between two slave owners in 1842 when Myers bought a slave—Stephen—whom he hoped to take to Kentucky. However, Stephen was "unwilling" to go, as he had a wife on the plantation of Mr. Robert. The case was resolved to Stephen's benefit when Myers exchanged him for two of Robert's slaves.[37]

The Columbia slave owner John Guignard also encountered difficulties in attempting to minimize the problems caused by his cross-plantation slaves. Recognizing the unhappiness of his slave, also called Stephen, Guignard chose to hire Stephen's abroad wife for two dollars per month, thus uniting the couple.[38] Stephen was lucky. His owner was sympathetic to his plight and took action to ensure that he could live with his wife. Perhaps he was a favored slave, indulged by Guignard, who would have had no qualms about treating Stephen better than the majority of his slaves. When it came to the treatment of rank-and-file individuals in abroad unions, though, it was a different story—most did not undertake such considerate action to unite them with their spouses.

More commonly, slaveholders' actions illustrated a desire to improve the efficiency of their plantation while also facilitating the relationships of those they held in bondage. Contented slaves made better workers, and it did owners no harm if they presented a benevolent face. Owners would sometimes swap slaves to facilitate marriages, but only if they liked the sound of the spouse that they would be receiving in return for a more problematic slave. For example, the day after he decided to take the abroad wife of Stephen, Guignard devised an alternative plan that was more beneficial to him. He wrote to his father: "Barber's Charlotte I found sick over at Davis's where she has been for a few days. I think her of little or no account in the field and would like to swap her for a better. (Perhaps you could trade her for Stephen's wife whom I have not seen, but Stephen describes her as a good cook and house wench)."[39] Guignard realized that instead of merely hiring Stephen's wife, he could obtain her as his own by swapping for her the unproductive, sickly Charlotte.

Likewise, the South Carolina WPA respondent Rebecca Jane Grant described her father's owner, Tom Wilmington, as a "Christian gentleman" because he apparently tried to buy Grant, her mother, and her siblings so they could all reside together. However, Wilmington may have had other motives: in buying the wife and children of one of his slaves it was extremely likely that his stock of slaves would be increased in the future.[40] Moreover, when owners did consent to buy or hire the spouses of their slaves, they expected plenty of gratitude in return. The Dorchester County planter and lawyer David Gavin was disgusted when one of his slaves, Team, ran away from his plantation despite having been bought by Gavin so that he could be united with his wife, mother, and siblings. Gavin wrote: "I think the scoundrel has used me mean."[41] The clear expectation was for Team to be grateful to his master for keeping his family together.

Sometimes owners mentioned cross-plantation marriage arrangements in their plantation rulebooks, and generally their words were couched in disapproving terms. The Sumter planter John B. Miller, who owned between thirty and forty slaves, imposed various regulations on slave behavior in his rulebook. His slaves were not allowed to leave their homes to attend religious meetings at night, and he preferred his field hands not to marry those from the Big House.[42] Miller also wrote that his slaves were "not to leave plantation without a ticket and that to express the place they are to go to and how long to be absent and not to be for any greater distance than a few miles without my express orders, except to the nearest church. Tickets to be given alone by me, wife or son. . . . No negro but those connected to my negroes and of good character to be allowed on plantation and they must have a ticket for that purpose from their owners to be brought to me except them that have a wife or husband on the plantation."[43]

The list of plantation rules in the papers of the Conway-Black-Davis family refers indirectly to cross-plantation links. Overseers were advised to "prevent night visits in the week, and put an end to late hours. Let 'early to bed and early to rise' be the word."[44] Similarly, the Charleston planter

Andrew Flinn worried about night visits and slave mobility. His plantation book stated that no slaves were to be allowed out of their houses after
nine o'clock in summer and eight o'clock in winter.[45] Flinn also compiled
a list of ten punishable offences: running away represented the ultimate
crime; second came drinking alcohol; third was the theft of hogs, followed
by stealing in general; leaving the plantation without permission came in
fifth; and sixth was absence after horn blow; having an unclean house or
person was seventh, followed by the neglect of mules, tools, and work.
Flinn wrote that the highest punishment for these offences should not ex-
ceed fifty lashes in one day.[46] His list of punishable misdemeanors illustrates just how concerned owners were about issues relating to off-plantation courtship and marriage. Similarly, in his autobiography I. E. Lowery
detailed the courtship and marriage rules of his master, Mr. Frierson, who
always advised his slaves to marry someone on their own quarters. He told
them that if they followed this advice they would not be parted. However,
if they chose to ignore their master and wed off-plantation, they would be
at risk of being separated by "nigger traders." Frierson was clearly trying
to influence his slaves by presenting same-residence marriage as the easier, less precarious option.[47]

Charles Manigault took a harsh line on cross-plantation marriages,
simply dictating that his slaves could not marry those on other holdings.
This is illustrated in a letter to his overseer, in which he wrote: "I allow
no strange negro to take a wife on my place."[48] Manigault probably felt
that the large size of his rice plantation meant that he did not need to
"allow" his slaves to make abroad marriages. He had around one hundred
slaves living in his Gowrie plantation on Argyle Island in the Savannah
River, and this would have given them a wider choice of potential spouses
than those on other, smaller holdings.[49] William Dusinberre, in his richly
detailed study of slavery in the rice areas of the low country, states that
several abroad marriages existed at Manigault's Gowrie plantation when
he bought it in 1833. However, through his enforcement of the above rule,
cross-plantation unions became rare, with dire consequences for the slave
population at Gowrie. However, this did not concern Manigault, who prioritized plantation discipline over the family life of those he held in bondage. Despite the relatively large numbers of slaves living at Gowrie, Dusinberre argues, the harshness of plantation life (including disease, death,
and enforced separations) meant that the pool of potential marriage partners was actually very small. Manigault therefore simply replaced the
marital hardship caused by abroad marriages with another—that of a limited marriage market. This resulted in many choosing to wed someone
considerably older than themselves.[50] Family life for slaves at Gowrie

must have been hard, but the important point is that the desire to find a spouse was still paramount.

Some among the minority who owned more than one plantation allowed their slaves to live in abroad marriages provided that they owned both individuals. James Henry Hammond, for example, wrote in his plantation diary: " 'Negroes living on one plantation and having wives at the other can visit them only between Saturday night and Monday morning.' "[51] However, Hammond also stated: " 'No marriage will be allowed with negroes not belonging to the master.' "[52] By trying to limit cross-plantation unions to those between his own slaves, Hammond was, like most masters, exercising his degree of control. Likewise, a few owners allowed only cross-plantation marriages between their own slaves and those of their white relations. In his autobiography, Jacob Stroyer related the story of how his sisters, Violet and Priscilla, married two men belonging to the brother of Stroyer's master.[53] Such practices inevitably heightened the degree of control that owners held while also enabling them to reaffirm their caring self-image. They could take a paternalistic pride in the existence of both black and white family ties throughout their extended familial networks.

The WPA and full-length slave narratives suggest, however, that it was not the norm for slaves who lived in cross-plantation marriages to belong either to the same owner or to those who were related. Out of fifty-three abroad unions in the South Carolina WPA sample, only four involved spouses whose owners appear to have been related. John Franklin of Spartanburg County lived with his mother on the plantation of Benjamin Bobo, whereas his father lived on the plantation of Bobo's brother-in-law, Henry Franklin.[54] Lucinda Miller and her mother belonged to Mat Alexander, but her father belonged to Mat's brother, who "lived two or three plantations away."[55] A Winnsboro slave, Bill Leitner, and his mother belonged to Robin Brice, while his father belonged to John Partook Brice. Leitner said: "Daddy have to have pass to come to see mammy," although he did not indicate the relationship between the two owners.[56] Neither did Sam Polite, enslaved on St. Helena Island, who testified: "My fadder b'long to Mister Marion Fripp and my mudder b'long to Old Mister B. Fripp."[57]

Owners' attitudes toward cross-plantation marriages were dictated largely by the size of their holdings.[58] An individual who held only a few slaves, including females of childbearing age, would most likely have encouraged these females to marry off their place of residence *in the absence of any potential partners at home*. Since any offspring of the female slave would have substantially increased one's stock of slaves, those in possession of smaller slaveholdings had a vested interest in encouraging their slave women to marry elsewhere. On the positive side, this would have given slaves a broader social world beyond the confines of their immediate environment, and it may also have contributed to the independence of female slaves from their husbands, a point argued by Deborah G. White, who claims that many slave couples saw benefits in cross-plantation marriages. Spouses did not have to witness each other's abuse, and many women gained strength from the independence offered by abroad unions: "If men were not always present to fall back on, women were compelled to develop methods of dealing with domestic responsibilities and crises."[59] Alternatively, though, evidence from slave sources suggests that abroad marriages were a source of much anxiety for slave women, who worried for the safety of their husbands when visiting. They must also have felt guilty if their husbands made illicit visits only to be caught and whipped.

It has been argued that slave women felt pressurized into marrying someone off-plantation rather than no one at all. Perhaps they were aware of the fact that they and their children were economic assets for slaveholders and that owners might sell them if they proved reluctant to increase their supply of slaves.[60] The South Carolina WPA respondent Nancy Washington (detailed previously) had to look for a spouse away from the farm where she lived because there were no possible marriage partners on her quarters.[61] However, female slaves resented any attempts by their masters to force them into wedlock, desiring instead to marry someone of their own choosing. While most women would have preferred to marry off their place of residence than not to marry at all, they sought husbands because the love, support, and companionship of a spouse mitigated against the harsher features of slave life, despite the emotional risks that entering wedlock entailed.

## The Slaves' Perspective

One indication of the typical slave's attachment to family is the absence, in the WPA testimony and elsewhere, of reference to anything like a widespread desire for voluntary separation (divorce). Other supporting evidence includes the dread of white threats to the family and the resilience not only of same-residence marriages but also of cross-plantation unions. It is striking that the South Carolina WPA narratives make virtually no reference to voluntary separation between slave spouses. Several narratives refer to living with stepparents, but in none of these cases was an original slave union broken voluntarily. Of the ten respondents who had stepparents, three had white fathers, and John C. Brown had a white mother.[62] The death of a parent accounted for two cases,[63] and a further two had had a parent sold away.[64] In the remaining two cases there was no testimony concerning the circumstances in which natural parents had been lost.[65]

The case involving Emanuel Elmore is particularly revealing. Elmore reported that his father married Jenny after his mother, Dorcas, was sold away from their home in Spartanburg to Alabama. Eventually, though, Dorcas managed to find her way back home. Elmore explained: "When she did get back to Col. Elmore's [the master's] place, she was lanky, ragged and poor, but Col. Elmore was glad to see her and told her he was not going to let anybody take her off. Jenny had cared so well for her children while she was off, that she liked her." In an unusual move, all resided in the same house until the death of Elmore's mother.[66] The desire to live according to their own norms and to provide a stable environment for their children appears to have taken precedence among his family.

Turning from stepfamilies to female-headed families, the absence of voluntary separations is again significant. Of the twenty female-headed families reported by the informants, two gave no details other than that they lived only with their mothers.[67] A further seven testified that they and their mothers had been sold or given away, so separating them from their fathers.[68] Another five, one of whom was Robert Smith, enslaved in Union County, revealed that their father had been sold away.[69] Smith recalled: "My ma was Chlorrie Greer, and my pa was Bob Young. His white folks ca'ed him off somewhars and I never see'd him [again]."[70] Of the remaining six female-headed families in the sample, the ex-slaves had white fathers and unmarried mothers.[71] Female-headed families in the South Carolina narratives can be best defined as broken two-parent families, families that had been disrupted by owners.

Slaves who ran away also offer some clues about the nature of male-female relationships, since it is likely that couples with strong ties of affection would have been less inclined to run away than those in unhappy marriages. Interestingly, the number of WPA informants who mentioned runaway slaves was rather small (thirty-one, representing 9.3 percent). Few of these indicated the motives for escape, with most commenting only that runaways were whipped upon their return. Recent research has suggested that slaves who did escape were running to, not from, family members. For example, in their pioneering study, John Hope Franklin and Loren Schweninger noted that the desire to be reunited with spouses, children, and parents was widespread among slaves who escaped from their owners.[72] Take the case of Emanuel Elmore's mother, Dorcas, detailed above. She ran away from her new owner in Alabama to be reunited with her husband. Elmore testified: "She said that she stayed in the woods at night. Negroes along the way would give her bread and she would kill rabbits and squirrels and cook and eat in the woods. She would get drunk and beat anyone that tried to stop her from coming back."[73]

The gender dimension of runaway slaves is also significant: of the South Carolina respondents, only nine (6.2 percent) commented on female runaways, while twenty-two (11.6 percent) indicated that those who escaped were men, supporting the findings of Franklin and Schweninger that it was young, single male slaves without family ties or attachments who were most inclined to escape.[74] However, there were notable exceptions, including Linda Brent, who escaped to the northern states after spending years hiding in the roof of a small shed at her grandmother's house. Being able to watch her children from her hideout undoubtedly gave Brent some much-needed strength to cope with her ordeal.[75]

Occasionally, slave couples got the opportunity to run away together, though obviously this involved considerable risks, since black couples were more likely to attract attention than were single blacks.[76] The minutes of the Ebenezer Baptist church of Florence County detail the case of a slave, Philip, who in 1829 absconded from his master. A fellow slave, London, informed the church that Philip had told him he was going to Charleston, from where he planned to leave South Carolina by sea in the hope of obtaining his freedom. However, the captain of the boat refused to take Philip's wife, and Philip was unwilling to leave her. They therefore decided to return home together.[77] Rather than providing evidence of weak and unstable partnerships, the experiences of runaways illustrates the opposite—that couples strove to be together.

Slave testimony suggests that husbands in cross-plantation unions made great efforts to visit their wives and families. Trips were usually made on weekends, and sometimes a midweek meeting might be managed, provided that the distances involved were not too great. Indeed, Sunday visiting appears to have been closely associated with slaves. Caleb Coker's sister, Maria, of Darlington County, mocked the beau of their sister, Lizzy, for "negro like, making his visits on Sunday nights."[78] Disappointingly, comments on how far the WPA respondents' fathers traveled for such visits were rare. However, the distance related by Millie Barber seems to be representative. She stated: "Well, my pa b'longin' to one man and my mammy b'longin' to another, four or five miles apart [in Fairfield County], caused some confusion, mix-up, and heartaches. My pa have to git a pass to come to see my mammy. He come sometimes widout de pass."[79] At a practical level, since journeys had to be made by foot, slave men could not be expected to walk for more than a few miles to see their loved ones, especially when the return journey had to be made before the start of an arduous working day. Walking for many miles without a permit was also a highly risky undertaking for slave men, because the longer they were away from their quarters the greater was the chance of being caught.

In visiting their loved ones, we can see not only the strength of the relationships between slave couples but also a gender division in slave life. It was, for the most part, men who were expected to visit their wives and girlfriends.[80] This exposed them to a bigger risk than females of being caught and punished by patrollers. Deborah G. White raises this issue in relation to female slave independence. She argues that because husbands tended to visit wives, it was more acceptable for men to be seen off-plantation. The movement of slave women away from their quarters was therefore more limited, which proved a liability when it came to running away.[81] White focuses on some of the negative consequences of cross-plantation marriages for female slaves, but she fails to emphasize the great burden placed upon male slaves who wished to visit wives or girlfriends, and in so doing risked often severe physical punishment.

Despite carrying a considerable burden as risk-takers, slave men could extract some virtues from life in an abroad union: they were often spared witnessing their spouse's abuse, they extended their social world in regularly leaving their quarters, and they also had a break from the boredom of their everyday routine.[82] However, the WPA testimony does not support this somewhat positive view of cross-plantation marriages. A persistent theme among the informants is the trouble and risks that husbands and fathers encountered in visiting their families. In particular, they risked beatings at the hands of the patrollers. Julia Woodberry of Marion explained how slave men would have to carry a pass: "You see, de nigger men would want to go to see dey wives en dey would have to get a [per]'mit from dey massa to visit dem."[83] Manda Walker vividly recalled the slaves' dread of these patrols when she told her interviewer about the time her abroad father stayed beyond the leave that was written on his pass and was unfortunate enough to encounter them: "They [the patrollers] say: 'De time done out, nigger.' Pappy try to explain but they pay no 'tention to him. Tied him up, pulled down his breeches, and whupped him right befo' mammy and us chillun. I shudder, to dis day, to think of it."[84] Numerous other respondents also testified to the dread of patrollers and to the courage of lovers, husbands, and fathers in running the gauntlet of patrols.[85] An Anderson County slave, Will Dill, for example, had an uncle who would sneak off at night to visit a girl, giving them the slip.[86] Charlie Grant of Mars Bluff stated that he would not dare leave his quarters to visit anyone without a permit from his master, for fear of being whipped.[87] The low-country ex-slave Ben Horry said that when visiting a girl on the plantation of Benjamin Allston, a pass was vital: "Got to have paper. Got to carry you paper. Dem patroller put you cross a log! Beat you to death."[88]

Slave owners sometimes insisted gently, sometimes violently on the need for a pass, and the types of permits considered acceptable also varied. One slave autobiographer, Sam Aleckson, describes the visit of a slave, Mingo, to his sweetheart, Dolly. Mingo had to show his pass to Dolly's owner, Mr. Ward, who took exception to the fact that the permit did not indicate where Mingo was to visit. He informed Mingo that he never allowed any slave on his land with such a pass and that next time he must obtain one that clearly stated that he was to visit the Ward plantation.[89] John Edwin Fripp's plantation journal contained the blunt entry: "Gave Peter 25 lashes for going to the [St. Helena] island without permission."[90] Similarly, the Darlington slaveholder Ada Bacot wrote in her diary: "I find some of my young negroes have been disobeying my orders, they were found away from home without a pass, I hope I may be able to make them understand without much trouble that I am mistress and will be obeyed."[91]

When planters such as Charles Manigault completely forbade their slaves from marrying off-plantation, a small minority of slaves might still have chosen to wed in this way. The desire to marry someone of their own choosing was crucial for slaves, and some may have been willing to risk the wrath of owners and patrollers by visiting loved ones illicitly. This course of action, though, was extremely dangerous; owners controlled the visiting rights of their slaves through the granting of passes, and being caught without permission mostly had severe repercussions. The issue of visiting rights, as has been shown, was hotly contested between masters and slaves, since even those who had lived in abroad unions with the permission of their owners were still subjected to the indignity of limited visiting rights and the necessity of obtaining a pass.

The persistence of the theme of visiting suggests something of the vigor of cross-plantation marriages. Going to see loved ones or anticipating a visit from a suitor or spouse also provided slaves with a source of excitement under an often monotonous regime. It gave the enslaved something to look forward to at the end of the arduous working week, a chance to share affection and sexual relations, to be cheered up, amused, and entertained. Undoubtedly this gave slaves a sense of hope for the immediate future.[92] Furthermore, the fact that males took the role of visitor, with its attendant risks and hardships, suggests the position of husbands and fathers as protectors and risk-takers: the wives, with their day-to-day childcare responsibilities, were the visited.

The testimony of the WPA informant Charlie Davis, describing his parents' relationship when enslaved in Fairfield County, gives a sense of his father as the family protector and the affection between spouses. Davis regarded his parents as role models in the realm of romantic love. He said: "Mammy said dat de patrollers was as thick as flies 'round dese plantations all de time, and my daddy sho' had to slip 'round to see mammy. Sometime they would ketch him and whip him good, pass or no pass. De patrollers was nothin' but poor white trash, mammy say, and if they didn't whip some slaves, every now and then, they would lose deir jobs. My mammy and daddy got married after freedom, 'cause they didn't git de time for a weddin' befo'. They called deirselves man and wife a long time befo' they was really married, and dat is de reason dat I's as old as I is now. I reckon they was right . . . 'cause they never did want nobody else 'cept each other, nohow. Here I is, I has been married one time and at no time has I ever seen another woman I wanted."[93] Slave sources overwhelmingly show a pattern not of neglect of family life by slaves but of the central role of familial affection in slave communities. This contrasts with the notion that slave husbands were routinely misogynist, putting their interests before those of their wives and taking a perverse pride in abusing and mistreating women.[94]

## Slave Spousal Antagonisms

The pattern of positive relationships between spouses is reinforced when the nature of antagonism between male and female slaves is explored. Intimacy between husbands and wives can be difficult to uncover, especially in the WPA testimony, where the ex-slaves appear to have been reluctant to divulge much information about their marital relationships. Spouses were certainly subject to complex issues of discord that could result in verbal or physical abuse, including the tiredness caused by working for owners as well as for their families, the stresses caused by trying to raise children within bondage, the threat of sale or separation, and the fear of sexual assault upon enslaved women by white men.[95] These factors caused tensions between couples and must undoubtedly have caused some to lose their tempers or to seek comfort in the arms of another. Unfortunately for the historian, testimony that illustrates slave marital strife is rare.

Disharmony within marriage for people of color is, however, apparent in the postbellum period, when some ex-slaves used the Freedmen's Bureau to make complaints about spouses to whom they had been married under bondage. The records of the Freedmen's Bureau have been used to illustrate the strength of slave partnerships, since many freedpeople approached the bureau in the hope of tracing those from whom they had been forcibly separated. Others went to get their marriages validated before American law.[96] However, a less significant though still important trend relates to couples who used the opportunities that freedom gave to relinquish unhappy partnerships. Some freedpeople used the bureau to conciliate in spousal disputes or as a means of escaping from a problematic marriage. Evidence contained within these records suggests that some of the problems that plagued the partnerships of slave men and women had begun during slavery and, therefore, that their marriages could be rocky and tempestuous.

The opportunity for freedom in a general sense was accompanied, for some, by the desire for freedom in a more personal sense. A Texan WPA informant, Rose Williams, had been forced by her master to live with a man she did not love. Shortly after freedom, she told her interviewer, he had to leave.[97] Similarly, Lucy Skipwith used the openings provided by emancipation to leave her husband, Armistead, with whom she had lived "a life of trouble" in Greene County, Alabama.[98] It is difficult to evaluate the reasons behind Lucy's marital strife, but the fact that she had borne two children to white men could have led to friction between her and Armistead. That their own first child died young must also have put the couple under stress.[99]

Complaints that were made to Freedmen's Bureau officials in South Carolina illustrate similar causes of marital strife. These have been well documented by Leslie A. Schwalm, including significant incidents of family violence. For example, Clarinder told bureau agents how her husband, Bungie, had been unfaithful, yet when she reproached him he whipped her.[100] A girl named Amaretta complained that her father had attacked her mother. Similarly, a young man reported a father who had beaten the whole family. Laney described how Caesar, her husband, had whipped her over her back and shoulders. While Schwalm acknowledges that "we have no way of estimating the extent of frequency of domestic violence among freedpeople," the fact that it is mentioned at all is significant for any study of gender relations among ex-slaves and slaves.[101] Although they were sometimes hidden from the eyes of whites, antagonism between spouses did exist.

Another useful historical source for investigating slave spousal disputes can be found within the testimony given to the disciplinary committees of antebellum biracial Baptist churches. Like other southern denominations, Baptist churches used discipline to protect and control the religious lives of slaves: "Because secular law did not regulate slave mar-

riages, the churches did; ministers performed marriages and church discipline committees regulated them, granting divorces and remarriages
with only a tenuous justification from biblical and church authority."[102]
Church disciplinary committees normally met about once a month, with
witnesses or victims reporting on a member's behavior and a committee
then deciding on the appropriate course of action to take. For this study,
the collection of antebellum Baptist church records held on microfilm at
the South Carolina Department of Archives and History was consulted to
examine the reasons behind hostilities between enslaved couples and the
subsequent actions taken by the disciplinary committees.[103] It was found
that among both slave and white couples, the most frequent cause for
marital strife was adultery, though bigamy also occasionally crops up
among slave members.[104] Furthermore, slave and white members appear
to have been equally at risk of excommunication if found guilty of adultery, and this was not something to be taken lightly. Word of misdemeanors was likely to have reached not only church members but wider
slave communities.[105]

However, the complexities of the slaves' situation means that cases
of slave "adultery" tended to require a deeper investigation. The initial
impression given from these records was that slaves were extremely immoral and adulterous. But the status of the spousal relationships of those
excommunicated for adultery is often unclear. For example, on 18 April
1852, the discipline committee of Antioch Baptist church of Society Hill
declared: "Louisa, a servant of Brother Bird was reported for having married and her husband living." She was excluded from the church on 20
June of that year.[106] However, it is not known *where* Louisa's husband was
living. Perhaps he had been sold away; perhaps they had been informally
separated for some time. Similar questions might be raised about Affy, a
slave member of Ebenezer Baptist church in Florence County, who was
charged with "having married another while her former husband was still
living."[107] Indeed, it appears as though the charge of adultery could be
brought against slaves who had aggrieved their owners merely as a reason
to punish them by means of excommunication. In the Barnwell church,
"Brother Collins gave information . . . that his Negro fellow Solomon who
is a member of this church has acted in a very outrageous manner, that he
lately attempted to strike him, that he lives in adultery . . . it was decided
that he be excommunicated from the church."[108] In this case, slave religiosity appears to have been used as a means of control. Enslaved members of Baptist churches appear to have had every right to fear that their
masters could accuse them of crimes such as adultery if they crossed

them. More implicitly, this also suggests that claims of slave adultery may have been exaggerated in the church records.

Sometimes church discipline committees spent considerable time enquiring into the nature of spousal antagonisms among enslaved members. The Barnwell Baptist church appointed a committee to investigate the nature of the differences between the slave Clarion and his wife and reported that "in their opinion he has not been to blame for their separation but thinks it would be opening a door to[o] wide to permit him to take another wife."[109] The churches obviously had a dilemma in striving for certain levels of morality, on the one hand, and on the other hand acknowledging that slave marriages could run into difficulties that were caused not only by the breakup of relationships but also by the fact that owners could and did separate those they held in bondage if they so desired. This problem was even more pronounced when, as was sometimes the case, enslaved members belonged to white members.

Church committees sometimes had to face difficult questioning from slaves. "Big Sam," a member of the Elim Baptist church at Effingham, caused a committee to be set up after he "asked information of the church how he should proceed in reference to taking a wife, or what woman he should consider his wife."[110] Churches had to tread a fine line, knowing the precariousness of slave marriages and the often ambivalent attitudes of owners toward them. In this case, the committee does not appear to have reported any findings to the church. The Mountain Creek Baptist church of Anderson County excluded a slave member, Sambo, for "marrying a second wife and the first wife living *in reach* of him."[111] Obviously, it is the phrase "in reach" that is of significance. If Sambo had been separated from his wife by distance alone (most likely through enforced sale or separation) then it is likely that the church would have acted differently and allowed him to marry another. An unnamed slave member of the Hopewell Baptist church of Chester County was similarly charged with "taking up with another woman while he had a wife and family in another district from whence he came."[112] In this case, it is probable that the church would have had a different attitude toward the new relationship than that of the new master. While owners would be glad of the potential for future offspring that a new relationship might bring, the church inevitably felt it had a moral duty to respect the first marriage and family of the enslaved member.

These cases give clues about how churches sought to reconcile religious convictions with the day-to-day realities of a slave system. Janet Duitsman Cornelius has argued that, for the most part, churches refused to confront owners over the sale and separation of married slaves.[113] Sylvia R. Frey and Betty Wood have noted that some churches therefore adopted a relatively flexible approach to marriage vows, for example, by declaring that the marriage vow remained inviolate "until death or removal."[114] Margaret Washington Creel has regarded the churches as pharisaical, and it is true that there was an ultimate irony inherent in the disciplinary committees. Baptist slave owners, like many others, separated slave families regardless of their religious convictions. Thus, the way in which the committees treated slaves as though they had the freedom to make their own choices certainly displayed an element of hypocrisy.[115]

Female slave members do not appear to have been excommunicated for adultery any more than were men. However, there were cases where enslaved women were excommunicated for having children outside wedlock, suggesting that they were more likely than men to be excluded for reasons related to marriage and children.[116] Occasionally, too, the committees related instances of domestic abuse. Ephraim, a slave member of the First Baptist church of Darlington, was charged with having used violence against his wife, though he was excused.[117] The Philadelphia Baptist church of Pauline similarly received a charge against its female slave member, Betsy, for "striking her husband."[118] No instances of domestic violence inflicted either by women or men emerged from a reading of the South Carolina WPA narratives. However, it is true that this would be an issue the informants might have been reluctant to discuss with white interviewers, who themselves were unlikely to put questions of this nature to the ex-slaves.[119] The fact that it was not mentioned does not mean it did not happen, as evidence from Freedmen's Bureau and church records has shown. However, the existence of so many references to the affection between slave couples within the WPA testimony supports the claim that love and support between spouses was the norm.

Slave marital disharmony was, however, referred to in the manuscript source materials left by owners, and it was also mentioned once in the sample of full-length autobiographies when Charles Ball cited a female slave, Lydia, who did not enjoy the benefits of a supportive marriage. Lydia was married to an African slave who claimed he had once been a priest. He was not accustomed to performing any sort of work at home, and Ball wrote that "he now maintained, as far as he could, the same kind of lazy dignity that he had enjoyed. . . . This man was very irritable, and often beat and otherwise maltreated his wife, on the slightest provocation."[120] Ball seems to be suggesting that Lydia's husband beat her because he had an unusual African background, implicitly suggesting that the norm among American-born slaves was toward spousal support.

Often owners liked to get involved in the marital affairs of their slaves. While some undoubtedly tried to keep their marital affairs private, slaveholders generally preferred to believe that they were the ones who knew "what was best" for those they held in bondage. James Henry Hammond held "trials of divorce and adultery cases" whereby he ordered—often by means of a flogging—couples to stay together or to separate. He also whipped his black driver, Tom Kollock, for "interfering" with another slave's wife.[121] Unfortunately, though, the informal anecdotes of owners about their slaves' relationships are often so brief that they tend to raise more questions than they answer. The South Carolina mistress Emily Wharton Sinkler, for example, made reference to slave marital volatility when she wrote that her slave, Mollo, had complained that his wife was "continually fighting and scratching him," but she elaborated on this seemingly volatile relationship no further.[122] More poignantly, John Springs of Springfield plantation, York County, described to his son the death of their slave, Shadrock, who had committed suicide by hanging himself. Springs attributed Shadrock's death to the treatment he received at the hands of the "merciless woman he had for a wife."[123]

Owners sometimes referred to slave marital disharmony more explicitly when it impacted upon their own lives. A case of alleged domestic abuse by Jim, the slave husband of Maria, was detailed in one of the many letters of Elizabeth Franklin Perry to her husband. Perry's letter raises many issues, the first of which is the extent to which slave mothers sought to protect their children. Maria's mother, Winnie—enslaved to Mr. Couble—had visited Mrs. Perry and begged her for help. Jim had been abusing Maria, she alleged. He apparently "had beat her, broke her head, cut her face." Winnie said that Mr. Couble (Maria's former owner) would happily take her back with the consent of the Perrys, thus keeping her away from her abusive husband. On hearing this news, Mrs. Perry went to visit Maria and was shocked to find her living in squalor. "Everything about her [was] filthy, the floor not even swept, the beds, pails etc. . . . all dirty." Maria had a scar on her neck where Jim had hit her, but this did not concern Perry as much as the state of Maria's cabin. Therefore, instead of offering help, Mrs. Perry gave Maria advice about "doing better" in her domestic duties. Winnie had tried to help her daughter and had turned to Mrs. Perry for support. Mrs. Perry, however, seems to have regarded Maria's beating as justifiable because she was not adept in her role as a homemaker.

Mrs. Perry's lack of sympathy for her slave was further enhanced when she spoke to Maria's husband, Jim, who had no qualms in admitting that he had hit Maria three times—she deserved it, he claimed, before telling his mistress that he regretted ever marrying her. Jim described how Maria was obstinate, lazy, and dirty; she would not clean the house, nor wash or mend his clothes. Maria gave them meals on dirty plates "with peas all sticking to them." Worse, Jim claimed that he had to neglect his own field work to keep their cabin clean. He elaborated on the poor quality of work that she completed for the Perrys. While James (another troublesome slave) would work if he was watched, Jim alleged that "Maria you could not make work, and the more you coaxed and tried to please her the worse she was. She would not hoe or do anything." Charles, another of the Perrys' slaves, backed up Jim's assertions, after which Mrs. Perry gave her full support to Jim and, possibly because Maria was failing in her work for her owners as well as in her domestic responsibilities, decided that she wanted rid of her. She decided to take up the offer described by Winnie, whereby Mr. Couble would take Maria back. However, Mr. Couble indicated that Winnie had no authority to claim this, saying that "nothing would induce him to take Maria back, not if he were given five negroes along with her."

Enraged to learn that her husband had bought a lazy slave, especially when Mr. Couble suggested that he had informed Mr. Perry of Maria's problems at the time of purchase, Mrs. Perry directed her anger toward her husband: "I think it was astonishing you should think of buying her. . . . I want her sold to the first drover [slave trader] who passes . . . you are not strict enough with your servants, you can't make them work, and Mr. Couble says you are not a good manager of servants, and I have always said that. Now I have done with Maria, hoping you will sell her as soon as possible." Realizing that he had an opportunity to be freed from his troublesome wife, Jim also tried to induce his owners into selling Maria by telling Mrs. Perry that he would rather be sold than continue living with her.[124] It is ironic that Winnie's initial appeal to Mrs. Perry to help her abused daughter had consequences far worse than she could have anticipated. Since the bulk of domestic work fell on slave women, a failure to conform to expected gender conventions could have dire consequences, perfectly illustrated by Elizabeth Franklin Perry's lack of sympathy in this case.[125] Because she failed to perform her perceived "duties" in her own home, Maria was the victim of a sexual discrimination not unique to slavery. However, race is also important here: mistress and slave were separated by race, and this division may have prevented Mrs. Perry from empathizing with Maria's plight.[126]

Mistresses may have gotten more involved in their slaves' marital disputes than their husbands.[127] Aunt "JFP," of the Guignard family of Lexington County, desired to separate her slave, Hetty, from her husband, with whom she had a volatile relationship, by bringing her to work in the Big House. However, as with the preceding case of the Perrys' slave, Maria, self-interest appears to have played a significant role. Aunt JFP wrote that despite the fact that Hetty had begged to leave her husband, she should only be permitted to do so once the crop was laid.[128] Since it was illegal for slaves to read or write, it was rare for slaves to write to their owners. However, a few did master these skills, and the Lawton family papers contain a letter to "missus" from her slave, Lavinia.[129] Highly distressed about the separation of her daughter, Aggy, from her husband, Jimmy, Lavinia begged her mistress not to allow Jimmy to set up home with another female slave who was "worse than Mary Magdalene."[130] Lavinia's powerful pleading and her obvious religiosity suggests that she made a strong case in striving for the intervention of her owners. She described the other woman as "a devil . . . her sparkling black eye catching other wimmin's husbands." She then pleaded: "Dear Missis can't you take pity on Aggy and use your influence in stopping this wretched business."[131] The willingness of slaves to approach their owners for support in times of crisis is immediately apparent from this testimony. It also reveals the seriousness of marriage for many slaves and indicates that adultery was highly frowned upon. Unfortunately for historians, it is also a problem mostly obscured from view. Few explicit references to adultery (such as Lavinia's letter) exist either in owners' records or, as has been shown, in slave source materials such as the WPA narratives.

It was generally assumed by the wider society of the nineteenth-century South that since men, including slaves, were the heads of households, they had the ultimate control over their wives, including the right to beat them. Therefore, one way in which owners attempted to exert control over those they held in bondage was by removing or controlling this "right" from their slave men. For example, the rulebook of John B. Miller's plantation near Sumter contained the entry: "No man must whip his wife without my permission."[132] This suggests that wife battering did occur and that Miller believed he was denying his slave men the liberty to use physical violence on their spouses. Ironically, though, for the majority of slaves it was not through violence but through affection that couples managed to maintain their humanity and the desire for an independent community life.

Historical evidence ultimately suggests that domestic violence in slave communities was not a significant problem and that the norm was toward spousal support, although considering the nature of the institution under which they lived, it is not surprising that violence could sometimes erupt between husbands and wives. WPA testimony indicates that the threat of physical or sexual abuse came overwhelmingly from white men, not black men.[133] However, any evidence specifically relating to any *sexual* abuse that slave women received at the hands of their menfolk is notoriously difficult to discover. Scarcity of data has often meant that generalizations about male-female relationships under slavery have been made on the basis of preconceived notions about the nature of relationships between men and women. For example, bell hooks, who believes that "sexism looms as large as racism as an oppressive force in the lives of black women," claims that male slaves in the antebellum South did sexually abuse black women, and that in doing so they were imitating the behavior of white men.[134]

Susan Brownmiller has similarly argued that "it is consistent with the nature of oppression that within an oppressed group, men abuse women." She notes that a variety of men, from plantation masters, through lower-class whites, down to the black driver on a plantation, were all in a position to sexually abuse female slaves, since all played enforcer roles within the system of slavery.[135] However, Brownmiller displays only two pieces of evidence to back up her claims. One is from a Maryland advertisement for a runaway who had raped a slave woman.[136] The other comes from the journal of a Georgia mistress, Fanny Kemble. When Kemble questioned her husband's slaves about the paternity of their offspring, the name of a slave driver was frequently mentioned.[137] Despite Brownmiller's lack of systematic evidence on the rape of slave women by slave men, she does raise an important point when she mentions that the rapist in question was a driver. It may be suggested that elite males, who were in positions of power and authority over others, would have been the most likely to abuse enslaved women sexually.

Within the South Carolina WPA testimony, only one case of the possible rape of a slave woman by a slave man was mentioned, and it was described in a rather oblique way. Benjamin Horry reported that on his low-country plantation a slave driver would set the women tasks that were impossible to achieve. When they failed to complete them he would then send them to a barn. Talking to his daughter, Lillie, Horry said: "You getting this beating not for your task—for your flesh!" Horry indicated that he and his father had witnessed the appalling activities that took place in the barn at the hands of the driver, and he also felt that a combination of the driver's black skin and his enslavement were responsible for his actions. White overseers, he professed, acted differently because they had a vested interest in keeping their jobs.[138] Horry later divulged more information about the punishments inflicted by the driver. His own mother, he testified, once "won't do all he say." She had also refused to go to the barn, so the driver had given her more and more tasks, which of course she failed to finish. Horry's mother was then forced into the barn and strapped onto a contraption called "the pony" where she was spread out and tied to the ground. It must have been extremely painful for Horry to then relate how "she been give twenty-five to fifty lashes till the blood flow. And my father and me stand right there and look and ain't able to lift a hand!"[139] Implicitly, Horry might have been suggesting that his mother was whipped because she would not submit to the driver's sexual demands, and compounding the horror of this event is the fact that the woman's own son and husband bore witness to it.

The sense of helplessness expressed by Horry over this occurrence goes against the notion that the first instinct of males under slavery was toward self-preservation. Moreover, the testimony of other males held in bondage supports this claim. Jacob Stroyer felt a desire to protect his mother—compounded by frustration at his own helplessness—when a white groom whipped her.[140] The Virginia ex-slave Allen Wilson similarly described the physical punishment inflicted by an overseer (he does not say whether black or white) upon his mother, who was tied to a peach tree and whipped with cowhide. Wilson's anguish was clearly still raw, as he exclaimed: "Lawd, Lawd, I prayed Gawd dat someday he'd open a way fur me to protect mother."[141]

The dreadful experiences suffered by Ben Horry's mother support the claim that slave men (in this case a black driver) imitated the behavior of white men under slavery; since white men sexually abused slave women, some slave men, especially those in powerful positions, may have desired to do the same.[142] However, it is the extent to which slave men as a whole sexually abused slave women, compared with the much greater extent of such abuse slave women suffered at the hands of white men, that is significant. For this investigation the entire collection of WPA slave narratives (including some supplementary volumes) was examined using the *Index to "The American Slave."*[143] The sample therefore comprised several thousand narratives. All index entries for "Overseers, Drivers and Foremen (Black)" were consulted, along with all entries for "Sexual Practices, Slave" and "Slave Breeding." Apart from the South Carolina case just cited, only three other examples of slave women being sexually abused by male slaves were found. In the first case, the man in question was a black overseer, which again lends support to the proposition that slave men in positions of authority were more likely than others to harass women sexually. The respondent, Anna Baker of Mississippi, said that her grandmother had run away during slavery: "It was on 'count o' de nigger overseers. . . . Dey kep' a-tryin' to mess 'roun' wid her an' she wouldn' have nothin' to do wid 'em."[144]

In the second instance, Mary Gaffney of Texas said that she hated the man her master forced her to marry: "When I was married it was just a home wedding, fact is, I just hated the man I married but it was what Maser said do. . . . I would not let that negro touch me and he told Maser and Maser gave me a real good whipping, so that night I let that negro have his way."[145] It is not known whether Gaffney's husband would have sexually harassed her had his master not said that they were married. Perhaps he believed it was his "right" as a husband to impose himself on his wife, and Gaffney also seems to have acknowledged that she had to submit herself to him. The third case of sexual abuse—very similar to that described by Gaffney—also came from the Texas narratives and was related by Rose Williams, who said that she was forced by her master to live with another slave (Rufus) against her will. Initially she tried to fight off his sexual advances but relented when her master threatened her with the whip.[146] The fact that only four cases of sexual abuse by slave men were mentioned in the massive collection of WPA narratives (and no mention of black-on-black abuse was detailed in the full-length autobiographies used for this study) means that—despite the problems associated with the reluctance to divulge information—the risk of sexual abuse by slave men was small, especially when compared with the risk posed by white men.[147]

A somewhat crude comparison of the relative significance of black rape and white rape in the South Carolina WPA narratives shows that there were twenty-nine respondents who had knowledge of either the sexual abuse of slave women at the hands of white men or of sexual liaisons between slave women and white men.[148] This represents 8.7 percent of all respondents, compared with the 0.3 percent of respondents—namely, Horry—who knew of black-on-black sexual abuse. Even allowing for the fact that some of the sexual encounters between enslaved females and white males may have been voluntary relationships, when compared with the single incident of black-on-black sexual abuse related by the South Carolina ex-slaves, it can be said with relative certainty that the rape of slave women by white men was far more common than that by black men. Despite being protectors of and providers for their families, men held under bondage did not normally attempt to assert their gender dominance through physical or sexual abuse. The relationships between slave men and women can be best characterized as broadly egalitarian and supportive, and the norm within their communities was a climate of togetherness.[149]

Within the WPA narratives, examples of slave men trying to protect their wives against physical or sexual abuse at the hands of white men reinforces the claim that supportive relationships were typical. While it is true that a lack of evidence relating to slave husbands abusing wives could, in part, be because ex-slaves sought to hide these events, such abuse is so completely against the positive tone of the testimony that it seems inconceivable that it could have been a significant part of the inner thoughts of ex-slaves.[150] Instead, cases can be seen of husbands protecting wives, sometimes boldly, sometimes quietly. Philip Evans recalled a dramatic case of a husband protecting wife when an overseer insulted and beat his aunt. His uncle, Dennis, attacked the overseer before running away to the woods. As was common with many runaways, he stayed there for some time, only returning to the plantation at night when it was safe to get something to eat. However, Dennis took a great risk when he joined Evans's father on a wagon journey to Winnsboro and was pointed out to an officer. Evans recalled how he was clamped, jailed, and later taken to the town whipping post. His hands were put in stocks, and his feet were tied before he was stripped and whipped.[151]

Henry Gladney's father, known as "Bill the Giant," used to try to protect his wife from the advances of other slave men and once broke the leg of a man for "looking at her." His owner, John Mobely, intervened, threatening Bill with the whip. Fortunately, Gladney's mother begged that her husband be spared this punishment, and Mobely relented. Gladney recalled that she had been scared that her husband would run away if he had been punished in this way.[152] Similarly, in the narrative of "Wild Tom," contained within Tom Jones's autobiography, Tom killed an overseer who was responsible for whipping his wife to death.[153] The courageous stands of these men in trying to protect their wives is commendable. Perhaps, however, an element of caution should be expressed. Their behavior, if not violent, was certainly volatile, and one might question whether their aggressive actions were confined solely to those who mistreated their wives. Certainly in the case of Henry Gladney's father, who broke a man's leg merely for "looking" at his wife, it may be questioned what the outcome would have been if his wife had been the one "looking."[154]

This chapter has pointed to the numerical importance and resilience of cross-plantation unions. However, slaves had to fight for the freedom to live in these marriages; aside from practical considerations such as size of holding, owners had much to gain from imposing rules and regulations concerning abroad unions. It has been suggested that slaveholders sought to instill in their slaves a Protestant work ethic through systems of rewards and punishments. They "wanted devoted, hard-working, responsible slaves who identified their fortunes with the fortunes of their masters. Planters sought to imbue slaves with a 'Protestant' work ethic and to transform that ethic from a state of mind into a high level of production."[155] The imposition of rules concerning cross-plantation marriages was therefore an ideal vehicle for implementing these systems. Slaves might have been "allowed" to marry off their place of residence as a reward for good behavior, or they could have been prevented from doing so if they "behaved badly." It is questionable, however, how much owners' actions encouraged a "work ethic" whereby slaves were anxious to please. Since the enslaved sought to marry whom they chose regardless of their "behavior" in the eyes of their masters, systems of rewards and punishments would likely have increased slaves' resentment and distrust of their owners. This would have decreased the degree of accommodation between master and slave.[156]

It is also hard to reconcile attitudes toward cross-plantation marriages with the notion of paternalistic slave owners as described by Eugene Genovese. He wrote: "A paternalism accepted by both masters and slaves—but with radically different interpretations—afforded a fragile bridge across the intolerable contradictions inherent in a society based on racism, slavery, and class exploitation. . . . Paternalism's insistence upon mutual obligations—duties, responsibilities, and ultimately even rights—implicitly recognized the slaves' humanity."[157] However, slaveholders were paternalistic only when they wanted to be. Those who were truly benevolent with regard to slave marriage did allow their slaves to wed someone of their own choosing, regardless of where they lived or the impact this might have had upon life in the quarters. The majority, though, did not "indulge" their slaves in this way, preferring instead to put their own priorities about work and reproduction above any consideration of slave romantic love.

Owners' ambivalent attitudes toward cross-plantation marriages correlate with the more recent interpretations that have been espoused on their treatment of slaves. William Dusinberre and Michael Tadman have highlighted the importance of "privilege" in master-slave relations. In some cases, owners may have indulged certain slaves by buying their chosen partners, while the marriages of certain favored individuals would have been protected from sale and separation. Tadman has suggested that the marriages most likely to be protected were those of a subset of favored key slaves with whom owners felt that they had special bonds of affection and respect. It is likely that these were high-ranking house servants, with whom slaveholders had the most contact and were most likely to develop a deep sense of trust.[158] Tadman points to the "poverty of paternalism," emphasizing that there was little content in the paternalism of owners: "the term 'paternalism'—which in the end implies bonds of mutual affection and respect—seems to confuse more than it clarifies. It might be better, if retaining the term paternalism in the context of American slavery, to talk of a white *discourse* of paternalism" (italics added).[159] The existence of key slaves might explain the variety of attitudes that owners held toward cross-plantation marriages: firstly, it allows us to see that paternalism was a mask and that attitudes toward abroad unions, as far as rank-and-file slaves were concerned, were dictated by practical necessity and the desire to increase the supply of slaves rather than by a paternalist ethos; secondly, the concept shows that owners used those who did reside in cross-plantation marriages as evidence of their alleged benevolence. By suggesting that all slaves were free to make their own marital choices, owners polished their image as altruistic, caring masters.

Moreover, despite the fact that the spousal relationships of some "privileged" slaves would have been taken seriously by their owners, Dusinberre has warned that such "privileges" could easily be taken away. Charles Manigault depended upon this notion as a tool in governing his slaves. It was the free gift of the powerful master and could at any moment be withdrawn. "Manigault granted privileges in order to make his slaves more dependent on himself, not to convert his slaves into the independent possessors of customary rights."[160] Both Dusinberre and Tadman have done much to expose the notion of slaveholder benevolence as a myth. Most lived under a harsh system that was imposed upon them by their masters,[161] and it is important to remember that if owners wanted to forbid their slaves from forming cross-plantation unions, for the most part, they had the power to do so. Undoubtedly, this would have left slaves with a distrust of their owners and contributed to increasing animosity and psychological distance between the worlds of the two.

It is clear that owners only approved of abroad marriages when it suited them to do so. For smaller slaveholders, the advantages of such unions are clear, but for larger planters the picture becomes more complex. In general, with little to gain from such betrothals, owners were reluctant to grant their slaves this "privilege" and the increased degree of autonomy it could bring. Therefore, most of those who managed to live within a cross-plantation marriage either relied on their owners' approval or they trod a risky path in attempting to visit their spouses behind the backs of their masters and the patrollers. While for a tiny minority of slaves, their owners not only allowed off-plantation unions but also would either buy or hire out spouses to keep partners together, such cases were rare. Furthermore, even when they did occur, it was rarely for reasons of pure benevolence, except for the particularly indulged or key slaves. Mostly, owners would have desired either the labor or the fertility of an extra slave, though it is doubtful whether they gave their slaves that impression. An appearance of benevolence could work wonders in terms of plantation discipline.

## Notes

1. I am grateful to Betty Wood for her useful suggestions on using church records for historical research.

2. See Stampp, *Peculiar Institution;* Moynihan, *Negro Family;* Rainwater and Yancey, *Moynihan Report and the Politics of Controversy;* and Davis, *Women, Race, and Class,* chap. 1.

3. See Gutman, *Black Family in Slavery and Freedom.* William Dusinberre, in his study of the harsh rice regime of the low country, has also highlighted the strains faced by slave couples that lived apart. See *Them Dark Days,* 106.

4. Genovese, *Roll, Jordan, Roll,* 473.

5. Steckel, *Economics of U.S. Slave and Southern White Fertility,* 229.

6. Escott, *Slavery Remembered,* 50–52, 62.

7. Crawford, "Quantified Memory," 149–54.

8. Ibid., 151.

9. See Hudson, *To Have and to Hold,* 142–45. He suggests that Deborah G. White has been too positive about the nature of cross-plantation marriages and rightly points out that living in such unions did have considerable disadvantages. It will be argued here, however, that these problems notwithstanding, slaves prioritized marrying someone of their own choosing.

10. Brenda E. Stevenson, in *Life in Black and White,* and Carole E. Merritt, in "Slave Family and Household Arrangements," found high numbers of cross-plantation marriages.

11. Five respondents were married before the Civil War. Alfred Sligh was twenty-three years old in 1865 and was a field worker who resided with his wife, Sarah (Rawick, *American Slave,* vol. 3, pt. 4, 92–94). Gordon Bluford, a female, was twenty years old in 1865 and a house worker who resided with 250 other slaves and married Arthur Bluford, who belonged to the same owner (ibid., vol. 2, pt. 1, 62–64). Louisa Davis was 103 years old at the time of her interview. She was a house worker who had a cross-plantation marriage (ibid., 299–303). Nancy Washington was thirty-two years old in 1865 and worked in the house, then the field. Since her owner only owned her mother and siblings, she married abroad (ibid., vol. 3, pt. 4, 184–87). Finally, Albert Means, nineteen years old in 1865 and a field worker, testified that his wife, Jane, belonged to a different owner (ibid., vol. 3, pt. 3, 182–84).

12. These were Ryer Emmanuel and Will Dill. Emmanuel's mother appears to have been an important domestic and may have lived in the Big House. Dill, who belonged to Zeek Long, did not say why his parents resided separately. See Rawick, *American Slave,* vol. 2, pt. 2, 22–26; and vol. 2, pt. 1, 319–23.

13. The South Carolina WPA results can be compared with those from the full-length narratives. Only two autobiographers (Charles Ball and Tom Jones) comment on their own family structure upon reaching adulthood, both of whom resided within cross-plantation unions. However, of the ten writers who mention their parents' residential arrangements, four had parents who lived together; three had parents who had abroad marriages; and three were raised within female-headed households. Compared with the WPA results, a higher proportion of autobiographers lived within female-headed house-

holds. However, the percentages of those who lived within nuclear and cross-plantation families are roughly the same.

14. Rawick, *American Slave,* vol. 3, pt. 4, 184–87.

15. The South Carolina low country as it is used here refers to the coastal districts of Beaufort, Colleton, Charleston, Georgetown, and Horry. See Stauffer, *Formation of Counties in South Carolina,* 14.

16. See Crawford, "Slave Family," 345–47.

17. In this study, house servants were slightly more likely than field slaves to have parents who resided in nuclear households. The parents of field slaves showed a 50 percent split between these two marriage types. See chap. 3 for further details.

18. Escott, *Slavery Remembered,* 50–51.

19. Crawford, "Quantified Memory," 149.

20. Ibid., 155.

21. Malone, *Sweet Chariot,* 6.

22. Ibid., 14–16.

23. Ibid., 254.

24. Ibid., 227.

25. Ibid., 202 n.3.

26. Stevenson, *Life in Black and White,* 222. On matrifocality, see also White, "Female Slaves," 256; and Robertson, "Africa into the Americas?" 9–20.

27. Stevenson, *Life in Black and White,* 212.

28. Ibid., xii.

29. Merritt, "Slave Family," 85.

30. Ibid., 128.

31. Ibid., 112, 131, 219–21. Merritt uses this evidence to criticize Herbert G. Gutman's emphasis on the importance of nuclear families, claiming that his data is atypical due to the large size of the holdings he examined.

32. Ibid., 221.

33. Quoted in Malone, *Sweet Chariot,* 327 n.78.

34. Quoted in Hudson, *To Have and to Hold,* 142.

35. Letter to Benjamin Franklin Perry from Elizabeth Perry, 1 December 1852, Benjamin Franklin Perry Papers, SCL.

36. Rosengarten, *Tombee,* 155.

37. Catterall, *Judicial Cases Concerning American Slavery,* 403

38. See Letter to James S. Guignard from John Guignard [son], 19 October 1828. Guignard Family Papers, SCL.

39. Ibid., 20 October 1828, Guignard Family Papers, SCL.

40. Rawick, *American Slave,* vol. 2, pt. 3, 178.

41. See entry for 14 March 1856, David Gavin Diary, Southern Historical Collection (hereafter SHC).

42. "Negro Rules for Government," Cornhill Plantation Book, 1827–73, [Plantation of John B. Miller], McDonald-Furman Papers, WRPL.

43. "Rules for Government of Plantation," ibid.

44. List of Plantation Rules, February 1815, Conway-Black-Davis Family Papers, SCL.

45. List of Plantation Rules, Andrew Flinn Plantation Book, 1840, SCL.

46. Ibid.

47. Lowery, *Life on the Old Plantation,* 42.

48. Letter to Mr. J. F. Cooper [overseer at Gowrie] from Charles Izard Manigault, 10 January 1848, Letterbook, 1846–48, Charles Izard Manigault Papers, SCL.

49. For more on Manigault's plantations, see the introduction to Clifton, ed., *Life and Labor on Argyle Island;* and Young, "Ideology and Death."

50. Dusinberre, *Them Dark Days*, 106.

51. Quoted in Burton, *In My Father's House*, 163 n.50.

52. Ibid., 169 n.69. See also Faust, *James Henry Hammond and the Old South*, 85.

53. Stroyer, *My Life in the South*, 39.

54. Rawick, *American Slave*, vol. 2, pt. 2, 84.

55. Ibid., vol. 3, pt. 3, 191.

56. Ibid., 100–101.

57. Ibid., 271.

58. J. William Harris's study of slavery in the Augusta area, where slaveholdings were generally small, illustrates that most owners' attitudes to cross-plantation marriages were influenced by their size of holding. Here, most masters conceded the right to wed abroad. See *Plain Folk and Gentry in a Slave Society*, 44–47.

59. White, *Ar'n't I a Woman?* 154.

60. Weiner, *Mistresses and Slaves*, 136.

61. Rawick, *American Slave*, vol. 3, pt. 4, 184–87.

62. These were Adeline Brown (Rawick, *American Slave*, vol. 2, pt. 1, 127), Isiah Jeffries (ibid., vol. 3, pt. 3, 17), and Alexander Robertson (ibid., vol. 3, pt. 4, 31). Testimony of John C. Brown can be found in ibid., vol. 2, pt. 1, 127.

63. These were Andy Brice and George Fleming (ibid., vol. 2, pt. 1, 75; and vol. 11, 126).

64. These were Emanuel Elmore and Sena Moore (ibid., vol. 2, pt. 2, 6; and vol. 3, pt. 3, 209).

65. These were Charlie Davis and Hunter Hester (ibid., vol. 2, pt. 1, 245; and vol. 2, pt. 3, 331).

66. Ibid., vol. 2, pt. 2, 9. See also Hudson, *To Have and to Hold*, 168.

67. These were Jane Bradley and Pauline Worth. See Rawick, *American Slave*, vol. 2, pt. 1, 74; and vol. 3, pt. 4, 260.

68. These were Francis Andrews (ibid., vol. 2, pt. 1, 17), Thomas Campbell (ibid., 176), Thomas Jefferson (ibid., vol. 3, pt. 2, 20), Emma Jeter (ibid., vol. 3, pt. 3, 33), Jimmie Johnson (ibid., 53), Mary Scott (ibid., vol. 3, pt. 4, 81), and Josephine Stewart (ibid., 151).

69. These were John Collins (ibid., vol. 2, pt. 1, 224), Sim Greely (ibid., vol. 2, pt. 2, 290), Andrew Means (ibid., vol. 3, pt. 3, 182), Robert Smith (ibid., vol. 11, 294), and Aleck Woodward (ibid., vol. 3, pt. 4, 253).

70. Ibid., vol. 11, 294.

71. These were Ed Barber (ibid., vol. 2, pt. 1, 34), John Davenport (ibid., 240), Henry Davis (ibid., 260), Thomas Dixon (ibid., 324), Jack Johnson (ibid., vol. 3, pt. 3, 41), and Victoria Perry (ibid., 260).

72. See Franklin and Schweninger, *Runaway Slaves*, 52 and 57–63, for descriptions of slave spouses running to each other or escaping together.

73. Rawick, *American Slave*, vol. 2, pt. 2, 9.

74. Franklin and Schweninger, *Runaway Slaves*, 210.

75. See Jacobs, *Incidents*, chap. 21 (114–17).

76. Franklin and Schweninger, *Runaway Slaves*, 62.

77. See entries for March–July 1829, Minutes of Ebenezer Baptist Church, Florence County, South Carolina Department of Archives and History (hereafter SCDAH).

78. Letter to Caleb Coker from sister, Maria, 16 September 1844, Lide-Coker Family Papers, SCL.

79. Rawick, *American Slave*, vol. 2, pt. 1, 39.

80. The proposition that it was generally only male slaves who traveled to visit wives and girlfriends is supported by Orville Vernon Burton. See *In My Father's House*, 163. However, Dusinberre notes an example of an elderly slave (Daniel) whose wife (Miley)

was much younger than him. In this case, Miley was granted permission by Manigault to visit her husband. See *Them Dark Days*, 152.

81. White, *Ar'n't I a Woman?* 76.

82. See Stevenson, *Life in Black and White*, 231.

83. Rawick, *American Slave*, vol. 3, pt. 4, 238.

84. Ibid., 170–71.

85. For more on slave patrollers, see Hadden, *Slave Patrols*, esp. 116–17.

86. Rawick, *American Slave*, vol. 3, pt. 4, 319.

87. Ibid., vol. 2, pt. 2, 174.

88. Ibid., 304.

89. Aleckson, *Before the War*, 56.

90. Entry for 2 September 1858, John Edwin Fripp Plantation Journal, SHC.

91. Entry for 11 February 1861, Ada Bacot Diary, SCL. See also Berlin, ed., *Confederate Nurse*.

92. See Hudson, *To Have and to Hold*, 160.

93. Rawick, *American Slave*, vol. 2, pt. 1, 252.

94. See hooks, *Ain't I a Woman?* 35.

95. See Stevenson, "Distress and Discord," 117–18.

96. See, for example, Gutman, *Black Family in Slavery and Freedom*, esp. chaps. 1 and 9.

97. Rawick, *American Slave*, Supplement Series 2, vol. 10, pt. 9: *Texas Narratives*, 4117.

98. See Sterling, ed., *We Are Your Sisters*, 310.

99. See Miller, *"Dear Master,"* 21, 159.

100. Schwalm, *A Hard Fight For We*, 234.

101. Ibid., 260–66, contains these and other cases of marital strife that were reported to the Freedmen's Bureau.

102. Cornelius, *Slave Missions and the Black Church*, 37. See also "Slave Marriages in a Georgia Congregation."

103. A full list of the Baptist church records examined in this study is contained in the bibliography.

104. See, for example, minutes for 7 July 1844, Barnwell Baptist Church, SCDAH.

105. See Hudson, "'The Average Truth,'" 179–80.

106. Minutes for 18 April 1852 and 20 June 1852, Antioch Baptist Church, Society Hill, SCDAH.

107. Minutes for 3 October 1829, Ebenezer Baptist Church, Florence County, SCDAH.

108. Minutes for 1 September 1838, Barnwell Baptist Church, SCDAH.

109. Minutes for 4 October 1828, ibid.

110. Minutes for November 1858, Elim Baptist Church, Effington, SCDAH.

111. Minutes for June 1833, Mountain Creek Baptist Church, Anderson County, SCDAH.

112. Minutes for 1828, Hopewell Baptist Church, Chester County, SCDAH.

113. Cornelius, *Slave Missions and the Black Church*, 41.

114. Frey and Wood, *Come Shouting to Zion*, 185.

115. Creel, *"A Peculiar People,"* 245.

116. See especially the records of the First Baptist Church of Edgefield, SCDAH.

117. Minutes for 28 November 1858, First Baptist Church, Darlington, SCDAH.

118. Minutes for April–June 1839, Philadelphia Baptist Church, Pauline, SCDAH.

119. See Hine, "Rape and the Inner Lives of Black Women," for more on the "culture of dissemblance" that prevented black women from divulging personal matters to southern whites.

120. Ball, *Fifty Years in Chains*, 197. See also Morgan, *Slave Counterpoint*, 535.

121. See Faust, *James Henry Hammond and the Old South*, 85.

122. Letter to mother, 11 December 1843, Emily Wharton Sinkler Letters, SCL.

123. Letter from John Springs to John Blackstone, 13 November 1845, Springs Family Papers, SHC.

124. Letter to Benjamin Franklin Perry from Elizabeth Perry, 11 May 1846, Benjamin Franklin Perry Papers, SCL.

125. See chap. 3 for an analysis of the gender exploitation of female slaves in the realm of work.

126. On the role of racism in dividing mistresses and female slaves, see Fox-Genovese, *Within the Plantation Household*, 34–35.

127. Catherine Clinton argues that mistresses served as the "conscience" of the plantation and that female slaves would often appeal directly to mistresses to intercede with masters on their behalf. See *Plantation Mistress*, 187. See also Weiner, *Mistresses and Slaves*, 76–79, 121.

128. Letter to John Guignard from Aunt "JFP," 11 June 1860, Guignard Family Papers, SCL.

129. See Cornelius, *"When Can I Read My Title Clear?"*

130. Letter to "Missus" from Lavinia, July 1849, Lawton Family Papers, SCL.

131. Ibid. See also King, "'Rais Your Children Up Rite,'" 154. King notes that, although Lavinia makes her initial appeal to her mistress, she also beseeches her master to "view the matter as you would if they were yore children."

132. "Negro Rules for Government," Cornhill Plantation Book, 1827–73, McDonald-Furman Papers, WRPL.

133. See chap. 4 for a more detailed analysis of the sexual harassment and abuse inflicted upon slave women at the hands of white men.

134. See hooks, *Ain't I a Woman?* 15, 35. hooks was not writing as a historian but for the "widest possible audience," she claims. Hence, unlike in her Ph.D. thesis, she does not provide any documentary evidence to back up her assertions. See "A Class Sister Act," 20.

135. Brownmiller, *Against Our Will*, 157–58.

136. Ibid., 163.

137. Ibid., 167.

138. Rawick, *American Slave*, vol. 2, pt. 2, 305–6. See also Schwalm, *A Hard Fight for We*, 44.

139. Rawick, *American Slave*, vol. 2, pt. 2, 310–11. See also Van Deburg, "Slave Drivers and Slave Narratives," 727.

140. Stroyer, *My Life in the South*, 17–18. Other examples of male slaves acting in ways that dispute the notion that their first instinct was toward self-preservation can be found in Steward, *Twenty-two Years a Slave*, 13–14. See also King, *Stolen Childhood*, 97–98.

141. Testimony of Allen Wilson in Perdue, Barden, and Phillips, eds., *Weevils in the Wheat*, 327.

142. See hooks, *Ain't I a Woman?* 35. By stating that some slave men may have imitated the behavior of white men, I am not denying the fact that the abuse of slave women by slave men pales in comparison to the abuse of slave women by white men. It may also have been the case that enslaved men who sexually assaulted slave women were acting on their own volition and not imitating whites. On male slaves' internalization of white values, see Wyatt-Brown, "Mask of Obedience," esp. 1246. For claims that slave men abused females because of their sense of powerlessness and the pervasive violence of slavery as a whole, see Malone, *Sweet Chariot*, 229; and Patterson, *Rit-*

*uals of Blood,* 37. For more on drivers' abuse of female slaves, see Schwalm, *A Hard Fight for We,* 68.

143. See Jacobs, ed., *Index to "The American Slave."*

144. Rawick, *American Slave,* vol. 7, pt. 2: *Mississippi Narratives,* 13.

145. Ibid., Supplement Series 2, vol. 5, pt. 4: *Texas Narratives,* 1453.

146. Ibid., Supplement Series 2, vol. 10, pt. 9: *Texas Narratives,* 4117–23. Also of possible significance is the fact that Williams' master, Mr. Hawkins, had bought her and her family on the auction block. Williams was grateful to him for keeping her with her parents and desired to keep him happy.

147. Since female slaves were not protected from rape by law, cases of rape against slave women (whether by white men or black men) were rare before the law. However, Diane Miller Sommerville details some of the rare cases in which male slaves were brought before courts charged with sexually assaulting women of color. See "Rape Myth in the Old South," 493–94. The scarcity of cases in which male slaves were charged with raping female slaves is also considered in McLaurin, *Celia, a Slave,* 113–15. McLaurin found not one case of a white male charged with raping a slave in Catterall's *Judicial Cases.*

148. See chap. 4 for a fuller discussion of the extent of sexual abuse of slave women by white men in the WPA narratives.

149. Deborah G. White has argued that this equality was founded upon the complementary roles that were played by slave men and slave women. See *Ar'n't I a Woman?* 158.

150. See Hine, "Rape and the Inner Lives of Black Women," 915, for more on the reluctance of slave women to divulge personal information.

151. Rawick, *American Slave,* vol. 2, pt. 2, 36.

152. Ibid., 129–30.

153. See Jones, *Experience and Personal Narrative.*

154. I am grateful to an anonymous reader at the University of Illinois Press for raising this issue.

155. Fogel and Engerman, *Time on the Cross,* 147.

156. For further criticisms of the accommodationist theories of Fogel and Engerman, see Tadman, "Slave Trading and the Mentalities of Masters and Slaves" and "Persistent Myth of Paternalism." Also David et al., *Reckoning with Slavery;* and Gutman, *Slavery and the Numbers Game.*

157. Genovese, *Roll, Jordan, Roll,* 5. James D. Anderson argues that Genovese should have more seriously considered the impact of racism upon the development of potentially humane values in a slave society. See "'Aunt Jemima in Dialectics,'" 102. For a more recent appraisal of the views of Genovese, see Smith, *Debating Slavery.*

158. On the protection of the marriages of key slaves from sale, see Tadman, *Speculators and Slaves,* xix–xxxvii, and "Persistent Myth of Paternalism."

159. Tadman, "Persistent Myth of Paternalism," 21. For more on the recent historiography of paternalism under slavery, see Fredrickson, "Skeleton in the Closet." He argues that slave primary sources reveal such variation in plantation regimes that it is time to move beyond arguments over paternalism versus force in explaining the nature of slavery. Tadman's concept of key slaves goes some way toward doing this.

160. Dusinberre, *Them Dark Days,* 179.

161. Ibid., 206. See also Young, "Ideology and Death," 673–706.

# 3  Work, Gender, and Status

Aw de colored people wha' ne'er hab no work to do 'bout
de big house was field hand en day hadder ge' up at de
fust crow uv de cock in de morning. . . . Coase dey eat dey
break'ast 'fore dey leab de quarter. Effen de sun look lak it
wuz gwinna shine, de o'erseer 'ud send dem in de field to
work en dey'ud stay in de field aw day till sun down in de
evenin'. Carry dey basket uv victual en pot 'long wid em
en cook right dere in de field.

—Genia Woodberry, an ex-slave

This chapter focuses on the work that slaves performed for
owners and their own families. It also examines the extent to which labor
was segregated by gender to assess the implications of work patterns on relationships between enslaved men and women. Finally, the relationship
between work and slave social status is explored, especially the role played
by gender in acquiring high-status positions. Owners imposed gender divisions in the tasks they gave their slaves, but the size of holding and the
crop that was produced also influenced work patterns. Furthermore, harvest time was a period when gender divisions at work became blurred because slaves of both genders often performed hard field labor such as cotton picking at this busy time. Very few South Carolina WPA respondents
informed their interviewers about their size of residence or the crop that
they grew when enslaved, making quantitative analysis impossible. However, this chapter will consider the variety of work patterns among South
Carolina slaves and the impact of labor upon their familial relationships.

Rice was grown on the very large plantations of the South Carolina
low country, where some of the richest slave owners in the United States
resided.[1] Here, the evolution of the task system (in which slaves were given

a measured amount of work to do within a given period of time) from the late eighteenth century onward gave the enslaved some degree of control over their working day.[2] They had an incentive to work productively so that they could gain more time for themselves. Laboring under the task system therefore enabled slaves to find time to devote to their families after work for owners was completed. Women in particular must have appreciated any extra time, although, with many tasks to complete at home, their "off times" were also characterized by hard work.[3] The experiences of slaves who lived under the task system can be contrasted with those who resided on plantations that grew cotton or tobacco, where work was most often governed by time, and most slaves labored under the gang labor system from "dawn till dusk."[4] The lives of slaves on small, up-country holdings differed again. Their work lives could be equally intensive, but mostly it was divided between laboring in their owners' houses and in the field. Finally, although most urban slaves and those who labored solely within the Big House on plantations were spared the daily grind of field labor, it will be shown how their working lives could be equally arduous.

Gender segregation restricted opportunities for male-female bonding while toiling for the master. This meant that the opportunities for socialization within the cultural life of slave communities, as detailed in chapter 1, were especially valuable. Females' childbearing roles meant that gender was also significant for the types of work performed for families after that for owners was completed. Work for families, while being gendered, was also relatively egalitarian in terms of content, with both men and women working hard to support and provide for their families in the face of the oppressive regime. This realm of the slaves' lives clearly shows the strength of the support between spouses. Such labor also contributed to the social space between the lives of slaves and owners, thereby enhancing the autonomy and psychological independence of slave communities.

Despite these relatively egalitarian relations, female slaves were undoubtedly the victims of gendered oppression; bearing the brunt of domestic work, they often had extra tasks to perform for their masters while also shouldering the burden of childcare responsibilities. This chapter examines the "triple exploitation" of slave women and its impact upon white and black notions of status within enslaved communities. It is important to contrast the ways owners and slaves defined status, since differences in their views reveal much about the gulf between their distinct and separate worlds. So far as slaves (but not owners) were concerned, high status was associated with those slaves who performed important roles within their own communities.

## The Work Patterns of South Carolina Slaves

Many of the South Carolina WPA informants did not work, or else completed only light tasks during slavery. Further, when considering those who did labor for their owners (and also the work undertaken by the respondents' parents), house servants are substantially overrepresented. House slaves may have dominated because the interviewers, when searching for ex-slaves to interview, inevitably contacted those known either to them or to other whites, most likely those with whom they had had the most interaction under slavery.[5] This bias does not, however, diminish the usefulness of WPA testimony as a historical source. It might be expected that former house servants would be less forthcoming about life under the peculiar institution and that they would be more inclined to paint a positive picture of slave-owner relations, but this was found not to be the case.[6] Despite the overrepresentation of house servants who may indeed have been more likely to relate fond anecdotes of their white owners, this study found significant mental and emotional distance between masters and slaves to be the norm.[7] However, because the majority of the WPA respondents and their parents performed house or skilled labor, they were not, for the most part, typical slaves. This contrasts with most other evidence relating to the work patterns of slaves, where it is generally accepted that between 75 and 80 percent of men and women labored in the fields.[8]

The preponderance of house servants within the South Carolina narratives was coupled with an overrepresentation of those who performed no work during slavery. Both factors can be attributed to the age of the respondents at the time of interview. Before the age of five, few slaves labored for their owners.[9] Thereafter, most tended to perform only small tasks or to run errands within the Big House before switching to field work at adolescence (normally between the ages of twelve and thirteen).[10] Typical were the recollections of Ellen Swindler, enslaved in Newberry County, who testified: "We children had to work around the home of our master 'till we was old enough to work in de fields, den we would hoe and pick cotton."[11] Since the average age of the South Carolina informants in 1865 was only ten years, most would either have not worked or would have fallen into the "odd jobs and errands" category.

A total of 146 of the 334 South Carolina respondents told their interviewers about their occupations during slavery, representing 43.7 percent of all informants. Of these, seventy-eight were men (41.1 percent of all males), and sixty-eight were women (47.2 percent of all females). For the purpose of clarity, their occupations were divided into three broad categories. It was found that 49.3 percent of the ex-slaves who commented on work performed house-related or skilled tasks; they shall also be referred to as domestics.[12] A further 34.3 percent labored in the field.[13] The remaining 16.4 percent said they did not work under slavery. There was also a marked gender difference in the occupational patterns of the informants, with more females than males working as domestics (67.6 percent of women, compared with 33.3 percent of men). This was probably a reflection of the desirability of young, female house servants by owners. Only 20.6 percent of the female ex-slaves worked in the field, compared with 46.2 percent of the males. Also worthy of note is the fact that more men than women said that they did not perform any work during slavery (20.5 percent of the males, compared with 11.8 percent of the females). It may tentatively be suggested that the quality of life for young boys may have been somewhat higher than that of young girls, since the latter were more likely to work and more likely to labor in the relative isolation of the Big House than the former.[14]

The occupations held by the parents of the WPA informants are also significant. Through an examination of parental occupations, the gender differences in the work patterns of slave men and slave women as a whole can be examined (rather than gender differences in the work patterns of predominantly young slaves). The jobs held by 105 parents of the respondents could be established; of these, sixty-eight related to mothers' occupations and thirty-seven to fathers'. As with the informants themselves, these were divided into two broad categories of house and field jobs. For both parents, the field-related group included only general field hands and those who looked after animals. However, among those who worked in the house or who held skilled positions, there was considerably more variety. Included in this category for the fathers of the respondents were drivers, blacksmiths, coachmen or carriage drivers, foremen, general house servants, carpenters, "headmen," makers of shoes and other leather goods, and overseers.

Mothers who worked in the house or held skilled positions included cooks, general house servants, seamstresses, midwives, nurses, and laundresses. It is noteworthy that the respondents' fathers held a more varied range of skilled positions than did their mothers. However, the work patterns of parents again shows a marked skew toward domestics, with 78.4 percent of fathers and 58.8 percent of mothers performing house and skilled labor.[15] The only conclusion that can be drawn from this is that the South Carolina WPA testimony, in so far as work is concerned, is strongly skewed toward those who carried out house-related or skilled jobs. In particular, the data for fathers seems to reflect an especially strong bias toward such slaves.

Full-length autobiographies often include more detail on work patterns than WPA testimony. However, they also display a bias toward house or skilled slaves. For example, Tom Jones worked both in his owners' house and also at their store, while performing field work at some stages of his life.[16] Charles Ball labored in the field, although he was eventually promoted to the position of overseer.[17] Moses Roper served as a domestic slave upon reaching adulthood.[18] Jacob Stroyer took care of horses as a child, but when older he worked as a carpenter before being sent to wait on officers fighting in the Civil War.[19] Likewise, Sam Aleckson served as an "officer's boy" in the Confederate army.[20] Finally, I. E. Lowery was a house slave who actually slept in the same room as his master and mistress.[21] Female autobiographies display a similar bias toward domestics. Linda Brent was a house servant who lived in the home of Dr. Flint. However, when she refused his sexual advances she was sent to work on his son's plantation as punishment.[22] Mattie J. Jackson, Lucy A. Delany, and Kate Drumgoold were all house slaves.[23] Annie L. Burton, a child during slavery, wrote that she lived on a plantation but performed no work.[24] Moreover, all the female autobiographers lived outside South Carolina. Coupled with fact that few mention the size of the holdings on which they lived, these considerations make it harder to evaluate the lives of rank-and-file field slaves who toiled on plantations in antebellum South Carolina from this evidence alone. Slave source materials, in the realm of work, are more useful when consulted alongside the records left by owners.

When comparing the quality of life of field slaves with those who labored in the house, the relative isolation of domestics, caused by them being separated from their wider communities, must be taken into account. House slaves, while not having to endure the arduous daily grind of outdoor field work, were often victims of isolation. Jessie Sparrow, enslaved in Marion County, described to her WPA interviewer how her mother was cut off from her wider community. She was taken away from her family when only a child and prevented from mixing with most other blacks. Raised in the Big House, she even had to sleep on a pallet at the end of her mistress's bed.[25] Isolation of this kind could also expose female domestics to greater risk of sexual abuse at the hands of their owners or other white men of the household.[26] The harshness of the regime notwithstanding, field slaves, in contrast, had more opportunities to bond with others and to develop shared work camaraderie away from the prying eyes of whites, as the comments made by Genia Woodberry at the beginning of this chapter illustrate. Similarly, Charles Ball described in his autobiography being part of a great gang who set out to work together in the field. They walked and talked together for nearly a mile.[27] Work times therefore provided opportunities for slaves to socialize with each other. Moreover, since the concern here is the extent to which the working lives of the mass of slaves led to close relationships within gender groups and across gender lines, an exploration of the work lives of field slaves is vital.

Deborah G. White has argued persuasively that the sex-segregated work patterns facilitated female bonding and the development of a gendered culture that enhanced their sense of womanhood.[28] Being in such close proximity all day certainly did provide opportunities for field slaves of the same gender to forge strong relationships, and White's claims are reinforced by the testimony of the WPA respondents. Gus Feaster gave a vivid description of female hoe workers. He stated: "Seed as many as a dozen hoe-womens in de field at one time. Dey come when dey finished breakfast and de plows had got a start. Dey used mulberry skins from fresh mulberry saplins to tie around dere waists fer belts."[29] Jane Johnson also illustrated sex-segregated work patterns when she said: "Most of de grown slave women knocked off from field work at dinner time on Saturdays and done de washin' for de rest of de slaves."[30] Nelson Cameron created an image of physically strong female field workers and an almost idyllic childhood on the plantation of Sam Brice near Winnsboro. He described the "little niggers runnin' 'round in deir shirt-tails and a kickin' up deir heels, while deir mammies was in de field a hoeing and geeing at de plow handles, workin' lak a man."[31] A sense of gendered camaraderie, therefore, was certainly an important component of field work, providing companionship and relief from oppression. Away from the field, though, testimony suggests that spousal relationships assumed primary importance.

A quantitative investigation into the relationship between work and marriage reinforces these findings. As chapter 1 has illustrated, the opportunities for courtship that arose after labor for owners was completed were of immense significance. It is true that most married within their occupational group—house workers wed fellow domestics, and those who toiled in the field also tended to marry each other. Slaves of the opposite sex but the same occupational grouping did, therefore, manage to find some time to socialize and to court one another during the working day. However, South Carolina WPA testimony illustrates that a significant minority of marriages brought field and house slaves together, which suggests the existence of important networks reaching throughout slave communities. The WPA evidence was examined to assess any correlation between the occupations of slave spouses. Due to the young age of the respondents, though, only one, Louisa Davis, enslaved in Fairfield County, gave both her occupation and that of her spouse.[32] Evidence obtained on the marital patterns of their parents is therefore more helpful. Seventeen informants related the work undertaken by both parents, eight (47.1 percent) of whom said that both were domestics. Three (17.6 percent) testified that both labored in the field, while six (35.3 percent) said that while one parent held a house or skilled position, the other was a field hand.[33]

The size of this sample is undoubtedly small and again displays a bias toward house or skilled workers. However, it is clear that while slaves tended to marry those who held similar positions, over one-third of the sample testified that their parents' marriage crossed the house-field divide. Slaves did not segregate themselves into parallel communities based upon the work they performed and did find opportunities to mix with each other outside the working day. As was seen in chapter 1, weekend dances and frolics were particularly significant in so far as courtship and marriage were concerned, allowing links to be forged across—as well as between—slave quarters.

The size of holding could have affected choice within marital markets, but the fairly high level of marriage across occupational lines suggests that slaves retained the ability to look beyond their immediate work environment and to form attachments within their broader community networks.[34] Where slaveholdings were small, the pool of potential spouses could be restricted, which sometimes resulted in an increased tendency to marry abroad.[35] Furthermore, the practicalities of occupation were also important. For example, the relative isolation of domestics may have contributed to the fact that they tended to marry those who held similar positions. House slaves mostly lived in quarters or a yard near to their owners' houses, if not within the Big House itself, and this obviously impacted upon slaves' social lives. Similarly, urban slaves tended to reside within the homes of their masters or those to whom they had been hired out—a common occurrence in cities.[36] However, in contrast to domestics who lived on plantations, urban slaves had more opportunities to socialize with each other, not least because being hired out offered the chance to meet other slaves who worked in comparable capacities.[37]

For field hands, the situation was different because they mostly lived in their own settlements. Anne Simons Deas described such quarters in her fictionalized reminiscences: "The Hill is where the field hands live. . . . It is a little village of two rows of double-houses, with a wide street between. . . . A partition divides each house in half, and the chimney is in the middle."[38] It has been shown how field slaves, especially those who labored on large plantations, had more opportunities to mix within a wide social sphere, their greater distance from owners giving them more opportunities to mingle with those belonging to different masters. This might explain the slightly larger tendency for field workers to reside within abroad marriages, as will later be illustrated. The high incidence of viable cross-plantation unions (discussed in chapter 2), together with the secondary pattern of a significant rate of marriage spanning different occupations, suggests that complex marriage markets worked in important ways to sustain slave-community solidarity and autonomy.

Because the South Carolina WPA narratives and published slave autobiographies were skewed toward slaves and enslaved parents who performed house-related tasks, an examination of the records left by South Carolina slaveholders can be useful in overcoming this bias. Owners' manuscripts include many references to slaves who worked in the field and to the sex-segregation in the tasks they completed.[39] Field slaves were, for the most part, separated into gendered gangs, and watching them digging trenches and sowing seeds fascinated Anne Simons Deas. She described how the trenchers made long straight lines in the soil, then, "Some little way behind them came the sowers, *all women,* with their skirts tied up, and carrying the seed-rice in handle baskets, open-mouthed bags, or even in their aprons. With the regularity of machines, their hands went into the receptacles, and with a long, graceful, far-reaching, and apparently careless sweep of the arm, they sent the rich yellow grain flying through the air straight into the trench" (italics added).[40] The low-country rice planter Louis Manigault also referred to the division of tasks according to gender: "The women are leveling the dirt from the new quarter drains dug in 37 acre square, and the men are clearing ditches in the swamp."[41] Indeed, there was a strong association between growing rice and female labor in the low country. Leslie A. Schwalm argues that because women were more likely to hoe than men, it became defined as an exclusively female task.[42] It has also been suggested that black women brought many of their rice-growing skills to the New World from Africa.[43]

The plantation journals of other South Carolina slaveholders frequently refer to the division of tasks according to gender. For example, entries in the journal of the Georgetown District rice planter Ben Sparkman included: "The fellows were employed in cutting up logs in [the] 29 acre field. The women in cutting down bushes in [the] potato field."[44] A few days later, Sparkman wrote: "The women were cutting down bushes in [the] 31 acre field. On Wednesday morning . . . they planted potatoes. The fellows, with the exception of the ploughman, were employed . . . at Wilson's place, in mending brakes in banks, with the help of women on Wednesday evening."[45] Similarly, the journal of the Beaufort County cotton planter John Edwin Fripp fits the pattern of tasks being divided according to gender: "Ordered . . . [Peter] to take in the few ripe peas, to strip the May corn tomorrow, and when they get through, gin out the yellow cotton etc., to work the slips with the women etc. and start the men cutting."[46] He later wrote: "Men digging canal in woods. Women listing cow penned land in swamp field."[47]

Evidence obtained on the work performed for owners supports the propositions that, for the most part, men and women worked in sex-segregated gangs and that they also tended to perform different tasks. Furthermore, because owners saw male labor as superior, it was men who performed the most arduous work, while women tended to complete lighter tasks such as hoeing. Harvest time may have provided an exception to this rule, with all slaves helping to reap the crops before winter. However, the harvest was not only a time for hard labor but also for celebration and festivity. The excitement generated by corn-shuckings, for example, illustrates that slaves saw this type of labor as atypical. As has been shown in chapter 1, matters of courtship assumed a high priority at such events, in part because males and females relished the rare opportunity to work and to celebrate together. Overall, while historical evidence supports White's theory of a female (and also a male) gendered solidarity forged through work, the fact that nearly all men and women desired the love and support of a husband or wife reveals much about the primary importance of spousal bonding within slave communities. At the end of the hard working day, they sought the love and comfort of their husbands, wives, and children.

## Gender Exploitation

The exclusive oppression faced by female slaves has provoked considerable scholarly debate. Angela Davis claimed in 1971 that slavery could not infer privilege on black men vis-à-vis black women: "The man-slave could not be the unquestioned superior within the 'family' or community. . . . The attainment of slavery's intrinsic goals was contingent upon the fullest and most brutal utilization of the productive capacities of every man, woman and child. They all had to 'provide' for the master."[48] In her analysis of the construction of black womanhood, Davis shows how slave women and men were equal as workers: they were both exploited by owners. Female slaves were also excluded from the ideology of true womanhood that idealized white women through its emphasis on piety, purity, submissiveness, and domesticity.[49] However, it remains true that bondage did subject women to gendered oppression, not least because they experienced the "double-day" before most other women in American society.[50]

Evidence presented here contradicts the assertion that slavery rendered men and women equal as workers. It is true that both were exploited, but the sex-segregation of slaves by owners illustrates how female labor was often regarded as inferior to that of men. Moreover, men had more opportunities than women to obtain skilled or prestigious positions that gave some degree of job satisfaction and helped to break the monotony of the everyday routine. Many historians have questioned the extent to which owners treated male and female laborers equally. Elizabeth Fox-Genovese has claimed that while "no slave holder refrained, out of respect for female delicacy, from letting a slave woman exercise her full strength," slave women were more inclined to work with other women, since owners reserved certain types of heavy tasks for men.[51] Thus, "masters . . . had differing expectations for the quantities of work that slave men and women should be expected to perform."[52]

Fox-Genovese's analysis of the gender divisions operating in the work lives of slave men and women is similar to that of Deborah G. White, who states that "despite their limited sensitivity to regarding female slave labor . . . owners did reluctantly acquiesce to female physiology . . . men were given the more physically demanding work unless there was a shortage of male hands."[53] Certain important tasks were reserved for men, and furthermore, while slaves of both genders would work in the fields during planting, growing, and harvesting, men completed the hard labor of preparing the fields for cultivation by ditching and embanking.[54] Marli F. Weiner writes: "Although slaveholders rarely had scruples about charging black women with physically demanding tasks, their assumptions about gender often influenced the assignments they made." Owners also worried that having men and women working together would disrupt the routine of the working day.[55] In this respect, gender discrimination toward female slaves would seem to be in their own interests, since they were given the less arduous tasks. However, such bias could also operate against women. It will later be shown how female slaves were limited in their opportunities for occupational mobility because of their gender.[56]

Slaveholders' records testify to their belief in the greater physical prowess of slave men. The plantation journal of Georgetown district rice planter Ben Sparkman describes how slave women used to work alongside elderly men: "The six fellows cut wood. The *women and two old fellows* cut down the corn stock in [the] 31 acre field" (italics added).[57] Only "inferior" men were expected to perform the same duties as women. The sexual division of labor assigned by Sparkman therefore reflects the dif-

fering physical capabilities of enslaved men and women as well as the belief in the superiority of male labor. Moreover, slaves may have internal-
ized this notion, as an extract from the diary of a clergyman, Samuel Cram
Jackson, illustrates. He related a story of a slave man who was instructed
by his master to undertake grinding work. He refused, however, and "the
next morning [he was] found in the woods hanging. He would not do
women's work."[58]

Because slaveholders regarded female labor as inferior to male, it was
men who held the majority of skilled occupations on plantations. The
South Carolina WPA respondent Genia Woodberry provided extensive
descriptions of skilled slave occupations on her plantation in Marion
County, including a description of the work of slaves in the "shoe house,"
the "gin house," and the blacksmith's shop. Male slaves ran all of these.[59]
Woodberry only mentioned two female slaves as being of central importance to the operation of the plantation: "Gran'mudder Phoebe," who was
in charge of the plantation dairy, and Patience, who "help do aw de weav-
ing fa de plantation."[60]

Most often it was men who gained positions of authority over their
peers. Charles Ball, for example, describes how, when hoeing and weeding
a cotton field, certain slave men were designated as "captains" by the overseer, "each of whom had under his command a certain number of the other
hands. The captain was the foreman of his company, and those under his
command had to keep up with him."[61] Male slaves were also aware of the
fact that their work was regarded as superior in both content and status
to the work of women. At one point in his autobiography, Ball states: "I
hung down my head, and felt very much ashamed of myself when I found
that my cotton [picking] was so far behind that of many, even of the
women, who had heretofore regarded me as the strongest and most powerful man of the whole gang."[62] Moses Roper was punished by his master
by being chained—with a forty-pound weight tied around his neck—to a
slave woman who had run away. Roper was humiliated and embarrassed
at the difficulties he had in completing the same work as her. He wrote:
"I would rather have suffered 100 lashes than she should have been thus
treated; he kept me chained to her during the week, and repeatedly flogged
us both . . . and forced us to keep up with the other slaves, although re-
tarded by the heavy weight of the log-chain."[63]

Slave women were also expected to perform extra, gender-specific
tasks for their owners such as sewing, knitting, or making clothes. This
imposition reveals much about contemporary notions of the types of work
that were regarded as intrinsically female. One slaveholder, Thomas Ble-

wett, stated that on rainy days, his slave women were expected to stay indoors and sew clothes.[64] Similarly, the Charlestonian plantation mistress Margaret Ann Morris made frequent reference in her diary to giving her female slaves fabric to make into clothes after their work in the field was over. The following entry is typical: "I gave each of the women servants a yard of long cloth to make an apron."[65] Likewise, Lucy Carpenter recalled a visit to James Chesnut's plantation in a letter to her brother, William Blanding. She wrote: "It was four o'clock, we passed many of the negroes returning from their labors . . . walking leisurely, the females knitting."[66]

In a letter to her husband, Elizabeth Franklin Perry gave a lengthy description of the visit of a slave, Milly, to her two daughters, Caroline (owned by a neighbor, Mrs. Lynch) and Delia (owned by the Perrys): "Very differently situated did she [Milly] find Caroline, who she went to see and passed one night with. She said Mrs. Lynch gave her . . . very little to eat, and that all the clothes she had on would not be enough to make an apron, and after working out all day, when she comes home at night from the fields, she has to spin a yard of cotton, which would take her until ten o'clock, and Mrs. Lynch won't let her have the bed clothes to sleep on. . . . She must be treated very badly. . . . She and Delia both cried at the thought of Caroline's situation."[67] Elizabeth Perry condemned Mrs. Lynch's harsh treatment of her slave and must have taken pride in her own comparative benevolence. Ironically, though, as will be shown later in this chapter, another of Mrs. Perry's slaves, Eliza, was also highly dissatisfied about the extra tasks she had to complete on weekends. Perhaps Perry favored Milly and Delia over Eliza; certainly she did not profess to see any similarities between the situation of Caroline and that of Eliza.

The South Carolina WPA narratives also contain frequent examples of women having to weave or spin in addition to performing other tasks, often under the direction of the plantation mistress, who generally took control over domestic production.[68] Josephine Bristow, enslaved in Marion County, described how enslaved women used to spin and weave when it was raining and they could not work in the field.[69] Similarly, Adeline Grey described helping her mother weave at night. She said: "Used to give a brooch [hank] or two to weave at night. I'se sometimes thread de needle for my Ma, or pick out de seed in de cotton, an make it into rolls to spin."[70] Margaret Hughes, although not specifying females, recalled how "De grown up slaves had to work in de field all day and then at night they spin cloth and make their clothes."[71] Because enslaved women had to complete these extra tasks, their lives often comprised more menial and apparently neverending lists of jobs when compared with the lives of men.

In this respect, slaves who lived on big plantations (such as those in the low country) may have had an easier time: these holdings were so large that a group of women would often work as seamstresses or laundresses full-time, thus sparing others from performing such tasks at the end of a long day's labor in the field.[72]

Slave men also had more opportunities than women to hold jobs that their owners saw as prestigious. Although some female tasks did carry status—notably the occupations of seamstress, cook, and midwife, all of which held places of considerable social standing on plantations—men held the majority of the high-ranking positions.[73] It has also been shown how the fathers of the South Carolina WPA respondents held a wider variety of house or skilled positions than did their mothers—another example of discrimination against women. Slave men worked as mechanics, carpenters, tanners, shoemakers, carriage drivers, coachmen, and coopers, to name a few. It is likely that owners did not want to spend time and money in training women to perform these roles only for their work lives frequently to be interrupted by childbearing and rearing.[74]

Female slaves were therefore victims of a gender oppression reflected in the occupational hierarchies. Robert W. Fogel and Stanley L. Engerman have quantified that on large plantations around 20 percent of slave men and women were exempt from field labor. However, while most of these women worked in the Big House or in such quasi domestic positions as seamstresses and nurses, the men had more opportunities to work as artisans (including blacksmiths, carpenters, and coopers) or semiskilled craftsmen (including coachmen, gardeners, stewards, and house servants).[75] Similarly, Leslie A. Schwalm argues that women formed the backbone of the field-labor force on rice plantations and that the few specialized positions slave women did occupy brought few of the relative advantages (such as mobility, cash, or power) enjoyed by men.[76] Betty Wood has developed this theme, noting how occupational opportunities for slave women were related to plantation size. On large plantations women could be employed full-time as cooks, maids, washerwomen, nurses, midwives, and seamstresses.[77] Those on smaller holdings, however, had different experiences and often had to perform a wide variety of tasks in addition to laboring in both the house and the field.

It is significant that slave owners generally believed that it was the plantation cook, the stereotypical "Mammy" figure, who held the highest social status upon plantations. The plantation cook was undoubtedly an important slave, although as someone who labored for whites rather than for peers, her status may have been lower in the eyes of slaves. Characterized as Mammy, she reinforced the owners' belief in their benevolent paternalism. In the 1970s, Eugene Genovese described her as follows: "Primarily, the Mammy raised the white children and ran the Big House either as the mistress's executive officer or her *de facto* superior. Her power extended over black and white so long as she exercised restraint, and she was not crossed. She carried herself like a surrogate mistress—neatly attired, barking orders, conscious of her dignity, full of self-respect."[78] More recently, it has been suggested that rather than representing reality, Mammy was more important as a stereotype that existed within white minds for rationalizing bondage. Mammy and her stereotypical opposite, "Jezebel," reflected the dominant white views of gender roles among the enslaved.[79] Elizabeth Fox-Genovese writes: "Mammy represented the harmonious nature of the slave regime. Reflecting motherhood and reproduction, she displaced sexuality into nurture, and she also illustrated the ultimate devotion of black women to whites."[80]

Unsurprisingly, it is within owners' records and conservative slave narratives that most references to Mammy are found. In the following extract from the reminiscences of Mary Esther Huger, most high-status slaves were men, with the exception of the Mammy figure, "Maum Sarey," and the dairymaid, Marianne. This extract also illustrates some of the familial ties that linked "high-status" slaves on this plantation, and it will be shown later how slaves and owners both played a role in training young slaves to perform certain types of work. Huger wrote:

> When I was a child, our servants were Ketch—an old grey headed negro and Johnnie, whom he had trained. When Ketch was too old and tired of work, Johnnie, then a young man, took his place, and had the cook's son, Smart, to train. Smart's father was Old Smart the cook . . . he was required to leave the kitchen and work in the garden, near by, where his wife was a regular garden woman named Hew. Many cooks were employed as gardeners for some hours daily, as it was not good for them to be all the time in a kitchen. Besides these there was Maum Sarey—who had been my mother's maid and had a house quite near us in the yard. She was first maid and seamstress, and made all our clothes when we were children. Then there was always one, and sometimes two girls, to help in housework and sewing. Then the pastry cook and dairy-maid Marianne. . . . Then Johnnie's mother was the washerwoman and had a girl to help her, and then there was Old Sam the coachman, and Maum Sarey's son Bertram the hostler, he afterward became coachman.[81]

Anne Simons Deas also described Mammy in her reminiscences. She wrote: "There are three women servants—seamstresses and chambermaids—besides 'Mauma,' the children's nurse who is everything by turns, and is, next to family, the most important personage in the household. . . .

She is her Mistress's right-hand, and can do everything, from nursing the sick to clear-starching and making the most delicious pie-crust you ever ate."[82] Recollections such as these highlight the close relationship between the white slaveowning family and the Mammy figure. Slavery is presented as a harmonious institution in which capable, contented female slaves are happy to toil for their owners in an important domestic capacity.

Interestingly, the image of Mammy was not described in the South Carolina WPA testimony. This omission emphasizes the fact that while the Mammy stereotype was essential for whites, she was more peripheral in most slave communities. She can, however, be found in certain full-length slave autobiographies, especially those with a conservative emphasis. I. E. Lowery's provides a good case in point. He fondly describes his Mammy figure, "Granny the cook": "Granny, though she was black, considered herself to be the mistress on that plantation. She thought that her color was no fault of hers, but circumstances (part of the time Mr. Frierson having no wife) and efficiency, made her head of the household. When Granny gave orders those orders had to be obeyed. White and colored respected and obeyed her."[83] Close relationships between owners and certain elderly, skilled female slaves certainly did exist, though these friendships should not be taken as representative of the norm among slave-owner relations. The majority of rank-and-file field slaves did not have close ties with those who held them in bondage. Neither should the role of the Mammy figure be taken to illustrate the high social status of females within slave communities, since it was generally owners rather than slaves who awarded her a high status. Instead, as will be shown, slaves awarded status to those who worked for their own communities in addition to performing tasks for whites.

## Childbearing and Rearing

Evidence found within the WPA testimony stresses the importance of and status granted to a certain minority of female slaves. For example, elderly midwives are well documented in these narratives, often being referred to as "grannies." The origin of this term is unclear, but a possible explanation is connected to the fact that these women did tend to be skilled, elderly, respected slaves.[84] Often a granny would replace the role of the white doctor in childbirth. As the Fairfield County ex-slave Millie Barber stated: "De fact is I can't 'member us ever had a doctor on de place; just a granny was enough at childbirth."[85] Similarly, Phillip Evans of Winnsboro said: "I help to bring my brother Richard, us calls him Dick, into de world. Dat is, when mammy got in de pains, I run for de old granny on de place to come right away."[86] Ellen Godfrey also spoke of the granny. She recalled: "Never have a doctor, granny for me yet. My Mary good old granny. Catch two set o' twin for me."[87]

The role of the midwife, or granny, illustrates the prevalence of self-sufficiency and community networks among slave women; in childbirth they turned to their own rather than to their owners. Testimony on grannies therefore backs up the claim that performing tasks that were of intrinsic benefit to their own communities as well as to owners most likely conferred a high social status upon the enslaved. Although midwives were not perceived by slaveholders to be of as high a social standing as certain slave men or the Mammy figure, they were still seen as important individuals. Elizabeth Franklin Perry, for example, made frequent reference to the slave midwife "Mom Phillis" in the letters she wrote to her husband from their Greenville home. On one sad occasion she informed him of the death of a newborn slave: "I am sorry to tell you that Eliza's child did not live a day. It was five weeks or more to[o] soon, and owing to her falls I suppose, was outwardly bruised and inwardly hurt, and also Mom Phillis not being here in time, might have been bad for it. From the fact of it being born alive I wrote to you in good spirits, thinking it would live, for Mary's that was so delicate lived five or six weeks, and perhaps longer if she had been careful, but Niny came to see Eliza a few hours after, and as soon as she saw it, said she did not think it would live."[88] Another time, Perry wrote of their slave woman, Sindy, who had recently given birth to a girl: "I sent first for Mom Phillis, and Mom Phillis afterward begged me to send for Dr. Crook so he was with her."[89] Childbirth was sometimes a shared responsibility between elderly slave women and white male doctors. When complications arose, Mom Phillis asked for the doctor to provide assistance.[90]

The childcare responsibilities of female slaves also impinged heavily on their work lives. While pregnant women were generally released from their responsibilities in the field, as the following WPA respondents illustrate, they were often assigned alternative tasks, such as spinning or carding. Gracie Gibson, enslaved in Richland County, described how "some of de old women, and women bearin' chillun not yet born, did cardin' wid hand-cards; then some would get at de spinnin' wheel and spin thread."[91] Similarly, Adeline Jackson of Winnsboro testified: "women in family way worked up to near de time, but guess Doctor Gibson knowed his business. Just befo' de time, they was took out and put in de cardin' and spinnin' rooms."[92] Henry D. Jenkins commented that at his home in Sumter County, his master, Joseph Howell, "made us all work; women in de perils of child birth drapped cotton seed and corn kernels. Dr. Turnipseed, dat was our doctor, 'low dat light labor lak dat good for them."[93]

Other ex-slaves mentioned that women had time off after childbirth, but perceptions varied considerably. Millie Barber claimed: "Slave women have a baby one day, up and gwine 'round de next day, singin' at her work lak nothin' unusual had happened."[94] Susan Hamlin of Charleston also suggested that slave women did not have much time off after childbirth: "In de days of slavery woman wuz jus' given time 'nough to deliver dere babies. Dey deliver de baby 'bout eight in de mornin' an' twelve had to be back to work."[95] As an urban slave, Hamlin may have unwittingly been describing how the amount of rest given to house slaves living in towns differed from that given to slaves on plantations. More typically, Ryer Emmanuel, enslaved on a plantation in Marion County, claimed that women had a month off work after childbirth. She recalled: "Always when a woman would get in de house, old Massa would let her leave off work en stay dere to de house a month till she mended in de body way. Den she would have to carry de child to de big house en get back in de field to work."[96]

Sam Polite also said that slave women generally had a month's respite, stating that on the Fripp plantation on St. Helena Island, "W'en 'ooman hab baby he hab mid-wife for nine day and sometime don't haffa wuk for month w'en baby born."[97] It appears, overall, that slave women felt they were not given enough time to recover after giving birth and that in caring for babies and working for their owners, their lives were filled with a constant stream of pressures and demands. Maggie Wright, enslaved in Newberry County, illustrated this point well when she said: "He [the overseer] wanted us to work all day when we had been up de night befo' rocking babies."[98]

Evidence contained within owners' records suggests, in keeping with Ryer Emmanuel's assertion, that slave women were generally allowed about a month off work after having their babies. John Edwin Fripp of St. Helena Island backed up the claims of the WPA informant Sam Polite when he stated in his plantation journal: "Pat . . . will be out on Monday as it's [her baby is] a month old."[99] Elizabeth Franklin Perry, similarly, wrote to her husband: "Minerva was taken sick, and in a short time was delivered of a girl, and both doing well. She will now be up . . . in a month. . . . You ought to be thankful that your property is gradually increasing as you now have an additional negro. Minerva's children do not interfere with her work, as Mary's baby did."[100] In addition to conveying how difficult life was for female slaves, Perry's sentiments illustrate that slave children were ultimately economic assets to owners. It appears that Minerva was more adept at coping with the hardships caused by laboring for owners and raising children than was Mary.

In his plantation rulebook, John B. Miller of Sumter District wrote of pregnant slaves: "Such women as may be near being confined must be put only to light work, and after delivery and able to go about, must be put to light work for a time."[101] Andrew Flinn also wrote in his plantation book: "Pregnant women and sucklers must be treated with great tenderness, worked near home and lightly. Pregnant women should not plough or lift, but must be kept at moderate work until the last hour if possible. Sucklers must be allowed time to suckle their children from twice to three times a day according to their ages. At twelve months old children must be weaned."[102] Working through their pregnancies and returning to work soon after childbirth undoubtedly impacted upon slave women's quality of life. While their owners sought to find a middle ground between their short-term economic interests (having all their slaves working hard) and their long-term economic interests (protecting the health of their unborn and newly born slaves), enslaved women were clearly the losers in this search for compromise, bearing and rearing children in addition to performing their everyday tasks.

The South Carolina WPA respondents made frequent comments on the nature of childcare provisions under slavery. Henry Brown suggested that on plantations it was the preserve of young and elderly female slaves who would care for babies in a "negro house": "At one o'clock the babies were taken to the field to be nursed, then they were brought back to the negro house until the mothers finished their work, then they would come for them."[103] Ryer Emmanuel also described how one elderly woman would mind the plantation children "till night come."[104] On larger holdings, the plantation nursery appears to have been a common feature. For example, at James Gadsen's large rice plantation, Pimlico, on the Cooper River, the nursery had seventy children up to the age of fifteen. It is likely that the older children shared some responsibility in caring for the younger ones. Although most caregivers were female, males also sometimes had responsibility for the children in the nursery.[105] Separation from their children must have been hard for mothers, who often were only allowed to return to suckle their infants.

However, when childcare was not provided, the burden upon slave mothers could be greater still. The WPA respondent Henrietta Fields described the plight of her mother, struggling to care for her children in addition to performing field labor: "My Mother'd set down an' tell us all about how she'd have to struggle to git 'long wid allus little chillun. Dey'd put us little uns in de baskets and set um in de edge of de field."[106] Charles Ball also makes reference to female slaves leaving their children in the field. He writes that as he began work in the morning, he observed several women carrying young children in their arms; they laid them in the shade by a fence or under cotton plants. When the slaves went to get water, "they would go to give suck to their children, requesting some one to bring them water in gourds, which they were careful to carry to the field with them."[107]

The types of childcare available therefore varied and were influenced by numerous factors. Wealthy owners with many slaves could often afford the luxury of a nursery, staffed by their slaves in a full-time capacity. Others, however, left their enslaved women to cope as best they could with the struggle to work full-time and to care for their offspring. The system of labor implemented by owners was also significant. Those who toiled under the gang system often had their break times regulated by masters or overseers, who would grant short intervals where mothers could nurse their infants. Under the task system, where specific jobs were set, or for those who lived on small holdings, women often had more flexibility when it came to feeding their babies.[108]

Female slaves undoubtedly missed their children during the long working day, and the time they spent with them during the evenings and on weekends was very precious. Leslie A. Schwalm has warned historians against romanticizing the family life of enslaved women, writing that their "social and reproductive" labor should be examined as critically as the work they performed for their owners.[109] However, the difficulties of bearing and rearing children notwithstanding, the supportive network of the slave community and the love, support, and joy that women gained from their spouses and children must have gone some way to alleviate the burdens placed upon them. In the realm of work for owners, the lives of women were undoubtedly more arduous than those of men. Gender divisions meant that males and females tended to labor separately, with men performing the heaviest tasks. However, enslaved women often had extra work to complete for their masters despite the additional burdens that childbearing and rearing imposed. Moreover, men also had more opportunity for occupational mobility within the slave regime.

## Work Performed by Slaves for Their Families

How did work for families shape family responsibilities and gender relations? Tasks performed for their families by slave men and women reflected gendered patterns within slave communities and impacted on their quality of life. South Carolina WPA testimony has proven valuable in investigating the tasks completed by slaves in this realm, with forty-eight of the 334 informants (14.4 percent of all respondents) relating some of the duties that they undertook to support their families after sundown.[110] Their recollections were broken down into five categories: gardens or patches, fishing and hunting, making clothes, washing, and raising animals. A total of 43.7 percent of the male respondents and 43.7 percent of the females who testified in this realm said that they helped work the family garden or patch, and it is significant that these percentages are the same. Tending gardens or patches of land had become common in South Carolina from the 1820s onward among slaves on both large and small holdings.[111] Moreover, tending the garden was a task in which all of the family—men, women, and children—participated. This shared responsibility provided important opportunities for male-female (as well as parent-child) socialization and bonding. As Genia Woodberry, enslaved in Marion County, recalled: "It jes lak I tellin' yunnah my Massa gi'e he colored peoples mos' eve't'ing dey hab en den he 'low eve'y family to hab uh acre uv land uv dey own to plant."[112] Charlie Davis also said that his master gave every family a garden that they could tend together all day Saturday.[113]

The ex-slaves' testimony broadly supports the proposition of Betty Wood, who, in her study of the informal slave economies of low-country Georgia, found that the slave garden tended to be a shared responsibility. She writes that "the division of labor on gardens reflected the outcome of negotiation between husband and wife, parents and children. More often than not it was shared work, rather than the exclusive responsibility of any one family member."[114] Similarly, Larry E. Hudson Jr. has argued persuasively for the importance of the slave family as an economic unit. He claims that "without assistance from family members, individual slaves would have struggled fully to exploit the land they tilled and other means of reducing their dependency. Throughout the state slaves worked in family groups and pooled their efforts."[115] Sam Polite, enslaved on St. Helena Island, testified that produce from slave gardens, including animals that were raised, could be sold for money to buy supplementary goods. He recalled: "Whe' you knock off wuk, you kin wuk on your land. Maybe you might hab two or t'ree tas' ob land 'round your cabin what Maussa gib you for plant. You kin hab chicken, maybe hawg. You kin sell aig [egg] and chicken to store and Maussa will buy your hawg. In dat way slabe kin hab money for buy t'ing lak fish and w'atebber he want."[116] Polite was lucky that his owner, "Mister Fripp," allowed his slaves to partake in these activities. This acquiescence may have been a consequence of the fact that he owned a large sea island rice plantation with more than a hundred slaves. Those on large plantations did not have to divide their time between house and field work to the same extent as those on small holdings. Further, the harshness of the rice regime notwithstanding, laboring under the task system could have allowed Polite's family more time to devote to such enterprises.

Other types of work undertaken on behalf of families show marked gender divisions. Fishing and hunting contained a strong male bias, since these were roles traditionally regarded as the preserve of men. While none of the women fished or hunted, 96.9 percent of the male ex-slaves mentioned that they partook in these activities. Women dominated when it came to making clothes and washing. Only 6.2 percent of the men, representing two informants, said they made clothes, and none washed, while 37.5 percent of the women made clothes, and 18.7 percent remembered washing them.[117] John N. Davenport's comments are typical. He stated that on his quarters in Newberry County, "Sometimes de fellows would slip off and hunt or fish a little on Sunday. Women would do washing on Saturday nights, or other nights."[118] Finally, only two ex-slaves (6.2 percent), both of whom were male, said they raised animals. In general, with the exception of laboring in their gardens, which was very much a family enterprise, the work performed by slaves for their families conforms to traditional white norms about conventional gender roles. Men undertook the more arduous physical tasks, while women's work revolved around the home.

Within the sample of full-length slave autobiographies, too, much information was given on the work that slaves performed after sundown. Jacob Stroyer reminisced about slave boys hunting on a Sunday,[119] and Charles Ball provided extensive descriptions of the types of work performed by slaves to support their own. Highly talented, Ball made wooden trays and bowls that he sold to support the family (Nero, Dinah, and their children) he lodged with. He wrote: "Before Christmas, I had sold more than thirty dollars worth of my manufactures; but the merchant with whom I traded, charged such high prices for his goods, that I was poorly compensated for my Sunday toils, and nightly labors; nevertheless, by these means, I was able to keep our family supplied with molasses, and some other luxuries, and at the approach of winter, I purchased three coarse blankets, to which Nero added as many, and we had all these made up into blanket-coats for Dinah, ourselves, and the children."[120] Ball also described how slave families supported themselves and each other in growing and exchanging produce. He stated: "We were supplied with an abundance of bread, for a peck of corn is as much as a man can consume in a week, if he has other vegetables with it; but we were obliged to provide ourselves with the other articles necessary for our subsistence. Nero had corn in his patch, which was now hard enough to be fit for boiling, and my friend Lydia had beans in her garden. We exchanged corn for beans, and had a good supply of both."[121]

Conventional norms, then, dictated that women should perform tasks about the house but also that men were expected to undertake certain types of work to support their families. This is well exemplified by Ball's comments on the husband of his friend Lydia. An African priest who maltreated his wife, this man did not perform any work other than that for the master. Ball describes him in somewhat derogatory tones: "He was compelled by the overseer to work, with the other hands, in the field, but as soon as he had come in to his cabin, he took his seat, and refused to give his wife the least assistance in doing anything. She was consequently obliged to do the little work that it was necessary to perform in the cabin, and also to bear all the labor of weeding and cultivating the family patch or garden."[122]

Despite the sharing of responsibilities, there is no doubt that the majority of female slaves faced additional burdens when it came to working for their families. Take the case of the slave Eliza. Her mistress, Elizabeth Franklin Perry, described in a letter to her husband how she had instructed Eliza to work every Saturday. In return, another one of the Perry's slaves, Delia, would wash the clothes of Eliza's family. Eliza was unhappy with this decision and suggested to Mrs. Perry that Delia would most likely resent washing the clothes of another woman's family. Besides, Eliza complained, she needed time to work for herself and to care for her children. Working on Saturdays would prevent her from doing this. Greatly angered by Eliza's outburst, Mrs. Perry replied that she was being given one whole day a week (Sunday) on which she could wash her family's clothes and that Eliza was actually a very poor washer. Her children always wore dirty clothes. Eliza then accused Mrs. Perry of not giving her enough clothes for her children, but ever sharp, Mrs. Perry responded by claiming she had given Eliza fabric and that it was her responsibility to make it up into clothes. Eliza retorted that "[s]he had no time to work for herself, that she could not see to wash at night, her eyes were bad, and after getting her supper and putting her children to sleep, there was very little time until nine o'clock, the hour you [Benjamin Perry] said she must go to bed, and after working all day steadily for me, she was not able to work at night."[123]

Eliza's complaints expose the "triple burden" that was placed upon female slaves: they were victims of gender oppression in that they had to perform work for their owners (often including "extra" work such as spinning or sewing), they had tasks to complete at home for their own families, and they also had to shoulder the heavy burden of childbearing and much of the responsibility of child rearing. Furthermore, women's role in raising children impacted upon every area of their life, including their work and their status. It led owners to see females as less valuable workers and less suitable for training in certain types of occupations. All these factors translated into a form of gendered oppression that had a significant impact on the lives of slave women.

## Social Structure within Slave Communities

How did slave men and women gain status and prestige in the eyes of their contemporaries, and how did these processes impact upon male-female bonding and relationships between slaves and owners? The social structure of enslaved communities has attracted scholarly interest for some time. Writing in the 1930s, E. Franklin Frazier's comments now appear patronizing and dated. He claimed that it was masters who created social divisions among slaves by placing certain individuals in positions of authority over others. He argued that house slaves held higher social positions than field slaves and, furthermore, that "mulatto" slaves were more likely to perform housework than those with darker skin. Frazier also claimed that because of their light coloring and the nature of their tasks, mulatto slaves were of the highest standing in slave society. Moreover, increased contact with the whites of the Big House meant that these mainly mulatto house servants adopted the "superior" white forms of "life, language, traits and habits" and that they supposedly constituted a type of hereditary caste.[124]

Frazier has been criticized for examining social structure within slave communities only as owners perceived it. The fact that slaveholders put certain individuals to work in the house does not automatically mean that their peers awarded them a higher social standing, despite what slaveholders liked to believe. From the 1970s onward, historians have attempted to analyze the social structure of slave communities from the point of view of the enslaved. A key example from this literature is Eugene Genovese, who analyzed the concept of what he terms "the legend of the house-slave elite." House servants were not regarded as a hereditary caste. Instead, he argues, whites favored domestics because they underwent significant training and were hard to replace.[125] Furthermore, within slave communities house slaves were not automatically recognized as being of high social standing. Indeed, as has been shown earlier, while some preferred housework, other slaves preferred to labor in the fields. Only whites assumed that their slaves would desire a job in the Big House.[126] In his quantitative investigation of WPA testimony, Paul D. Escott similarly questioned the notion that house slaves were more likely to identify with their owners than with others held in bondage.[127] Escott and Genovese reach similar conclusions about slave status, and both are critical of the assumption that slaves derived their communities' social structure from the work that they were assigned by whites.[128]

In noting that the WPA respondents were anxious to please white interviewers, Escott draws attention to one of the major problems of using their testimony in any investigation into slave social structure. Informants who were domestics or whose parents worked in the house were keener than those linked to field work to mention their occupation (or their parents' work) to their interviewers. Such a pattern might have reflected a desire to impress, in turn reflecting white perceptions of status within slavery. The ex-slave Rosa Starke, of Winnsboro, touched on white notions of the higher status of domestics: "A house nigger man might swoop down and mate wid a field hand's good lookin' daughter, now and then, for pure love of her, but you never see a house gal lower herself by marryin' and matin' wid a common field-hand nigger. Dat offend de white folks, 'specially de young misses, who liked de business of match makin' and matin' of de young slaves."[129] Starke pointed to white manipulation of marriage patterns, suggesting that slaves tended not to marry those from different occupational categories for fear of "offending" whites. However, it would seem that her comments are atypical: most slaves married whom they wanted to marry, regardless of their job, although as has been shown, at a practical level, slaves from the same occupational grouping may have had more chances to mix with each other. Starke's comments therefore tell us more about what white owners wanted to believe about the social structure of slave communities than about the actual social structure itself.

## SLAVE OWNERS AND SOCIAL STRUCTURE

Establishing owners' perceptions of social structure among their slaves is of vital importance in illustrating how the worldviews of slaves and masters were at odds and how slave communities strove to act upon their own cultural norms. Slaveholders rationalized bondage by defining a minority of those they held as favored key slaves. Michael Tadman has argued that, for the typical owner, certain elite slaves (the driver and his wife and one or two senior domestics) were, psychologically and ideologically, of critical importance. Masters, he argues, could congratulate themselves that they treated these "worthy" (key) slaves with benevolence, and this allowed them to treat "less worthy" (non-key) slaves with indifference and racist contempt. This process, Tadman argues, was critical for the maintenance of the owner's benevolent self-image, which did not necessarily reflect the way they treated most of those they held in bondage.[130]

The nature of the relationship between the work completed by slaves and that by their parents is also important in any consideration of status, since a pattern of slave children following in their parents' occupational footsteps would suggest that owners favored certain individuals or families when it came to ascribing tasks. In his study of the WPA narratives, Stephen Crawford found that 79 percent of the daughters of house servants in his sample held domestic positions as their initial adult job, allowing him to claim that slave daughters generally worked in the same capacity as their mothers.[131] Some slaves may have had input into the types of tasks they performed. Parents often influenced their children, while others had set ideas about what types of work they found preferable. Jacob Stroyer described how he was unhappy about being taken to work in the field, having previously taken care of his master's horses. He successfully complained to his mistress, protesting that his deceased master had said that he could become a carpenter. He wrote: "I was informed by one of the slaves, who was a carpenter, that she [his mistress] had ordered that I should go and work at the trade with him. This gave me great joy."[132] Charles Ball, on his own initiative, made a weir across a river to catch fish. He was subsequently put in charge of supplying the whole plantation with this foodstuff.[133]

In the realm of female labor, Deborah G. White has written that "becoming a cook or seamstress or midwife sometimes involved more than just having the favor bestowed on one by the master or mistress. Skills were sometimes passed down from one generation to the next within a slave family."[134] Consequently, certain slave girls might have become domestics because their mothers taught them valuable skills or as a result of them expressing a desire to work in this capacity. Some therefore served as "informal apprentices to their mothers."[135] Certainly, many mothers taught their daughters. In her autobiography, Lucy A. Delany describes how she was sold to Mrs. Mitchell to work as a house servant. However, since Delany's only previous job had been looking after children, she wrote: "I had no more idea how it was to be done than Mrs. Mitchell herself. But I made the effort to do what she required, and my failure would have been amusing had it not been so appalling." Delany therefore asked her mother for help in showing her how to clean clothes properly.[136] The ultimate decision as to the tasks slaves performed, however, did rest with slaveholders. For example, Jacob Stroyer could not have worked as a carpenter had his mistress not given her consent. Similarly, Lucy Delany was chosen to labor in the house despite having no previous knowledge of this realm of work. Regardless of slave sentiments, owners often employed slaves in similar positions to their parents.[137]

The tasks performed by parents and children in the South Carolina WPA narratives were compared using the same broad categories used earlier in this chapter, and it was found that occupational patterns were usually strongly influenced by owners. Small sample size was a problem when it came to comparing the work of fathers and children, with only sixteen respondents mentioning their father's work as well as their own.[138] Furthermore, only two—a house servant and a field hand—stated that their fathers labored in the field.[139] The others all said that their fathers performed house or skilled work. Bias toward domestics, coupled with the small sample size, therefore makes it impossible to gain useful evidence on the likelihood of young slaves following the occupations of their fathers.

A comparison of the work of the informants with that of their mothers proved more fruitful. The sample size was larger, with forty-one respondents who commented on their own labor also mentioning that of their mothers.[140] Thus there was not such a pronounced bias toward domestics in this sample. There was also a correlation between the tasks performed by the informants and those of their mothers: 71.3 percent of those who worked in the house had mothers who did the same, while 61.5 percent of field hands had mothers who labored in the field.[141] Those who performed no work were also more likely to have mothers who worked as house or skilled slaves (61.5 percent) than field hands (38.5 percent).

These findings are important in an assessment of social structure as defined by owners. Slaveholders ascribed house servants a higher status than field slaves, and high-status, skilled house slaves who held close relationships with owners were more likely to have children who would move into senior domestic positions. Conversely, some rank-and-file field hands would never have the opportunity of working in the Big House or having children who did. Such differences were cultivated over generations; slave owners believed in and strove to create a house-servant "elite," reserving certain positions for favored families (from whom a core of key slaves would emerge), thereby creating and maintaining close relationships between themselves and a minority of those they held in bondage.

However, it is also important to remember that even the privileged were subject to the indignities of living under a system of oppression. William Dusinberre has shown that on the Manigault plantations of the low country, "the privilege of holding a relatively good job could easily be lost. . . . Privilege granted was readily withdrawn."[142] He therefore suggests that many desired high-status positions for individualistic or familial reasons. Being a favored slave could bring material rewards to families. It also enabled them to escape the harshness and monotony of the regime, since unskilled work could be boring and repetitive. Dusinberre writes that although such aims were "not inspired by devotion to the welfare of the whole slave community," they should not be seen as "less admirable for being this-worldly and individualistic." These slaves were "combating through their own personal development their masters' impulse to render slaves wholly powerless and dishonored."[143] Moreover, seeking privilege for the benefit of their families is surely to be commended in illustrating just how much slaves valued their relationships with their spouses and children.

There is some evidence in the South Carolina WPA narratives to suggest that house slaves had a greater likelihood of living in nuclear, rather than cross-plantation, families, although the sample size is small. There were thirty-seven respondents whose parents both held house or skilled occupations who also commented on their family type. Of these, twenty-seven (72.9 percent) lived in nuclear households, and ten (27.1 percent) in cross-plantation families. This compares with the eighteen respondents who came from families where both parents labored in the field. Nine of these resided within nuclear families, and nine within cross-plantation, representing 50 percent each. As was seen in chapter 2, owners sometimes indulged house slaves by buying their chosen partners. It has been suggested that the marriages most likely to be protected were not simply those of domestics as a group but especially the subset of key slaves with whom owners felt that they had special bonds of affection and respect.[144] For many, though, working in the Big House would have had more pressures and inconveniences than owners cared to admit. Since slaves strove for autonomy in their personal affairs, being in close proximity to whites could be restrictive. This reinforces the point that it was owners rather than slaves who ascribed a high status to those who performed housework. They strove to divide their slaves along status lines, and in trying to generate an elite they also took comfort in their self-image as benevolent masters who treated "worthy" slaves well.

As well as awarding domestics a higher status than field hands, owners also saw house servants as more similar to themselves, and they took pride in the close relationships they shared. The Darlington owner Ada Bacot touched on these ideas in her diary: upon hearing that a mistress had been smothered in her bed at the hands of her own slaves, Bacot feared violence from her own field workers. Significantly, though, she was not scared of her domestics. Bacot wrote: "We none of us know when we are safe. I have some [slaves] about me that I fear it would take very little to make them put me out of the way. I don't mean any of my house servants for I think they are very fond of me."[145]

Because owners saw their house servants and certain favored slaves as more like themselves, they often allowed them special "privileges" and "rewards." The WPA respondent Rebecca Jane Grant, enslaved in Beaufort County, mentioned a significant example: "De drivers and de overseers, de house servants, de bricklayers and folks like dat'd go to de white folk's church. But not de field hands."[146] It may, however, be questioned whether the majority of slaves would have wanted to go to the "white folk's" church. Other informants were also aware of the "privileges" that whites might grant to house but not field slaves. John Collins, the child of a field hand from Chester County, testified: "Marster didn't have many slaves. Best I 'member, dere was about twenty men, women, and chillun to work in de field and five house slaves. Dere was no good feelin's twixt field hands and house servants. De house servants put on more airs than de white folks. They got better things to eat, too, than de field hands and wore better and cleaner clothes."[147] Similarly, observers often noted how well-dressed the slaves were within the city of Charleston.[148] Since most worked as domestics and lived within the houses of their owners, having smartly attired slaves reflected well on slaveholders, and it is also likely that the slaves themselves appreciated a touch of luxury. However, for many these material benefits came with a high price: isolation, loneliness, and a separation from the wider slave community.

SLAVES AND SOCIAL STRUCTURE

Owners sought to create disunity among their slaves by awarding them unequal privileges, but despite the encouragement of these divisions, the slaves' own notions of status, which were not based upon being favored by whites, limited the effectiveness of such tactics. Slaveholders did not, for the most part, succeed in splitting their slaves along status lines. Indeed, the enslaved strove for autonomy in their marital, residential, and cultural arrangements regardless of their work. As has been shown, the occupations of seamstress, cook, and midwife all held places of considerable social standing for female slaves.[149] Notably, these positions required considerable amounts of skill that could be transferred over generations. Further, they were all occupations that benefited slave as well as white communities. For men, the positions of blacksmith, carpenter, or shoemaker, for example, possessed the same characteristics, requiring talents that were of use to many slaves. This differentiated them from general house servants, and it also indicates that community values rather than straightforward "skills" were important considerations when ascribing status.

Moreover, since it took a considerable amount of time to become competent in the positions listed above, it is likely that social structure within slave communities was also influenced by age.[150] How slaves defined social status differently from their owners has been investigated by Larry E. Hudson Jr., who argues that it was the increased use of cash in slave quarters in the antebellum period (for example, through selling produce from slave gardens) that facilitated the development of status divisions. Status was therefore linked to economic autonomy from whites and also to the provision of services to the enslaved.[151] Hudson suggests that a type of meritocracy for entrepreneurial slaves existed on plantations: "However humble their beginnings, industrious slaves, be they skilled or unskilled, house or field, young or old, male or female, could, if they desired, aspire to positions of power and influence in the slave quarters."[152]

Much of the initial research into the social structure of slave communities as defined by slaves (rather than by owners) has come from John W. Blassingame, who made the original claim that "slaves reserved the top rungs of the social ladder for those blacks who performed services for other slaves rather than for whites."[153] He placed conjurers, preachers, midwives, and root doctors (all of whom were likely to have been rather elderly) at the top of his social structure; while exploitative drivers, live-in houseservants with many years of service, voluntary concubines, and informants languished at the bottom.[154] Slave communities held conjurers in awe, as many WPA informants testified. Thomas Harper of Fairfield County said: "There was a conjurer in our neighborhood who could make you do what he wanted, sometimes he had folks killed."[155] Similarly, Sallie Layton Keenan, enslaved in Spartanburg and later in Mississippi, recalled: "When my paw, Obie, wuz a courtin, a nigger put a spell on him kaise he was a wantin' my maw too. De nigger got a conjure bag and drapped it in de spring what my paw drunk water from. He wuz laid up on a bed o' rheumatiz fer six weeks."[156]

Slaves who used their alleged spiritual powers for positive purposes were elevated to the highest positions. Gus Feaster reminisced that old women on his plantation served as "root doctors" by making herbal remedies. He testified: "Dem old womens made pine rosin pills from de pine rosin what drapped from de pine trees and give de pills to de folks to take fer de back ache."[157] Similarly, Solomon Caldwell remembered how his mother used to make the herbal medicines on their quarters: "I 'member my ma would take fever grass and boil it to a tea and have us drink it to keep de fever away. She used branch elder twigs and dogwood berries for chills."[158] The importance of Christianity also meant that religious leaders commanded considerable respect and high social status. Within the WPA sample, 132 individuals commented on religion, representing 39.5 percent of all respondents. Only two of these professed to be nonbelievers, with all others expressing positive sentiments.[159] As Affie Singleton recalled, slaves used to sing at night "didn't my soul feel happy when I come out the wilderness leaning on the Lord." Overall, WPA evidence suggests that slave preachers held positions of high status within their communities.[160]

Clearly, considerable differences existed between the ways in which slaves and owners ascribed social status. Slaveholders rationalized bondage by awarding domestics a high status, since favoring certain key house and skilled slaves and treating them well reaffirmed their belief in their own benevolence. Slaves who commanded positions of social prestige within their own communities, however, were those who held skills that were of benefit to their peers as well as white owners. House and field slaves displayed different marital patterns, but even so, one-third of the South Carolina WPA respondents married someone from a different occupational grouping, and slaves showed considerable independence of thought when choosing whom they wanted to wed (regardless of the whims of their owners and the residential arrangements that marriage might entail). Despite the efforts by owners to control the lives of those they held in bondage and indoctrinate a few key individuals into their own white world, slaves showed initiative and a robust desire to live according to their own norms and customs.

Work was highly gendered, but some female slaves assumed leading roles in their communities. Women's childbearing and child-rearing roles made profound differences between the lives of men and women, placing heavy burdens upon females. However, while enslaved women were victims of gender discrimination because they had to perform specific types of work for their families in addition to laboring for owners and their childcare responsibilities, men also had their own particular duties and obligations. The work that spouses performed for families was therefore very much a shared responsibility. Furthermore, it was the strength of the relationships between them that facilitated this joint approach. In caring for their families, the work roles for men and women were different but also relatively egalitarian. Take, for example, the reminiscences of Tom Jones in his slave narrative: "Father and mother tried to make it [their cabin] a happy place for their dear children. They worked late into the night many and many a time to get a little simple furniture for their home and the home of their children; and they spent many hours of willing toil to stop up the chinks between the logs of their poor hut, that they and their children might be protected from the storm and the cold."[161] While evidence on work shows a high level of gendering, it also indicates significant links across slave communities and significant sharing within the family. Once slaves had settled into a stable union, both partners labored together, albeit sometimes in different ways, to provide for their own and to make their lives as comfortable as possible. Clearly, status differences according to gender must be understood within a context of broad cooperation.

## Notes

1. For more on wealthy slave owners who lived on the Waccamaw River, All Saints Parish, see Joyner, *Down by the Riverside*, 34.

2. On the evolution of the task system, see Hudson, *To Have and to Hold*, 2; Edgar, *South Carolina*, 313; Berlin, *Many Thousands Gone*, 166–67; and Morgan, *Slave Counterpoint*, 179–87.

3. Leslie A. Schwalm has argued that, paradoxically, this increased the burdens upon slave women who labored under the task system. See *A Hard Fight for We*, 4.

4. James Henry Hammond, after inheriting the Silver Bluff plantation on the Savannah River, was anxious to abolish the task system his slaves were accustomed to. He felt that they worked too quickly and too carelessly in their quest for free time. Hammond was determined to only use the gang labor system. See Faust, *James Henry Hammond and the Old South*, 74–75.

5. Escott, *Slavery Remembered*, 13.

6. Similarly, Escott found that the potential bias toward house servants did not constitute a methodological problem: "Astute commentators have warned that the predominance of house servants and young slaves could produce overly fond memories of the master . . . and of the relationships between whites and blacks. The author has found few such memories in the narratives, and many of quite a different kind" (ibid., 16–17).

7. Ibid., 27.

8. See Fogel and Engerman, *Time on the Cross*, 39–40. Herbert Gutman and Richard Sutch, however, believe that Fogel and Engerman underestimated the number of field slaves. See Gutman and Sutch, "Sambo Makes Good," 77–80.

9. See Weiner, *Mistresses and Slaves*, 8; and Schwartz, *Born in Bondage*, 108.

10. Within the South Carolina WPA narratives, thirteen of the 146 respondents who related their work under slavery said that their labor changed from housework to field work during bondage. Most of these also said that this shift occurred between the ages of twelve and thirteen. Other historians have found that around these ages there was a major shift from housework to permanent field work. See Crawford, "Quantified Memory," 55; Weiner, *Mistresses and Slaves*, 8–9; and Schwartz, *Born in Bondage*, 132–34.

11. Rawick, *American Slave*, vol. 3, pt. 4, 156.

12. This category includes general house servants, child minders, bodyguards, carriage drivers, carpenters, and midwives.

13. This category includes general field hands, those who cared for animals or scared birds, and respondents who fetched water or wood to the field.

14. These assertions reinforce the claims of Stephen Crawford and Marli F. Weiner that male and female slaves underwent different childhood work experiences from age five onward. Girls were more likely to perform work at an earlier age and were also more likely to labor in the Big House. See Crawford, "Quantified Memory," 47–50; and Weiner, *Mistresses and Slaves*, 8–9.

15. This compares to the 21.6 percent of fathers and 41.2 percent of mothers who labored in the field.

16. Jones, *Experience and Personal Narrative*, 10–11.

17. See Ball, *Fifty Years in Chains*, 301, for a description of his role as an overseer.

18. Roper, *Narrative of the Adventures*, 70.

19. See Stroyer, *My Life in the South*, 17, 32, 34–35, for descriptions of the work he performed when enslaved.

20. Aleckson, *Before the War and after the Union*, 87.

21. See Lowery, *Life on the Old Plantation*, 15.

22. Jacobs, *Incidents*, 44, chaps. 14–16.

23. See Jackson, *Story of Mattie J. Jackson*, 26; Delany, *From the Darkness Cometh the Light*, 24; Drumgoold, *Slave Girl's Story*, 10.

24. Burton, *Memories*, 3.

25. Rawick, *American Slave*, vol. 3, pt. 4, 121–22.

26. See chap. 4 for a discussion of the sexual abuse that Linda Brent suffered at the hands of Dr. Flint.

27. See Ball, *Fifty Years in Chains*, 116–18.

28. White, *Ar'n't I a Woman?* 121. See also Weiner, *Mistresses and Slaves*, 13.

29. Rawick, *American Slave*, vol. 2, pt. 2, 50.

30. Ibid., vol. 3, pt. 3, 49.

31. Ibid., vol. 2, pt. 1, 173.

32. Ibid., 299–303. Davis was a house servant whose husband worked in the field.

33. Paul D. Escott also found a high level of same-occupation marriage among slaves in *Slavery Remembered*, 61.

34. William Dusinberre argues that marriage was the principal institution that dissolved the line between privileged slaves and field hands. He claims that a high turnover in certain jobs was important here, as will later be shown. See *Them Dark Days*, 199.

35. On marriage markets, see also Crawford, "Quantified Memory," 188; and Hudson, *To Have and to Hold*, 142–43.

36. Two WPA respondents were enslaved in Charleston (Susan Hamlin and Amos Gadsden). Both referred to the hiring out of slaves within the city: Hamlin was enslaved to Edward Fuller and lived on St. Philip Street. She was hired out to Mr. McDonald on Atlantic Street. See Rawick, *American Slave*, vol. 2, pt. 2, 226–27. Gadsden spoke of neighbors hiring out slaves (ibid., 92).

37. See chap. 1 for more on the freedoms afforded urban slaves.

38. Anne Simons Deas, "Two Years of Plantation Life," 28, SCL.

39. See also Burton, *In My Father's House*, 181.

40. Anne Simons Deas, "Two Years of Plantation Life," 124, SCL.

41. Letter to Charles Manigault from Louis Manigault, 4 March 1854, Manigault Family Papers, SCL. Also quoted in Clifton, ed., *Life and Labor on Argyle Island*, 177.

42. Schwalm, *A Hard Fight for We*, 21.

43. Judith A. Carney has argued that the association of rice sowing with female labor had its origins in African society. See *Black Rice*, 120–21. Philip D. Morgan also claims that African slaves contributed to the development of South Carolina's rice economy in *Slave Counterpoint*, 183. The evolution of rice cultivation in the low country is also considered in Berlin, *Many Thousands Gone*, chap. 6.

44. Entry for 9 April 1853, Ben Sparkman Plantation Journal, SHC.

45. Ibid., 12 April 1853.

46. Entry for 24 August 1857, John Edwin Fripp Plantation Journal, SHC.

47. Ibid., 2 February 1858.

48. Davis, "Reflections," 7.

49. See Welter, "Cult of True Womanhood," 115. For more on the polarity between ideologies of black and white womanhood under slavery, see Carby, *Reconstructing Womanhood*, chap. 2; and Fox-Genovese, *Within the Plantation Household*, 50–51. Fox-Genovese draws attention to Sojourner Truth's "Ar'n't I a Woman?" speech, in which she called into question the notion of womanhood in the experience of slave women.

50. See Dill, "Fictive Kin, Paper Sons, and *Compadrazgo*," 153.

51. Fox-Genovese, *Within the Plantation Household*, 172–74.

52. Ibid., 176–77.

53. White, *Ar'n't I a Woman?* 121.

54. See Joyner, *Down by the Riverside*, 45.

55. Weiner, *Mistresses and Slaves*, 12–13.

56. Jacqueline Jones has advocated this proposition in *Labor of Love, Labor of Sorrow*, chap. 1.

57. Entry for 18 December 1854, Ben Sparkman Plantation Journal, SHC.

58. Entry for 10 December 1832, Samuel Cram Jackson Diary, SHC.

59. Rawick, *American Slave*, vol. 3, pt. 4, 223.

60. Ibid., 222.

61. Ball, *Fifty Years in Chains*, 118–19.

62. Ibid., 147.

63. Roper, *Narrative of the Adventures*, 16.

64. Entry for 29 September 1855, Thomas Blewett Plantation Book, SCL.

65. Entry for 15 May 1864, Margaret Ann (Meta) Morris Diary, SHC.

66. Letter to William Blanding from Lucy Carpenter [sister], 23 January 1849, William Blanding Papers, SCL.

67. Letter to Benjamin Franklin Perry from Elizabeth Perry, 29 November 1843, Benjamin Franklin Perry Papers, SCL.

68. Weiner, *Mistresses and Slaves*, 9–10.

69. Rawick, *American Slave*, vol. 2, pt. 1, 100.

70. Ibid., vol. 2, pt. 2, 206.

71. Ibid., 327.

72. Joyner, *Down by the Riverside*, 75.

73. White, *Ar'n't I a Woman?* 129.

74. See Jones, *Labor of Love, Labor of Sorrow*, 18. Leslie A. Schwalm has also noted the high number of male artisans in low-country rice plantations in *A Hard Fight for We*, 32.

75. Fogel and Engerman, *Time on the Cross*, 39.

76. Schwalm, *A Hard Fight for We*, 45.

77. Wood, *Women's Work, Men's Work*, 106.

78. Genovese, *Roll, Jordan, Roll*, 355–56.

79. On stereotypes, see chap. 5. See also Fox-Genovese, *Within the Plantation Household*, 291–92; and White, *Ar'n't I a Woman?* chap. 1.

80. Fox-Genovese, *Within the Plantation Household*, 292.

81. Mary Esther Huger Reminiscences, SCL.

82. Anne Simons Deas, "Two Years of Plantation Life," 7, SCL.

83. Lowery, *Life on the Old Plantation*, 51–52.

84. See Weiner, *Mistresses and Slaves*, 19.

85. Rawick, *American Slave*, vol. 2, pt. 1, 39.

86. Ibid., vol. 2, pt. 2, 35.

87. Ibid., 162.

88. Letter to Benjamin Franklin Perry from Elizabeth Perry, 30 November 1850, Benjamin Franklin Perry Papers, SCL.

89. Ibid., 29 March 1852.

90. See Schwartz, *Born in Bondage*, 34–35.

91. Rawick, *American Slave*, vol. 2, pt. 2, 114.

92. Ibid., vol. 3, pt. 3, 3. See also Schwalm, *A Hard Fight for We*, 59; and Weiner, *Mistresses and Slaves*, 10.

93. Rawick, *American Slave*, vol. 3, pt. 3, 24.

94. Ibid., vol. 2, pt. 1, 39.

95. Ibid., vol. 2, pt. 2, 236.

96. Ibid., 12.

97. Ibid., vol. 3, pt. 3, 273. See also Schwalm, *A Hard Fight for We*, 43.

98. Rawick, *American Slave*, vol. 11, 316.

99. Entry for 16 June 1857, John Edwin Fripp Plantation Journal, SHC.

100. Letter to Benjamin Franklin Perry from Elizabeth Perry, 30 June 1848, Benjamin Franklin Perry Papers, SCL.

101. Cornhill Plantation Book, 1827–73, McDonald-Furman Papers, WRPL.

102. Andrew Flinn Plantation Book, 1840, SCL.

103. Rawick, *American Slave*, vol. 2, pt. 1, 119.

104. Ibid., vol. 2, pt. 2, 12–13.

105. See King, *Stolen Childhood*, 13–14; Kemble, *Journal of a Residence*, 359–60; and Schwartz, *Born in Bondage*, 69–72. The South Carolina WPA respondent Rebecca Jane Grant said that old men would sometimes care for children (Rawick, *American Slave*, vol. 2, pt. 2, 179). See also Jones, "Cultural Middle Passage," 103, 108, for an example of a Florida plantation where an elderly slave couple shared responsibility for the children in the nursery.

106. Rawick, *American Slave*, vol. 11, 124.

107. Ball, *Fifty Years in Chains*, 122.

108. See Schwartz, *Born in Bondage*, 63–65.

109. See Schwalm, *A Hard Fight for We*, 47.

110. For a discussion of the lives of slaves after sundown, see Rawick, *From Sundown to Sunup*. In the South Carolina WPA evidence, men made thirty-two comments on work for families, and women made sixteen.

111. See Hudson, *To Have and to Hold*, 10; and Saville, *Work of Reconstruction*, 7.

112. Rawick, *American Slave*, vol. 3. pt. 4, 219.

113. Ibid., vol. 2, pt. 1, 246.

114. Wood, *Women's Work, Men's Work*, 41.

115. Hudson, *To Have and to Hold*, 32–33. See also chap. 2, "The Family as an Economic Unit," 32–78.

116. Rawick, *American Slave*, vol. 3, pt. 3, 272.

117. Of course, it is likely that the number of women who washed their family's clothes was nearer to 100 percent, but not all respondents thought this worthy of mention to their interviewers.

118. Rawick, *American Slave*, vol. 2, pt. 1, 241.

119. Stroyer, *My Life in the South*, 46–47.

120. Ball, *Fifty Years in Chains*, 134.

121. Ibid., 133.

122. Ibid., 197. See also chap. 2 of this volume.

123. Letter to Benjamin Franklin Perry from Elizabeth Perry, "Monday afternoon," [no year], Benjamin Franklin Perry Papers, SCL.

124. See Frazier, "Negro Slave Family," 207–11.

125. Genovese, *Roll, Jordan, Roll*, 328–29.

126. Ibid., 331.

127. Escott writes: "Repeatedly in the narratives the former slaves spoke of the concern for each other that united their group and ignored the supposed attractions of the big house" (*Slavery Remembered*, 64).

128. Even so, Escott is somewhat critical of what he sees as Genovese's preoccupation with the minority of slaves on extremely large plantations who were status-conscious. He argues that Genovese underestimated the desire to satisfy white interviewers. See ibid., 63–64.

129. Rawick, *American Slave*, vol. 3, pt. 4, 148.

130. On the concept of key slaves, see the introduction to Tadman, *Speculators and Slaves*, and "Persistent Myth of Paternalism."

131. Crawford, "Quantified Memory," 63.

132. Stroyer, *My Life in the South*, 30–32.

133. Ball, *Fifty Years in Chains*, 203–5.

134. White, *Ar'n't I a Woman?* 129.

135. See Weiner, *Mistresses and Slaves*, 8.

136. Delany, *From the Darkness Cometh the Light*, 24–25.

137. Michael P. Johnson has argued that young slaves were "reared" to do the same kind of work as their parents. The children of house slaves gravitated toward work in the Big House, while the children of field hands tended to stay in the field. See "Work Culture and the Slave Community," 339, 342.

138. These included nine field slaves, four who did not work, and three house workers.

139. These were Margaret Hughes (Rawick, *American Slave*, vol. 2, pt. 2, 327) and Jessie Williams (ibid., vol. 3, pt. 4, 202).

140. This sample consisted of fifteen house or skilled workers, thirteen field workers, and thirteen respondents who did not work under slavery.

141. This compares to the 26.7 percent of house slaves whose mothers were field hands and the 35.8 percent of field slaves whose mothers were skilled or house slaves.

142. Dusinberre, *Them Dark Days*, 179.

143. Ibid., 195.

144. On the protection of the marriages of key slaves from sale, see Tadman, *Speculators and Slaves*, xix–xxxvii.

145. Entry for 21 September 1861, Ada Bacot Diary, SCL.

146. Rawick, *American Slave*, vol. 2, pt. 2, 184–85.

147. Ibid., vol. 2, pt. 1, 225.

148. Powers, *Black Charlestonians*, 21–22.

149. White, *Ar'n't I a Woman?* 129.

150. White notes that "the slave woman's status in the slave community seems to have increased with old age as a consequence of her service as caretaker of children, nurse, and midwife" (ibid., 129).

151. Hudson, "'All That Cash,'" 83.

152. Hudson, *To Have and to Hold*, 31.

153. Blassingame, "Status and Social Structure," 142. Paul A. Cimbala argues that slave instrumentalists, or "musicianers," also held an important position in slave social structure because they played an important role in Saturday night frolics. See "Fortunate Bondsmen."

154. See Blassingame, "Status and Social Structure," 150–51, for Blassingame's classification system of the internal social structure of the slave community. On exploitative drivers, see also Van Deburg, "Slave Drivers and Slave Narratives."

155. Rawick, *American Slave*, vol. 2, pt. 2, 240.

156. Ibid., vol. 3, pt. 3, 78.

157. Ibid., vol. 2, pt. 2, 55.

158. Ibid., vol. 2, pt. 1, 171.

159. One nonbeliever was M. E. Abrams, although she did believe in the power of spiritualism (ibid., 2). The other was John C. Brown of Winnsboro. Brown was the son of a white mother and lived with a stepmother who mistreated him. It was possibly these experiences that led him to hold negative views on religion (ibid., 130). See also chap. 4 of this volume.

160. Ibid., vol. 11, 283.

161. Jones, *Experience and Personal Narrative*, 6.

# 4 Interracial Sexual Contact

> The slave master's sexual domination of the black woman
> contained an unveiled element of counter-insurgency. . . .
> In confronting the black woman as adversary in a sexual
> contest, the master would be subjecting her to the most
> elemental form of terrorism distinctively suited for the fe-
> male: rape. Given the already terroristic texture of planta-
> tion life, it would be as potential victim of rape that the
> slave woman would be most unguarded.
>
> —Angela Davis, *Women, Race, and Class*

Chapters 4 and 5 examine the exploitation inflicted upon
slaves and the impact of this on male-female relations. Exploitation could
take many forms, including physical punishment, sexual abuse, or sale
and separation from loved ones. What is significant is that oppression
by owners stimulated the slaves' desire to create social space—distance
between their lives and those of their masters. Thus, although forms of
exploitation were often gender-specific, resistance to it was part of the
bonding process between slave men and women. This chapter investigates an area of oppression that affected females more than males—sexual contact with and abuse by whites. Such abuse of enslaved women
by white men constitutes one of the major differences between the lives
of slave men and women.

However, a parallel in the lives of male and female slaves also deserves
recognition; namely, the way in which both were stereotyped by whites
as being sexually promiscuous. It is highly ironic that slaves were defined
in this way, since slave marriages were neither protected through the law
nor religious bodies, and owners frequently broke up couples through sales

and separations. However, stereotyping served to rationalize interracial sexual liaisons in the minds of slaveholders, while removing the blame for sexual contact from white members of society (with the exception of poor white women). Stereotypical attitudes provide an important perspective from which to examine issues of sexual relationships and sexual abuse. After establishing the white mythmaking of black sexuality, what seem to be exceptional sexual liaisons are explored—those between white women and black men. More widespread patterns—sexual encounters between white men and slave women—are then considered, and it is argued that owners rather than overseers or other whites were the main abusers or white sexual partners of enslaved females. The significance of this upon relationships between slave women and the wives of slaveholders is then explored. Finally, possible links between sexual contact and manumissions are investigated, suggesting that the number of female slaves who sought to gain their freedom through sexual relationships with white men was actually very small; instead, they endeavored to survive their oppression by gaining the love and support of a spouse.

One major problem encountered when examining sexual relationships between whites and blacks revolves around the difficulty of establishing whether such liaisons took the form of voluntary relationships or forced sexual abuse. It cannot be assumed that all white women who were sexually involved with black men were victims of sexual harassment or abuse. Neither can it be taken for granted that all slave women involved in liaisons with white men were victims of harassment or enforced sexual relationships (although it will be argued that most sexual contact between enslaved women and white men was a result of exploitation). This chapter seeks to understand the motives behind all types of sexual contact to encompass voluntary and involuntary interracial liaisons.

South Carolina WPA testimony is used extensively in the construction of quantitative trends concerning the extent of interracial sexual contact. Moreover, their detailed textual information on such issues has also proven valuable. The full-length autobiographies are also extremely useful in this realm, especially the memoirs of Harriet Jacobs, which illustrate in detail the sexual harassment Linda Brent suffered at the hands of her master, Dr. Flint.[1] Manuscript materials left by owners are of more limited use because slaveholders often did not want to mention sensitive issues, or matters pertaining to sexual relationships may have been destroyed by later generations. However, the attitudes of slave mistresses toward issues of interracial sexual contact and abuse will be considered from a historiographical perspective.

## The Stereotyping of Male and Female Slaves

Whites stereotyped slaves of both sexes in their attempt to justify sexual encounters with them. The fact that the "Jezebel" image of slave women, brilliantly analyzed by Deborah G. White, bears a striking resemblance to the "Buck" character of slave men is immensely significant. White has argued that Jezebel was one of the most prevalent images of black womanhood in antebellum America. The counterimage of the ideal Victorian "Lady"—governed by piety, domesticity, and prudery—Jezebel was ruled by her libido.[2] Stereotyping female slaves in this way, therefore, emphasized promiscuity in much the same way as the male version of this character construction. Buck reversed the notion of the planter cavalier and, like Jezebel, was governed by his sexuality. Buck encoded white fears of black male virility, in particular the threat of black sexuality to white women. Elizabeth Fox-Genovese notes that this was "a fascinating reversal since the main interracial sexual threat was that of white predators against black women."[3]

Buck also contradicted the other stereotype to which male slaves were subjected—that of "Sambo," who represented an image of black male subservience and docility, serving to reassure whites of their ability to control their slaves.[4] Similarly, Jezebel was at odds with the other female slave stereotype of the "Mammy." Jezebel "legitimized the wanton behavior of white men by proclaiming black women to be lusty wenches in whom sexual impulse overwhelmed all restraint. The image eased the consciences of white men by suggesting that black women asked for the treatment they received."[5] By defining certain female slaves as Jezebels, white men could thereby excuse themselves from any blame involving involuntary sexual liaisons. Likewise, the Buck image removed the blame from certain white women involved in intimate relationships with black men.

The extent to which the stereotype of Jezebel eased the consciences of white men can be seen through the images of slave women they presented in their manuscripts records. John C. Gorman, a captain in the North Carolina infantry during the Civil War who was hospitalized in Beaufort, South Carolina, wrote in his diary: "Besides soldiers, there are but few whites, but a great many citizen negroes among them oceans of women, who live by harlotry and do little or no more work—They dress generally flashy and use the manners of their former mistresses. They live on easy equality with the Yankee women, are even impudent to them, and appear as if they felt they were their equals every way. Their state of morals, from what I have witnessed, is decidedly loose, and illicit intercourse is general. I often see the soldiers lounging in the shade in company with their dark-skinned mistresses, rollicking and playing with a freedom from all coyness or shame. They have their classes, a few, especially whose blood is intermixed with that of the white man, are the elite."[6] The image of black womanhood presented by Gorman displays many of the characteristics typically associated with Jezebel, including being light-skinned, impudent, and immoral. Gorman was compelled to conclude from his observations that these black women would be "kept" by their white lovers. Whether this was true or not is less significant than the fact that he supposed these women actually desired to be kept by white men. His assumptions therefore reveal much about the perceptions of black females by white men.

However, white men were not the only ones who held the Jezebel stereotype of slave women to be true. Many white women also utilized the image to remove blame from their husbands in cases of interracial sexual contact. In her diary, for example, the plantation mistress Keziah Brevard of Richland District illustrates the contempt that was felt by many white women at the alleged promiscuity of their female slaves. Brevard seems to have accepted a certain degree of promiscuity among her slave men as inevitable, but it was inexcusable for the women. She wrote: "They are not prepared for freedom, many of them set no higher value on themselves than the beasts of the field do—I know a family in five miles of me where there are six women who have and have had children for thirty years back and not one of them but [have] been bastards and only one ever had a husband. . . . I own many slaves and many of the females are of the lowest cast—making miserable their own fellow servants by meddling with the husbands of others—I am not excusing the males, but in the world they are not so degraded by such conduct as the females."[7] It is ironic that slave women bore the brunt of the blame for interracial sexual contact through being labeled as Jezebels. While it is true that slaves of both sexes could potentially be characterized as sexually promiscuous, such a characteristic was seen as especially in conflict with notions of femininity; the alleged sexual "weakness" of slave women removed them from the idealized image of womanhood represented by the white Lady.

Slave sources give a unique perspective on sexual encounters between white men and black women. The South Carolina WPA respondent Cornelius Holmes, although not explicitly referring to the Jezebel stereotype, suggested to his interviewer that female slaves offered a kind of "protection" to white women from enticement and seduction by white men. Holmes's grandfather had told him that the sanctification of white women was of vital importance to their society and that he had "never heard of a bad white woman befo' freedom." Implicitly, then, Holmes seems to be referring to the ways in which white men could act out their sexual desires upon female slaves and leave the chastity and overall "purity" of white women intact. Furthermore, casting black women as the polar opposites of white women also served to legitimize white men's behavior. Unfortunately, Holmes did not indicate to his interviewer the extent to which he felt sexual relations between white men and slave women were enforced.[8] However, he did unwittingly illustrate how the stereotype of Jezebel also allowed for the creation of the idealized Lady figure of white womanhood. Because Jezebel was there for the sexual pleasures of white men, white women could be elevated onto a pedestal: Here sat the Lady with all her connotations of purity, spirituality, and virginity, where they were viewed as "moral exemplars and counselors."[9]

In the full-length slave autobiographies only one reference to the alleged promiscuity of slaves could be found, and that was within the rather conservative narrative of I. E. Lowery. He states that his owner, Mr. Frierson, "had it understood on his plantation that there should be no little bastard slaves there. He gave it out that they were not wanted."[10] Significantly, the assumption of slave promiscuity came from the master rather than from slaves. Slave testimony does not suggest that those held in bondage lived within promiscuous communities; this image was, instead, one that was cultivated by whites for their own purposes. Whites defined those they held in bondage as sexually promiscuous so that they could absolve themselves of blame in cases of voluntary and involuntary sexual contact.

## Sexual Contact between White Women and Black Men

The lives of slave men and women differed in terms of how interracial sexual liaisons affected their relationships with whites. Hence, the records of white southerners can be especially revealing in an investigation of such relationships between white women and slave men. White evidence shows how the Buck stereotype manifested itself within their minds and how, in more general terms, black men were perceived as sexually threatening. In his diary, the lawyer and slave owner William Valentine referred to a black man accused of rape as a "monster," writing: "This day must be memorable to a certain poor respectable family in this county, on account of a horrible crime, revolting to human society, perpetuated on that family. This is a rape, an offence that calls up the highest sympathy and the strongest resentment. . . . This alleged rape was committed a day or two ago. Today there was an examination . . . of the *monster in the shape of a black negro*" (italics added).[11]

Fears of black male sexuality are also reflected in the following South Carolina judicial cases involving enslaved men who were charged with the intention to commit rape. In the first case, a slave named Lewis was also tried for burglary and assault and battery. It was alleged that he had forcibly entered the house of a white woman by "breaking open the door." The woman alleged he committed "an assault" on her and that she believed he intended to commit rape.[12] In the second case, Elizabeth Mitchell, a white woman, claimed that she was attacked in her mother's house by "a negro boy" who held her on the ground and choked her. He only let her go on the promise of money, after which Mitchell gave him a dollar. The accused slave, Nathan, was tried for assault, battery, and the intention to commit rape.[13] It is noteworthy that Nathan desisted once he had been given money and that it is not at all clear from the description given by Elizabeth Mitchell that he had intended to rape her. In the first case, however, the white woman explicitly stated that she believed she was to be raped. This seems to account for the differing punishments. Nathan was found guilty only of assault and battery and received the lesser sentence of a hundred lashes on the bare back. However, Lewis was found guilty of the intention to commit a rape, and he paid with his life, thus illustrating how seriously black male sexual violence was viewed in the antebellum South.

Characterizing black men as sexually threatening Bucks had broad implications, and white southerners expressed their alleged fear of black male sexuality in many realms of life, especially when their status quo was threatened. In claiming that a free black community would be sexually threatening to white women, for instance, slaveholders could (without losing their caring, paternalistic image) justify the harsh treatment of potential insurrectionaries. A link between the fear of revolt and that of black male sexuality is implicit in the following letter from Rachel Blanding, of Camden, to her cousin. She stated: "Our village and neighborhood has been in great confusion for two days owing to the fear of an insurrection of the blacks. . . . It was their intention to have set fire to one part of the town and while the attention of the people was taken up with that they meant to have taken possession of the arsenal which is filled with arms and ammunition and proceeded to murder the men but *the women they intended to have reserved for their own purposes*" (italics added).[14]

Fears of black male sexuality, especially with regard to the rape of white women, increased in the postbellum period in the southern states.[15] Since whites no longer owned blacks as property, the appalling physical treatment of black men at the hands of white men could continue through the elevation of the importance of the Buck stereotype. Racial persecution was therefore justified under the guise of "protecting" virtuous white

women. As Eugene Genovese stated: "The titillating and violence-pro-
voking theory of the superpotency of that black superpenis, while whis-
pered about for several centuries, did not become an obsession in the
South until after emancipation, when it served the purposes of racial seg-
regationists."[16] A textual reading of white manuscript materials seems
to confirmonfirm the notion that fears over black men's sexuality, characterized by Buck, increased over the nineteenth century. This was especially true in the aftermath of emancipation, when fears for the safety of
white women at the hands of newly freed black men were expressed. In
the following extract from an 1865 letter to Peter Glass, J. B. Glass wrote:
"A young lady at Greenwood was outraged a few days since by two negroes and a white man, and I have heard of much insolence and some
threats in this neighborhood. The visits to Sulphur Springs by ladies also
have been stopped since some of them met a burly negro man at the
Spring house who was very familiar."[17]

The "black rapist" stereotype could cause great panic in postslavery
society, and by contrast, it has been argued, the trials of slaves accused
of raping white women were relatively fair.[18] However, a brutal reminder
of the harshness of chattel slavery can be found in the cases of alleged
rape described in petitions to the South Carolina State Assembly. Slaveholders could petition the assembly for compensation for the value of
their slaves who were executed under the charge of rape. Typical is the
petition on behalf of Nathan Boon of Pickens County, asking for compensation for the execution of his nineteen-year-old slave man, Lem, who
had been found guilty of committing "a diabolical act" on a young white
woman named Jane Ross.[19] Cases such as this serve as a stark reminder
of the paramount importance of racial oppression in antebellum South
Carolina, especially when the differences between the treatment of black
men accused of raping white women and of white men who sexually
abused black women are considered. Racism allowed white men the opportunity systematically to abuse their female slaves, while black men
who were accused of raping white women often lost their lives.

The Buck stereotype was not the sole factor that came into play in rationalizing sexual liaisons between white women and black men. Gender
and class stereotyping (as well as racism) were also significant, and lower-
class white women were particularly vulnerable to being described as
"wanton." This image-construction process meant that more "respectable" white women did not have to accept any responsibility for their relationships with black men, whereas poor white women who were involved in interracial sexual encounters were frequently labeled deviant.[20]
Poverty, therefore, violated southern norms of white femininity, and Vic-

toria E. Bynum has argued that it defeminized poor white women in the same way that race defeminized black women.[21] Furthermore, by ascribing negative characteristics to poor white women—assuming that they were the only women who would be inclined to enter sexual relationships with black men—the Lady stereotype of the southern planter class could be upheld.

It was therefore rare in the extreme for an elite white woman to be suspected of having an intimate relationship with a black man. Women accused of such encounters were liable to receive harsh societal sanctions, as exemplified in the petition of a Barnwell resident, Marmaduke James, to the South Carolina State Assembly. James wished to divorce his wife, Ann, after she had given birth to a "mulatto child." His petition emphasized his "respectability," stating that he had "always supported and maintained a good name and character with, and among, all the good and honest people of Barnwell district." He also argued that it would be impossible for him to continue to live with his wife under the circumstances but that he hoped to remarry in the future and to have "the enjoyment of a family." James also provided a supplementary "Paper B" attached to his petition, in which a list of individuals certified that "we have seen the child of the said Ann James . . . that the father of the said child is a black negro."[22]

White women were severely sanctioned for relationships with black men. Ann James not only put her own respectability at stake but also that of her husband. Furthermore, comparing the treatment of Ann James with the attitudes of white men who engaged in sexual relationships with female slaves shows just how much white women were the victims of gender discrimination at the hands of white men. They would have been ostracized from their families and communities as a consequence of their interracial relationships regardless of whether they were enforced or voluntary.

The following case illustrates the immense shame these women must have felt in bearing children as a result of interracial encounters. Maria Cumming's brother had informed her that a woman had been found in the woods "in her underdress," with "an infant a few days old to which she was trying to administer nourishment although she said she had not eaten one mouthful since its *birth and the child was a black one.* She was taken to some person's house but positively refused to give her name. She was apparently so overcome by shame as to have wandered away from her home, wherever that may be, and when her child was born she had no assistance at all. Brother said . . . he could find out nothing of the person's name or family" (italics added).[23]

Sexual contact between white women and black men also impacted upon the children of their liaisons. Two children of such relationships whose poignant stories are worth quoting at some length are John C. Brown, a South Carolina WPA respondent, and Lucy Andrews, who petitioned the South Carolina State Assembly several times requesting that she be permitted to become a slave. The case of Brown is unusual. He lived on the Winnsboro plantation of Tom Dawkins during slavery, with some two hundred other slaves. Telling his interviewer that his mother was white, Brown said: "I never knowed my mammy. They say she was a white lady dat visited my old marster and mistress. Dat I was found in a basket, dressed in nice baby clothes, on de railroad track at Dawkins. . . . Marse Tom carry me home and give me to miss Betsy. Dat was his wife and my mistress. Her always say dat Sheton Brown was my father. He was one of de slaves on de place; de carriage driver. After freedom he tell me he was my real pappy."[24]

Life histories such as this offer a glimpse into the complexities of the interaction of race, gender, and class exploitations in antebellum South Carolina. It may have been the case that Brown's father did not want to reveal his identity to his son for fear of recriminations from his owners. The fact that his father was the carriage driver also offers suggestions about which male slaves were most likely to enter sexual relationships with white women. Brown's stepmother's hostility toward him may also have been a consequence of their loosely adoptive relationship.[25] Also of possible significance is the fact that Brown was one of only two WPA informants to express an ambivalent view of religion.[26] Perhaps his unfortunate upbringing accounted for his uncertain attitude toward faith. As he eloquently testified: "Adeline [his wife] b'long to de church. Always after me to jine but I can't believe dere is anything to it, though I believes in de law and de Ten Commandments. Preacher calls me a infidel. Can't help it. They is maybe got me figured out wrong. I believes in a Great Spirit but, in my time, I is seen so many good dogs and hosses and so many mean niggers and white folks, dat I 'clare I is confused on de subject. Then I can't believe in a hell and everlastin' brimstone. I just think dat people is lak grains of corn; dere is some good grains and some rotten grains."[27]

Occasionally, then, testimony from the children of sexual liaisons between white women and black men can offer poignant insights into the consequences of such cross-race encounters. Lucy Andrews, born of a white mother and black father in Lancaster District, petitioned the South Carolina State Assembly expressing a desire to be enslaved. She claimed to be isolated from both white and slave communities. Andrews had a slave husband and requested that she be made a slave of her husband's master.[28] In one of her first petitions she wrote that she was a sixteen-year-old mother and "that she is dissatisfied with her present condition, being compelled to go about from place to place to seek employment for her support, and not permitted to stay at any place more than a week or two at a time, no one caring about employing her." Andrews argued that she wanted to raise a family, yet was unable to support them. Perhaps playing on white sentiments, she professed to believe that "slaves are far more happy, and enjoy themselves far better than she does in her present, isolated condition of freedom, and are well-treated and cared for by their masters, while she is going about from place to place hunting employment for her support." She therefore "prays that your honorable body would enact a law authorizing and permitting her, to go voluntarily into slavery, and select her own master."[29] Andrews's emphasis on the benevolence of the slaveholding class is revealing and suggests a ploy to appeal to members of the State Assembly rather than a comment on the nature of slavery.

Five years later, Andrews was still fighting to be enslaved. By this time, she had borne three children, although one had died. Andrews's petition stated that she wished to belong to Henry H. Duncan, who "owns her husband Robbin, with whom she, together with her above mentioned children, [are] comfortably fixed and situated."[30] In part, Andrews's petitions were motivated by economic factors. Her impoverishment can be likened to that of other free people of color, many of whom faced financial difficulties and racial discrimination in the antebellum South.[31] For a minority, servitude may have seemed a more preferable option.[32] However, a desire to remain with her husband also appears to be paramount in Andrews's case. She desired to live with her husband even if that meant subjecting herself to bondage.

Overall, evidence relating to sexual liaisons between white women and black men is scarce.[33] Of the South Carolina WPA respondents, only John C. Brown had a white mother. Furthermore, in the slave autobiographies only one reference to a sexual encounter between white women and slave men was found. This incident was related by Linda Brent, who wrote that a slaveholder's daughter had "selected one of the meanest slaves on his plantation to be the father of his first grandchild. She did not make her advances to her equals, nor even to her father's more intelligent servants. She selected the most brutalized, over whom her authority could be exercised with less fear of exposure. Her father, half frantic with rage, sought to revenge himself on the offending black man; but his daughter, foreseeing the storm that would arise, had given him free papers, and sent him out of the state."[34] The motives of this woman are difficult to ascertain. For some reason, she may have wished to punish her father. It is also significant that she tried to protect the enslaved father of her child from her own father. Perhaps she had fallen in love with him, although, admittedly, this is not the impression given in Brent's account. The lives of slave men and women could therefore be very different in the realm of sexual exploitation; both were depicted as promiscuous by whites, but women seem to have been exposed to a much greater risk than men of direct sexual abuse by whites. Whites wove complex rationalizations around their sexual contact with blacks, and these encounters often left tragic victims in their wake.

## Sexual Contact between White Men and Slave Women

Intimate contact between white men and female slaves highlights similarities and differences in the lives of enslaved men and women. Primarily, enforced sexual encounters impacted much more directly on slave women than on men. It has been argued that their rape by masters was part of the institutional apparatus used by slaveholders in their attempt to subjugate their slaves.[35] Angela Davis, writing in 1971, claimed that the resistance of slave women to sexual abuse constituted an extension of the mechanisms of resistance they employed in their everyday lives, "a response to a politically tinged sexual repression."[36] However, encounters between white men and slave women are particularly difficult to establish through an examination of source materials left by whites. Owners rarely made references to such affairs in their letters and diaries. The personal papers of James Henry Hammond, edited by Carol Bleser, are unusual in that they detail his long-term relationships with two slave women. His first was with an eighteen-year-old Sally Johnson, his second with Johnson's daughter, Louisa, who caught Hammond's eye at the age of only twelve. Bleser notes that finding testimony of this kind that had survived "the natural instinct of heirs and executors" was "most surprising."[37]

The WPA testimony has perhaps a unique potential as a basis for advancing knowledge in this area. While white sources give only the most fragmentary and generally self-serving comments on these issues, and despite the fact that the WPA narratives leave major gaps because they were not originally designed to address questions of sexual liaisons, such evidence can still provide quantitative information on the extent of sexual contact with female slaves. They can also provide evidence on who (masters, overseers, or others) had the most intimate encounters with slave women, and they also suggest which slaves (field or domestic) were most likely to be harassed sexually.[38] A search of WPA evidence and slave autobiographies has also revealed that most sexual contact between white men and slave women took the form of enforced abuse, reducing many slave women to a life dogged by the threat, if not the reality, of such terror at the hands of their owners.

Using quantitative analysis to try to calculate the amount of sexual contact in the antebellum South has proven problematic, with any attempt to "measure" such intimacies being fraught with difficulties. Robert W. Fogel and Stanley L. Engerman, in *Time on the Cross*, attempted to provide quantitative estimations of the extent of what they term miscegenation under slavery. The widespread criticism of their results and their methodological techniques, however, serves as a stark reminder of the extreme caution needed when attempting this type of analysis. Fogel and Engerman concluded that there was a low level of miscegenation between white men and slave women, a proposition that was based on three broad claims: firstly, they argued that the racism and prudishness of owners prohibited them from seeking these types of liaisons; secondly, they maintained that the high age of slave women at first birth showed a lack of sexual interference; and thirdly, using data from census schedules, they suggested that there were only a small number of "mulatto" children in the slave South (7.7 percent).[39] Fogel and Engerman have been widely criticized for this oversimplistic analysis. Herbert G. Gutman and Richard Sutch have stated: "It should be noted immediately that neither this designation [mulatto] nor the term 'black' was officially defined by the Census Office and that the reports of the skin color of slaves were made by their owners."[40] Susan Brownmiller has also suggested that "any census statistic on the proportion of mulattoes on a plantation would be a most unreliable figure. In addition, why do Fogel and Engerman assume that a rape, even in a 'non-contraceptive society,' as they put it, is necessarily going to result in pregnancy and birth?"[41]

WPA evidence does, however, provide a basis for progress in investigating the extent of intimate contact. From the testimony of the respondents, it is possible to calculate a *minimum estimate* of the extent of sexual encounters in antebellum South Carolina by totaling all those who had either a direct or an indirect knowledge of sexual contact with whites (including those who only related broad anecdotes about such contact).[42] Included here are informants who stated that they had a white parent; respondents who said that they had some other blood link to whites; and those who mentioned issues of sexual contact or abuse in more general terms. A total of nine (2.7 percent of all informants) had a white parent, of which eight had white fathers and one had a white mother.[43] Interestingly, seven of these were male, but only two were female, implying that intimate interracial encounters were an area of life that men were more willing than women to discuss with their white interviewers. This in turn suggests an underestimation of sexual contact. A further sixteen (4.8 percent of all respondents) had some other blood link to whites,[44] and five more (1.5 percent) spoke of interracial sexual liaisons in more general terms.[45] This gives a total of thirty, or 9 percent of all informants, who had some knowledge of interracial sexual contact.

The nature of the sexual liaisons between blacks and whites is as significant as its extent. Consequently, slave experiences at the individual level are also worthy of consideration. WPA ex-slaves who had white parents tended to be reticent in explaining this to their interviewers. Most merely stated that their fathers were "white men."[46] Ed Barber told his interviewer: "My mother name Ann. Her b'long to my marster, James Barber. Dat's not a fair question when you ask me who my daddy was. Well, just say he was a white man and dat my mother never did marry nobody while he lived."[47] Similarly, Alexander Robertson testified that no one would tell him who his father was: "I have to find out dat for myself, after freedom, when I was lookin' 'round for a name. From all I hear and 'pear in de lookin' glass, I see I was half white for sure, and from de things I hear, I conclude I was a Robertson which have never been denied. Maybe it best just to give no front names."[48]

Adeline Brown and Victoria Perry were both fathered by white overseers. Brown's husband (John C. Brown) related his wife's story of her parentage: "Her daddy was a full-blooded Irishman. He come over here from Ireland and was overseer for Marse Bob Clowney. He took a fancy for Adeline's mammy, a bright 'latto gal slave on de place. White woman in them days looked down on overseers as poor white trash. Him couldn't git a white wife but made de best of it by puttin' in his spare time a honeyin' 'round Adeline's mammy."[49] Similarly, Victoria Perry, enslaved in Newberry, recalled that her father was a white man, an overseer, she suspected.[50] Two respondents were fathered by their owners. Jack Johnson stated explicitly that his master, Tom Reed, was his father and that he himself was his mother's only child. His master was kind to both of them, he said.[51] The up-country ex-slave Isiah Jeffries only implied that his master was his father, referring to himself as an "outside child."[52]

The testimony of the five respondents who spoke of interracial sexual encounters in more general terms was the most revealing. Ryer Emmanuel and Savilla Burrell discussed the impact of abuse on owners' wives; their comments are examined later. Thomas Goodwater, enslaved in the Mount Pleasant area, described how his owner, Lias Winning, tried to rape his mother, a field worker: "Lias 'inning wasn' a mean man. He couldn' lick pa cus dey grow up togedder or at least he didn' try. But he liked his woman slave. One day ma wus in de field workin' alone an' he went there an' try to rape 'er. Ma pull his ears almos' off so he let 'er off an' gone an' tell pa he better talk to ma. Pa wus workin' in the salt pen an' w'en Mr. Winning tell him he jus laugh cus he know why ma did it."[53] This case gives a sense of the resistance on the part of Goodwater's mother and also of the support she received from her husband. It therefore provides evidence on the strength of the relationships between spouses within the confines of the slave regime. Cureton Milling said that his master, Levi Bolicks, sexually harassed female slaves at their home in Winnsboro. He stated: "He take 'vantage of de young gal slaves. 'You go yonder and shell corn in de crib,' he say to one of them. He's de marster so she have to go. Then he send de others to work some other place, then he go to de crib." Milling also said that one such woman later had a mulatto boy.[54]

It appears that most sexual encounters between white men and slave women in antebellum South Carolina took the form of enforced abuse rather than voluntary liaisons. This not only contradicts the image of Jezebel that was so prevalent in white minds but it shows that the lives of enslaved men and women had the potential to differ markedly. It is likely that most men and boys did not live under the threat of sexual abuse at the hands of their owners, although life was undoubtedly hard for those involved in intimate relationships with white women.[55] Female slaves displayed a steely resistance, a strong desire not only to survive slavery but also to survive it through gaining the support and companionship of a spouse, which must be recognized as a remarkable achievement. These women also relied upon their wits. Gus Feaster said that the white overseer on his holding, Wash Evans, was "a wicked man. He take 'vantage of all de slaves when he git half chance." He then related an incident when he had been out picking berries with his friend, John, his mother, and his mother's friend, Lucy. Wash Evans rode up and began to argue with the two women. Feaster recalled how "dey kept telling him dat de missus want her berries and dat dey was 'ligious wimmins anyhow and didn't practice no life o' sin and vile wickedness. Finally he got down off'n his hoss and pull out his whip and low if dey didn't submit to him he gwine to beat dem half to death." At this point, Feaster and John ran away, although they could hear his mother and Lucy crying and pleading with Evans. From their hiding place, Feaster testified that Lucy and his mother "act like dey gwine to indulge in de wickedness wid dat ole man. But when he tuck off his whip and some other garments, my mammy and ole lady Lucy grab him by his goatee and further down and hits him over in de middle of dem blackberry bushes." His mother then went and told her mistress, who fired Evans.[56]

Feaster's mother and Lucy cleverly played up to the notion of Jezebel in tricking the overseer. In acting as though they were party to his "wickedness" they were able to catch him off guard and escape.

Overall, there were three incidents of sexual encounters between slave women and white overseers related in the WPA narratives, compared with four involving masters.[57] Although these numbers are small, they do not support the notion that the sexual abuse or harassment of slave women mostly took place at the hands of "lower-class" white men. However, a different impression is given from the examination of the records of slaveholders. The social-class implications of interracial sexual liaisons can be seen in the following extract from a letter written by the upstate resident J. M. Wallace, who recognized that an overseer was sexually harassing his women. Wallace attributed this to his "lowly" status, writing: "I have already had to turn off the man he [Mr. Rice] brought out [as an overseer], who was drunk there all the time with a crowd of *low associates disturbing his negro women* and riding his mules" (italics added).[58] Charles Manigault also grew distrustful of his overseers after two cases in which slave women bore his overseers' children. The first was in 1837, when the overseer of Silk Hope plantation, Thomas R. Heargroves, made pregnant "a girl of seventeen or eighteen named Elsey." The second was in 1857, when Leonard Ventners had a child with a field hand, Harriet.[59]

In assessing the types of white men that were most likely to have intimate encounters with slave women, issues of sexual contact at the hands of masters and overseers are worthy of investigation at a broader level. For this purpose, the entire collection of WPA slave narratives (including the supplementary volumes) was examined using the *Index to "The American Slave."*[60] All index entries for "miscegenation" were consulted to establish the relative propensity of masters and overseers to indulge in such liaisons. A total of twenty-two cases were found where informants expressed direct knowledge of sexual encounters between either their owner or their overseer and slave women. Of these, seven involved overseers, and fifteen (nearly 70 percent of the total) involved masters.[61] Appendix 2 shows that of the fifteen cases involving owners, six specified that the sexual contact was with house servants, and only one specified a field worker. In the seven cases involving overseers, two specified that the encounters were with house servants, while only one said that their overseer sexually abused a field worker.[62] These results suggest that masters were more likely to sexually abuse female slaves than were overseers. Hence enforced sexual encounters could not be attributed to lower-class white men. House servants were also, unsurprisingly, more at risk of abuse than were field slaves.[63]

Evidence found within slave autobiographies supports the broad trends that have been established from the WPA testimony. While no direct evidence of sexual relationships between slave men and white women was found (with the exception of the anecdote of Linda Brent), issues of sexual encounters between white men and enslaved women loomed large. Moses Roper stated that he "resembled Mr. Roper [his 'young master'] very much."[64] Similarly, Annie L. Burton was the daughter of a white man, a planter, she claimed. Burton wrote that she occasionally saw her father when he drove past the plantation. However, he never acknowledged her as his child, despite the fact that Burton's mistress would "take me by the hand and run out upon the piazza, and exclaim, 'Stop there, I say! Don't you want to see and speak to and caress your darling child?' . . . My mistress's action was, of course, intended to humble and shame my father."[65] One of the main themes within Harriet Jacobs's autobiography is the sexual harassment suffered by Linda Brent at the hands of her master, Dr. Flint. She wrote: "But I now entered on my fifteenth year—a sad epoch in the life of a slave girl. My master began to whisper foul words in my ear. Young as I was, I could not remain ignorant of their import. . . . He was a crafty man, and resorted to many means to accomplish his purposes. Sometimes he had stormy, terrific ways, that made his victims tremble; sometimes he assumed a gentleness that he thought must surely subdue. Of the two, I preferred his stormy moods, although they left me trembling. . . . I turned from him with disgust and hatred. But he was my master."[66]

The WPA evidence (being black evidence on the black experience) is probably the only available primary source for developing useful quantitative estimates on interracial sexual contact. It was found that small but significant percentages of slaves had white fathers. Several other (more tentative) trends were also discovered. Female slaves were more likely to be sexually abused by their owners than by overseers. Domestics were particularly at risk of rape, and Crawford found that slaves on smaller units (fewer than fifty slaves) were exposed to an even more acute risk.[67] The overall patterns therefore suggest that a significant minority of masters sexually abused their slave women. Looked at from the slaves' point of view, the threat of sexual harassment was very real. However, the percentage of those abused in this way would have been unlikely to dislodge the slaves' sense of family. Undeterred, they sought to overcome this unique form of oppression through the love and support provided by their spouses.

## The Impact of Interracial Sexual Contact upon Mistresses

The abuse of slave women by owners affected their relationships with white mistresses. It has been suggested that black and white women formed close relationships along gendered lines, across the divisions created by race and class. For example, Catherine Clinton argues that "[w]ives and daughters would often plead with planters for the humane treatment of slaves. Slaves understood this role of white women and would often appeal directly to the mistress to intercede with the master on his or her behalf."[68] In contrast, Elizabeth Fox-Genovese has emphasized the fact that racism created a gulf between mistresses and their female slaves. She makes the valuable point that white women could complain about slavery without necessarily opposing it as a social system. They did not accept the bourgeois claims of the (mostly northern) feminists about female universality across class and race lines.[69]

More recently, in her study of elite plantation women in South Carolina, Marli F. Weiner has argued that mistresses did seek to help their female slaves, most notably by intervening in cases of physical punishments. These women also interpreted the prevalent ideology of domesticity as justifying concern for the personal lives of those they held in bondage; they wanted to see themselves as good mistresses, as representing ideal womanhood.[70] However, while they genuinely cared for their slaves, identifying with them on issues such as childbearing, the fact that they could not imagine a world without slavery meant that even when mistresses expressed reservations about slavery and interracial sexual liaisons, they did so only privately.[71] Weiner's sensible points correlate with the opinion expressed by Anne Firor Scott some thirty years ago, that many southern women were actually "private abolitionists."[72] Both slave women and their mistresses, to varying degrees, can be seen as victims in the realms of interracial sexual contact.

Within the WPA narratives, two respondents mentioned the effect of sexual encounters between owners and female slaves upon their mistresses.[73] In addition, Gus Feaster's testimony, in which a white overseer (Wash Evans) tried to sexually abuse his mother, is revealing, since his mistress fired Evans.[74] However, when the sexual attackers were their own husbands, slaveholding women were caused great anguish and mostly reacted in a very different way. Evidence from the WPA narratives suggests that while they were undoubtedly distressed by such occurrences, mistresses directed their anger toward either the female slave victims or toward any resultant offspring. As Ryer Emmanuel of Marion County said: "Like I speak to you, my white folks was blessed wid a heap of black chillun, but den dere been an odd one in de crowd what wasn' noways like dem others. All de other chillun was black skin wid dis here kinky hair en she was yellow skin wid straight black hair. My Lord, old Missus been mighty proud of her black chillun, but she sho been touches [touchy] bout dat yellow one. I remember, all us chillun was playin' round bout de step one day whe' Miss Ross was settin en she ax dat yellow child, say 'Who your papa?' De child never know no better en she tell her right out exactly de one her mammy had tell her was her papa. Lord, Miss Ross, she say, 'Well, get off my step. Get off en stay off dere cause you don' noways belong to me.'"[75] Similarly, Savilla Burrell of Winnsboro testified that "Old Marse was de daddy of some mulatto chillun. De 'lations wid de mothers of dose chillun is what give so much grief to mistress. De neighbors would talk 'bout it and he would sell all dem chillun away from dey mothers to a trader. My mistress would cry 'bout dat."[76]

Reference was also made to the anguish felt by slaveholding women within full-length autobiographies. Moses Roper, the son of his "young master," recalls how he was attacked by his mistress—the young master's wife—after she found out his parentage: "She [his mistress] got a large club-stick and knife, and hastened to the place in which my mother was confined. She went into my mother's room with full intention to murder me with her knife and club, but as she was going to stick the knife into me, my grandmother happened to come in, caught the knife and saved my life. But . . . from what my mother told me, my father sold her and myself, soon after her confinement."[77] Linda Brent also writes of the persecution she faced from her "jealous mistress": "The mistress, who ought to protect the helpless victim, has no other feelings toward her but those of jealousy and rage." Later she claims: "I had entered my sixteenth year, and every day it became more apparent that my presence was intolerable to Mrs. Flint. Angry words frequently passed between her and her husband. He had never punished me himself, and he would not allow any body else to punish me. In that respect she was never satisfied; but, in her angry moods, no terms were too vile for her to bestow upon me."[78] As has been illustrated earlier, in contrast, Annie Burton had the support of her owner's wife regardless of the fact that her father was white. It is significant, though, that Burton's father was not her master—the husband of her mistress.[79] When their husbands fathered slave children, slaveholding women usually saw themselves as the primary victims. These attitudes, coupled with the resentment harbored against the abused women and their children, diminished the opportunities for mistresses to form close relationships with their female slaves.[80]

## Sexual Contact and Manumissions

It has been suggested that the sexual encounters between female slaves and white men meant that women stood a better chance than men of gaining their freedom and that females formed a substantial majority of manumitted slaves.[81] Sexual contact with whites, therefore, had the potential to cause yet another major difference between the lives of enslaved men and women. This raises the question of whether women held in bondage were tempted to seek their freedom through engaging in sexual relationships with white men. If they were, this would have had implications for slave family and community life. The notion that sexual liaisons between white men and slave women led to loving and meaningful relationships has contributed to the ideology of benevolent paternalism in the slave South, since assuming that most sexual encounters took the form of loving relationships diminishes the brutality of the sexual abuse of female slaves. Eugene Genovese's belief in the essentially paternalist nature of master-slave relationships in *Roll, Jordan, Roll*, for example, led him to conclude that "many white men who began by taking a slave girl in an act of sexual exploitation ended by loving her and the children she bore."[82] This may have been true, but it does not tell the whole story, because the responses of the girls themselves are also worthy of consideration. The evidence displayed here has strongly suggested that most sexual relationships were not consensual. If owners did display love and affection, for the most part enslaved women did not reciprocate, although some, such as Harriet Smith, whose experiences are detailed below, realized the futility of protest and resigned themselves to a lifetime of sexual abuse.[83]

Records left by owners who wished to free slave women with whom they had relationships (and sometimes their offspring, too) have sometimes been used as testimony to their benevolence. James Hugo Johnston wrote in 1937: "Fathers of such [mulatto] children would have been inhuman had they not sought to lighten the burden on their children. On examination of the wills of deceased slave owners it frequently appears that the deceased master is the father of certain slaves and seeks to make provision for his children."[84] The will of Philipe Noisette provides a typical example. Noisette petitioned the South Carolina State Assembly, requesting the manumission of his slave, Celestine, and the children they had together. His will requested that his executors "send the said woman Celestine and all her said issue, my children out of this state to some other state territory or county where they can there be made free."[85] Likewise, Archibald Grimke's mother, Nancy Weston, had three sons by her owner, Henry Grimke, with whom she began a long-standing relationship in 1847. It is noteworthy, however, that although Grimke had been making plans for her to live independently with her children in Charleston prior to his death, he made no effort to liberate her from bondage.[86]

Indeed, it appears that individuals such as Philipe Noisette were in a small minority. From an investigation into the records of slaveholders, few references are made to interracial sexual liaisons at all, let alone to white men seeking to free enslaved women with whom they were having relationships.[87] Far more typical was case of the slave woman subjected to a period if not a lifetime of sexual harassment—or worse, abuse—with no opportunities either for freedom or a "privileged" status. The experiences of Pauli Murray's ancestor, Harriet Smith, who gave birth to one child by her owner and another three by his brother, again testify to this ordeal.[88] Likewise, Linda Brent took a white lover (Mr. Sands) to prevent her owner (Dr. Flint) from forcing her to live alone in a cottage, where he would be free to sexually harass her. She hoped that Mr. Sands would rescue her from this desperate situation. However, despite the fact that Brent bore two children by him, Sands did not offer to buy or manumit her.[89] The sad experiences of these women support the proposition that even if they did enter relationships with white men in the hope of obtaining their freedom, female slaves were taking a huge risk. Many white lovers acted in the manner of Mr. Sands and made no effort to change the basis of their relationship with one who was enslaved. At other times, white lovers would settle down into family life with a white woman, or, alternatively, they would be forced by a jealous wife into selling their enslaved lover.[90]

The WPA evidence also shows that slave women who gained their freedom or quasi freedom though entering into sexual relationships with white men were rare in the extreme. Testimony for South Carolina contained no instances of slave women seeking or gaining freedom through liaisons with white men. Females were persistently in the majority among manumitted slaves, but rates of manumission (especially after 1820) were so low that sex did not provide a route to freedom.[91] Exceptionally, slave women might have gained protection and rewards short of freedom, but the overall tenor of the evidence from slave sources suggests that sexual contact with whites was much more likely to involve abuse than mutual affection. Love and respect was found in the relationships slaves had with their spouses.

This chapter has suggested fairly high levels of sexual abuse of slaves, especially of domestics by masters. Rather than seeking their freedom or special favors through intimate liaisons with white men, however, the vast majority of female slaves chose to try to cope with their oppression through their relationships with their spouses. While the extent and nature of the sexual abuse meant that, in this respect, the lives of enslaved women were more traumatic than those of men, the ties of attachment between couples is illustrated by the fact that men tried to protect their spouses against sexual abuse (as detailed in chapter 2) and also by their general condemnation of such attacks.

## Notes

1. See the introduction for more on whether Harriet Jacobs managed to resist the sexual advances of her master.

2. White, *Ar'n't I a Woman?* 28–29. The stereotyping of female slaves is also considered in Morton, *Disfigured Images*, chap. 1.

3. Fox-Genovese, *Within the Plantation Household*, 291.

4. See ibid., 291, for a detailed description of the Sambo stereotype.

5. Ibid., 292.

6. Diary-Memoir 1864, John C. Gorman Papers, WRPL.

7. Moore, ed., *A Plantation Mistress*, 39.

8. Rawick, *American Slave*, vol. 2, pt. 2, 296–97.

9. See Clinton, *Plantation Mistress*, 87–91, for an extensive description of the Lady stereotype.

10. Lowery, *Life on the Old Plantation*, 42.

11. Entry for 17 February 1838, William D. Valentine Diary, SHC.

12. *State v. Lewis (a slave)*, November 1849, in Catterall, *Judicial Cases concerning American Slavery*, 413.

13. *State v. Nathan (slave of Gabriel South)*, November 1851 (ibid., 428).

14. Letter to Hannah Lewis from Rachel Blanding, 4 July 1816, William Blanding Papers, SCL.

15. See Sommerville, "Rape Myth in the Old South," 485.

16. Genovese, *Roll, Jordan, Roll*, 461–62. See also Sommerville, "Rape Myth in the Old South"; and Fox-Genovese, *Within the Plantation Household*, 291.

17. Letter to Peter from J. B. Glass, 25 June 1865, Glass Family Papers, SCL.

18. See Bardaglio, "Rape and the Law in the Old South," 751, and *Reconstructing the Household*. See also Sommerville, "Rape Myth in the Old South." The case of the slave Nathan, found guilty not of rape but assault and battery (detailed earlier), provides evidence to support this claim.

19. See Nathan Boon, petition and supporting papers asking compensation for the execution of his slave on a charge of rape, 15 September 1829. Petitions to the South Carolina State Assembly, SCDAH.

20. See Clinton, *Plantation Mistress*, 210.

21. Bynum, *Unruly Women*, 6–7.

22. Marmaduke James, of Barnwell District, petition and supporting papers for a divorce from Ann Ross following the birth of a mulatto child, 1847. Petitions to the South Carolina State Assembly, SCDAH.

23. Letter to Julia A. B. Cumming from Maria Cumming, 11 March 1831, Hammond-Bryan-Cumming Family Papers, SCL.

24. Rawick, *American Slave*, vol. 2, pt. 1, 127.

25. Ibid., 127–30.

26. The other was M. E. Abrams (ibid., 2).

27. Ibid., 130.

28. Some free blacks who were in a more fortunate financial situation than Andrews attempted to buy their family members themselves. This suggests that family ties were of paramount importance to all blacks in antebellum South Carolina. See Koger, *Black Slaveowners*, chap. 4. He also argues that the slave conspirator Denmark Vesey, who

attempted to lead an insurrection in Charleston, South Carolina, in 1822, was motivated by his increasing frustration at the bondage of his wife and children (184–85). For more on the marriages of Denmark Vesey, see Egerton, *He Shall Go Free*, 77–83.

29. Lucy Andrews, free mulatto, petition to be allowed to return to slavery and to choose her own master, ca. 1858. Petitions to the South Carolina State Assembly, SCDAH.

30. Lucy Andrews, a free black of Lancaster District, petition asking that she and her children be allowed to become the slaves of Henry H. Duncan, 25 November 1863. Petitions to the South Carolina State Assembly, SCDAH.

31. See, for example, Berlin, *Slaves without Masters*, esp. chap. 7.

32. It is interesting to compare Andrews's petition with that of Lizzie Jones of Laurens District. Jones was a free woman of color who desired to become the property of Charles Lamotte. She petitioned the State Assembly on 31 January 1859, and her request was approved on 7 December 1859. See Petitions to the South Carolina State Assembly, SCDAH. Jones may have wished to be enslaved for economic reasons, although she might have been involved in an intimate relationship with Lamotte. Becoming his property may have enabled her to feel more permanently attached to this man. As such, her motives appear to have been very different to those of Andrews.

33. Although dealing with Virginia in the colonial period, Kathleen M. Brown considers interracial relationships between white women and black men and the status of free blacks in *Good Wives, Nasty Wenches, and Anxious Patriarchs*; see esp. chap. 7, "Born of a Free Woman: Gender and the Politics of Freedom."

34. Jacobs, *Incidents*, 80–81.

35. See Brownmiller, *Against Our Will*, 153.

36. See Davis, "Reflections," 12–14.

37. See Bleser, ed., *Secret and Sacred*, 18–19. See also Burton, *In My Father's House*, 186–87; and Faust, *James Henry Hammond and the Old South*, 86–87.

38. For more on the WPA narratives and their usefulness in uncovering issues of sexual exploitation, see Jennings, "Us Colored Women."

39. See Fogel and Engerman, *Time on the Cross*, 126–44, for their attempt at quantifying the extent of miscegenation in the slave South.

40. Gutman and Sutch, "Victorians All?" 149.

41. Brownmiller, *Against Our Will*, 171–72.

42. Any estimate is necessarily going to be a minimum since not all respondents who had intimate relations with whites (or who had knowledge of such contact) would be willing to relate their experiences to a white interviewer. It must also be remembered that using the number of ex-slaves who had a white parent as an indication of the extent of sexual contact will in itself be an underestimate, since not all sexual relationships resulted in offspring.

43. The following respondents had white fathers: Ed Barber (Rawick, *American Slave*, vol. 2, pt. 1, 35); Adeline Brown (ibid., 128); John C. Davenport (ibid., 240); Thomas Dixon (ibid., 324); Isiah Jeffries (ibid., vol. 3, pt. 3, 17–19); Jack Johnson (ibid., 41); Victoria Perry (ibid., 260–61); and Alexander Robertson (ibid., vol. 3, pt. 4, 32). John C. Brown (ibid., vol. 2, pt. 1, 127) had a white mother.

44. Ramsom Beckett (ibid., vol. 11, 59), Henry Davis (ibid., vol. 2, pt. 1, 260), and Isaac Suits (ibid., vol. 11, 301) were described by their interviewer as being of mixed race or mulatto. Another three respondents had some "white blood": Abe Harris (ibid., vol. 2, pt. 2, 242); Jim Henry (ibid., 206); and Cornelius Holmes (ibid., 294). John C. Brown (ibid., vol. 2, pt. 1, 127), Adeline Brown (ibid., 128), George Patterson (ibid., vol. 3, pt. 3, 226), Martha Richardson (ibid., vol. 3, pt. 4, 19), Rosa Starke (ibid., 147), and Delia Thompson (ibid., 160) mentioned either that one of their parents was mulatto or that one of

their parents had some "white blood." Two respondents, Susan Hamlin and Reuben Rosborough (ibid., vol. 2, pt. 2, 233; and vol. 3, pt. 4, 45), had white grandfathers. George Fleming (ibid., vol. 11, 138) said that his wife had a white father. Finally, Susan Hamlin told her black interviewer, Augustus Ladson, that she had a brother who was the son of her master, Edward Fuller (ibid., vol. 2, pt. 2, 233). For purposes of clarity in assessing the extent of sexual contact and abuse, where a respondent had more than one blood link to whites, they were included more than once in the sample.

45. The fact that issues of sexual contact and sexual abuse can be examined through the experiences of the parents and other relatives of the WPA respondents supports the proposition that these narratives can be used to investigate slave life as a whole rather than only slave childhood. Interestingly, Paul D. Escott and Stephen Crawford both found that around 6 percent of their respondents had white fathers. Escott also found that 0.5 percent had white mothers. See Crawford, "Quantified Memory," 159; and Escott, *Slavery Remembered*, 47. These figures were higher than the South Carolina sample, where only 2.4 percent acknowledged white fathers, and 0.2 percent acknowledged white mothers. The differences here appear to have arisen because Escott and Crawford both took their percentages from a subset of those who mentioned their father's color rather than from their samples as a whole. Crawford also found that slave women on small plantations were twice as likely to have a child by a white man than those on large plantations ("Quantified Memory," 160). His proposition may well hold true, but unfortunately, the small number of South Carolina respondents who commented on these issues made any correlation between race of father and size of slaveholding impossible to determine.

46. Ed Barber (Rawick, *American Slave*, vol. 2, pt. 1, 35), John N. Davenport (ibid., 240), Thomas Dixon (ibid., 324), and Alexander Robertson (ibid., vol. 3, pt. 4, 32) all said only that their fathers were white men.

47. Ibid., vol. 2, pt. 1, 35.

48. Ibid., vol. 3, pt. 4, 32.

49. Ibid., vol. 2, pt. 1, 128

50. Ibid., vol. 3, pt. 3, 260–61.

51. Ibid., 41.

52. See ibid., 17–19.

53. Ibid., vol. 2, pt. 2, 167. It is noteworthy that Goodwater related this incident to a black interviewer, Augustus Ladson.

54. Ibid., vol. 3, pt. 3, 194.

55. Orlando Patterson asserts that since homosexuality has existed in every known human society, it is highly likely that those with power over young male slaves would have exploited them. See *Rituals of Blood*, 289 n.70. However, instances of homosexual abuse of enslaved men by whites are, unsurprisingly, lacking in source materials. Harriet Jacobs hints at abuse of this kind in referring to a slave man, Luke, whose sickly master frequently beat him. She wrote: "As he lay there on his bed . . . he took into his head the strangest freaks of despotism; and if Luke hesitated to submit to his orders, the constable was immediately sent for. Some of these freaks were of a nature too filthy to be repeated" (*Incidents*, 192). See also Foreman, "Manifest in Signs," 78–79; and Gebhard, "Reconstructing Southern Manhood," 142.

56. See Rawick, *American Slave*, vol. 2, pt. 2, 57, 65–66.

57. Gus Feaster mentioned sexual abuse by overseers (ibid.). The two respondents fathered by white overseers were Victoria Perry and Adeline Brown (ibid., vol. 3, pt. 3, 260–61; and vol. 2, pt. 1, 128). Jack Johnson and Isiah Jeffries (ibid., vol. 3, pt. 3, 41; and vol. 3, pt. 3, 17–19) said that their masters were their fathers. Thomas Goodwater and

Cureton Milling (ibid., vol. 2, pt. 2, 167; and vol. 3, part 3, 194) mentioned that their masters sexually abused female slaves.

58. Letter to Ben H. Rice from J. M. Wallace, 17 February 1855, Wallace-Rice-Duncan Family Papers, SCL.

59. See Dusinberre, *Them Dark Days*, 112

60. See Jacobs, *Index to "The American Slave."*

61. It would have been interesting to evaluate the extent to which the teenage sons of owners engaged in interracial liaisons with enslaved women. However, none of the informants stated that the encounter they described involved the son of their owner. It is true that some may have actually been referring to the person commonly known as "young master," but as appendix 2 illustrates, this was not made clear in the testimony.

62. This includes those who had direct knowledge of sexual contact between their masters or their white overseers and female slaves. Those who simply related anecdotes on this subject—for example, by stating that "some masters abused their female slaves"—were not included. Interestingly, of the twenty-two respondents, eight were the children of their masters, and four were the children of their white overseers. See appendix 2 for further details.

63. These findings broadly correlate with the claims of Stephen Crawford, who argues that female domestics were twice as likely to bear a child by a white man than were those who labored in the field (see "Quantified Memory," 161). In the South Carolina WPA narratives, of the eight respondents who were fathered by white men, only two gave the occupation of their mothers. These were Thomas Dixon and Alexander Robertson (Rawick, *American Slave*, vol. 2, pt. 1, 324; and vol. 3, pt. 4, 32). Both performed housework. In the slave autobiographies, two wrote that they had white fathers, and both said that their mothers were cooks. See Burton, *Memories*, 7; and Roper, *Narrative of the Adventures*, 2.

64. Roper, *Narrative of the Adventures*, 2.

65. Burton, *Memories*, 7–8.

66. Jacobs, *Incidents*, 44

67. Crawford, "Quantified Memory," 160.

68. Clinton, *Plantation Mistress*, 187.

69. See Fox-Genovese, *Within the Plantation Household*, 338.

70. See Weiner, *Mistresses and Slaves*, 76–80.

71. Ibid., 93–96.

72. Scott, *Southern Lady*, 51.

73. These were Ryer Emmanuel and Savilla Burrell; see Rawick, *American Slave*, vol. 2, pt. 2, 14; and vol. 2, pt. 1, 150.

74. Ibid., vol. 2, pt. 2, 65–66.

75. Ibid., 14.

76. Ibid., vol. 2, pt. 1, 150.

77. Roper, *Narrative of the Adventures*, 2.

78. Jacobs, *Incidents*, 32.

79. See Burton, *Memories*, 7–8.

80. See Fox-Genovese, *Within the Plantation Household*, chap. 7.

81. See the introduction to Finkelman, ed., *Women and the Family in a Slave Society*, where Finkelman writes: "Some slave women had meaningful and loving relations with their owners. Women in these relationships, and the children they had, were more likely to be manumitted than any other slaves in the South. For this reason slave women as a group probably had a better chance of gaining freedom than slave men" (ix). Finkelman

does acknowledge, however, that the slave women manumitted by their owners through sexual relationships were "the lucky few" (ix). Similarly, Lois Virginia Meacham Gould argues that slave women in the gulf ports often participated in liaisons with their masters in the hope of obtaining their freedom, or at least to improve their living conditions and those of their children. She also argues that in New Orleans, the majority of manumissions were a direct consequence of relationships between slave women and white men. See "In Full Enjoyment of Their Liberty," 339, and "Urban Slavery-Urban Freedom."

82. Genovese, *Roll, Jordan, Roll*, 415.

83. Harriet Smith was the great-grandmother of Pauli Murray. She was enslaved in Orange County, North Carolina, to the Smiths—a prestigious local family. Harriet gave birth to one child by Sidney Smith and three more by his brother, Frank Smith. See Murray, *Proud Shoes*, 39–47. See also Clinton, "Caught in the Web of the Big House," 19–21.

84. Johnston, *Race Relations*, 220–21. This work was originally a doctoral dissertation in 1937.

85. Extract from the will of Philip Noisette, Noisette Family Papers, SCL. A copy of the will is also stored in the SCDAH, along with Noisette's petition to the State Assembly requesting the emancipation of his slaves.

86. Bruce, *Archibald Grimke*, 1–5. Since the laws of this time stated that manumitted slaves would have to be carried out of the state, it seems unlikely that Henry Grimke would have wanted to be parted from Nancy. Other allegedly consensual relationships between slave women and white men are detailed in Powers, *Black Charlestonians*, 27.

87. The major exceptions to this are the nineteenth-century petitions made to the South Carolina State Assembly by owners who desired to manumit certain slaves. Many of the petitions were written by men wishing to free their enslaved women, suggesting that sexual relationships were a major factor in manumissions. Their volume increased after an act of 1820 forbidding all emancipation except for those granted by act of the legislature. An act of 1841 imposed even more restrictions upon those wishing to free their slaves. It stated that the manumitted would have to be carried out of the state of South Carolina in order to secure their freedom. See Edgar, *South Carolina*, 307. Hence, petitions written after 1841 had to state that the slaves in question would be taken elsewhere. Other state legislatures also added obstacles to manumission over the antebellum period. See, for example, Schafer, " 'Open and Notorious Concubinage.' "

88. See Murray, *Proud Shoes*, 39–47.

89. Jacobs, *Incidents*, 85.

90. See White, *Ar'n't I a Woman?* 35.

91. On rates of manumission and its characteristics, see Koger, *Black Slaveowners*, chap. 3; Berlin, *Slaves without Masters*, 138–57; and McClelland and Zeckhauser, *Demographic Dimensions of the New Republic*, 16–17, 80–81.

# 5 *Enforced Separations*

---

> This man came up to me, and, seizing me by the collar,
> shook me violently, saying I was his property, and must
> go with him to Georgia. At the sound of these words, the
> thoughts of my wife and children rushed across my mind,
> and my heart beat away within me. I saw and knew that
> my case was hopeless, and that resistance was vain, as
> there were near twenty persons present, all of whom
> were ready to assist the man by whom I was kidnapped.
> . . . I asked if I could not be allowed to go to see my wife
> and children, or if this could not be permitted, if they
> might not have leave to come to see me, but I was told
> I would be able to get another wife in Georgia.
> —Charles Ball, *Fifty Years in Chains*

In this extract from his autobiography, Charles Ball poignantly
describes being forcibly separated from his wife and children in a chain
gang that was headed for South Carolina and Georgia before being sold in
Columbia, South Carolina. The impact of forced separations upon slaves
was undoubtedly immense, since they had to live under the constant
threat and sometimes the reality of being taken from their loved ones. This
chapter assesses the consequences of this threat upon the relationships between couples. Exploring the domestic slave trade and the structures of
families offers new insights into some of the implications of forced separations within slave communities. This chapter initially focuses on the
pressures that masters arbitrarily imposed on slaves through the various
ways in which they enforced the separation of families. Firstly, owners
could sell their slaves to long-distance traders, who would carry family
members out of South Carolina. A labor force was needed to grow cotton
in the new states of the emerging Southwest, including Alabama, Missis-

sippi, and Louisiana, and it has been estimated that two-thirds of a million people were moved through the interstate trade.[1] Secondly, slaves could be wrenched away from their families through local sales within South Carolina.[2] Finally, separations could result from family members being transferred as gifts or through nonsale divisions of slaveholdings between the heirs of an estate. This chapter also assesses the historiography of slave separations and offers some original quantitative information on separations based upon evidence obtained from WPA narratives.

Theoretically, this combination of pressures could have been devastating to any sense of family. However, through their cross-plantation family and community ties, many slaves managed to resist the potential threats to family and marriage viability. Local sales, gifts, and divisions of estates between heirs did mean, though, that family patterns were often multidimensional, with some family members belonging to the same owner, while others might belong to more or less distant neighbors. Evidence from slave autobiographies and white source materials are also utilized to assess owners' attitudes toward forced separations. However, it is slave (rather than white) evidence that is most important in revealing aspects of the complexity of family experience—aspects that have previously been little explored by historians. A pattern emerges of essentially nuclear families that often saw all members living on the same slaveholding, but which sometimes showed spouses, siblings, children, and other relatives dispersed across a more complex residential network that could span several miles.[3]

## The Scale and Nature of Separations

Slaves had to contend not only with forced separations through local or long-distance sales but also through being the subjects of gift between whites or of the division of estates between the heirs of a deceased owner. For example, it was relatively common for young boys and girls to be given to family members upon the marriage of an owner's son or daughter or upon the death of a slaveholder. Cheryll Ann Cody has noted how the dispersal of slave property came at two "transitions" in the life cycle of planter families, arguing that planters commonly presented large gifts of slaves and land at a child's marriage and additional legacies at death.[4] Similarly, Jane Turner Censer, in her study of North Carolina planters, has shown how they often made presents of slaves to newly married sons and daughters, which could considerably disrupt slave family and community ties, especially when the newlyweds lived some distance from their parents or outside the state. Although some planters would recognize the unwillingness of the slaves to leave, their own priorities always took precedence.[5]

It could be suggested, then, that the cumulative pressures on slave families were overwhelming. However, evidence obtained from the South Carolina WPA narratives and full-length autobiographies suggests that enslaved families were flexible enough to absorb such pressures and that the dominating fear within communities was of the slave trader and long-distance separation. Testimony of the WPA respondents and the autobiographers is used here to highlight just how greatly slaves feared being torn from their loved ones through long-distance, as opposed to local, separation.[6] Textual information obtained from slave source materials on the fear of long-distance sales and subsequent separations supports the proposition that forced separations through this manner represented a real threat to members of enslaved communities, justifying their dread of this experience. The slaves' trepidation is therefore of immense significance when investigating sales, since it would undoubtedly have created an immeasurable fear of losing a loved one. Spousal separations also affected more than husbands and wives; children, parents, and other kin also felt the impact of marriages being torn apart.[7]

In his study of slavery in the low-country rice swamps, William Dusinberre has presented a vivid picture of the devastating impact that sales could have on the community life of the enslaved.[8] He shows that of around five to six hundred Waccamaw slaves exchanged in four major transactions, "400 or 500 were removed from their old community and required to start life anew, elsewhere. Meanwhile a host of new slaves were imported into these (and other) Waccamaw plantations."[9] A fear of separations was undoubtedly instilled into slaves, and this must—by increasing the slaves' hostility to owners—have contributed to the psychological distance between the lives of the two. Overall, Dusinberre paints a more negative picture of slave-community survival than did Herbert G. Gutman, who, although not quantifying separations, had emphasized the resilience of the slave family despite the considerable pressures of sale.[10] Dusinberre suggests that slaves who tried to resist the particularly harsh rice regime were "only partially successful."[11]

Differentiating between local and long-distance sales is extremely valuable in seeking to understand the extent to which separations affected slaves. In *Speculators and Slaves*, Michael Tadman focused mainly on long-distance sales but also gave significant attention to those that were local in nature. These deals could either be private commercial transactions or arise through the process of the law (for example, in sheriff's sales for debt or in probate sales following the death of an owner). Tadman suggests that local sales were probably even more numerous than long-distance sales[12] and that some 60 percent of local sales were court sales (arising through the agency of sheriffs, probate judges, and the like), while the remaining 40 percent were private commercial transactions.[13] Local sales of various types clearly had the potential for considerable family disruption. Tadman suggests, however, that private sales of individual slaves and sales of small lots of slaves were likely to be more disruptive than the sale of whole substantial estates. In the case of the former, there was a tendency to sell in lots of mixed ages, including some families, but also those of limited labor value who would otherwise have been difficult to sell.[14]

Examples of these types of patterns in local sales appear in the records of owners. For example, Charles Manigault explained in a letter to his son why it was important to buy slaves from one gang. In the case of some local sales, many slave families were intentionally kept together, especially when the groups of slaves were large enough to appeal to wealthy planters such as Manigault. He wrote: "Where one buys 15 or 20 negroes it is of great importance to select them all from one gang. They then in a strange place have ties to bind them all together. But when you buy several small parcels and throw them all together among strangers they don't assimilate, and they ponder over former ties of family &c and all goes wrong with them."[15] Manigault's desire to buy from one group was motivated by self-interest; he believed that maintaining the slaves' sense of family would make them better, more contented workers. He was also prepared to take on elderly slaves in order to maintain family ties, as the following extract illustrates: "I have just returned from purchasing 19 negroes from the sale of Brisbane's gang. . . . There are 13 or 14 prime field hands, 6 men and 8 women price $623.70 . . . the rest promising children from 5 to 10. . . . There is an old man and an old women thrown in for nothing, as they wish to go with their family, making 21 in all."[16] The fact that the old man and woman would likely be able to perform small chores or care for children almost certainly would have crossed Manigault's mind. They cost him nothing while arresting possible discontent. Moreover, it is likely that the slaves involved would have preferred to labor for Manigault and remain with their families than to be parted from them at their late stage of life.

The following extract from a bill of sale for a gang of twenty-two slaves sold to the South Carolina planter James Henry Hammond also shows how local sales of gangs could be used to get rid of elderly or disabled slaves who would otherwise be difficult to sell. Both are represented in the following bill, although it is not possible to decipher potential familial relationships between the elderly and disabled slaves and others in the group. Hammond is unlikely to have paid a good price for the club-footed Dymass, the elderly Major with his sore leg, or Patience and Hector—both of whom were sixty-five years old. However, when thrown into a larger gang that contained more valuable slaves, they would have had some use, even if that were only looking after children or performing small chores. The list reads: "Adam about 27 years old and Mary his wife about 35, their son Hector about 12; Georgiana, 16, and her child; Faith, 22; Billy, 14; Black Henry, 20; Washington, 22; Jim, 10; Justina, 16; Steven, 14; Dymass, 28 (club footed); Dinah, 40; Harry, 27; Major, 50 (sore leg); Sue, 48; Monday, 50; Jenny, 60; Bungy, 50; Patience, 65; Hector, 65."[17]

Tadman argues that the interstate slave trade caused a far higher rate of family disruption than did local sales because the interstate traffic was highly selective (specializing in teenagers and young adults) and so was biased against family units.[18] Recently, however, Thomas Russell has disputed Tadman's claims, arguing that local sales were highly disruptive for slave families and that, like long-distance sales, they caused a high rate of family separations.[19] From an investigation of South Carolina court sales between 1823 and 1861, Russell claims that 52 percent of slaves sold at such events were sold individually. However, his sample is skewed toward the sale of small lots of slaves to pay off debts (at sheriff's sales and Master in Equity sales), a bias that exaggerates the extent of separations through local sale.[20] Hence, Russell's claim that the consequences of local court sales were devastating to slave families does not necessarily hold true. Furthermore, as will be shown, the existence of cross-plantation marriages and family networks also enabled slaves to survive the impact of local sales.[21]

## Separation of the WPA Respondents and Their Family Members

This chapter emphasizes the broad context of local sales (rather than offering a detailed analysis of the structure of sales). It is suggested that the family devastation implied by Russell's results was not in fact experienced due to the resilience of abroad marriages and the wider network of cross-plantation families. Significantly, the great dread of slaves was not local but long-distance sale. While separation of any kind was rarely welcomed, nearly all long-distance movement meant irreparable loss. However, cross-plantation networks (involving not only spouses but other family and community members) allowed slaves to cope with many of the pressures of local dispersal and sale.

Of the 334 South Carolina WPA informants, 118, or just over a third

(35.3 percent), spoke either of how they had been sold or given away or how they knew of slaves who had been subjected to forced separations. While the narratives are likely to underestimate their actual extent, testimony given on forcible separations can provide a useful estimate of the overall threat of enforced removal.[22] Unfortunately, while it was not possible to quantitatively assess the relative threat of local and long-distance separations because of a lack of information given in this area, general comments reveal much about forced separations, especially for the young. Families faced a real threat of being torn apart through sale or gift in later antebellum South Carolina. Gender differences in sales were also important; young females were more likely to be sold with their mothers, while young males were more likely to be sold alone. While some of the specific results are only suggestive, the overall evidence shows a high rate of separation.

Breaking down the respondents' testimony yields interesting results. Of the 118 who mentioned sales and separations, twenty-six (7.8 percent of all informants) had been subjected to forced separations—either through sale or gift—on their own. A further sixty-one (18.3 percent) mentioned separations within their families. Within these cases, nine testified that they were parted from their families along with their mothers, five mentioned that their whole family had been sold together, and six related how both parents were sold away from them. A further nineteen testified that their mothers were parted from their immediate families, while ten described how their fathers were sold away. Another twelve recalled the separation of other family members, including grandparents, aunts, uncles, or siblings.

Finally, thirty-one (9.2 percent of all informants) gave more general testimony on the forced removal of slaves. These respondents did not mention transactions involving themselves or their families but said that, for instance, their master sold slaves or that they witnessed slaves being sold. Adding these three sets of figures together makes it possible to provide a total estimate of forced separations. The chance of being torn apart from one's family was extremely real for South Carolina slaves, with 118 ex-slaves, a minimum of 35 percent of informants, knowing someone who had been subjected to such a divisive, stressful, and in many ways irrevocable event.

The eighty-seven (or 26 percent of all respondents) who were either sold themselves or had a family member sold represents a slightly higher figure than the findings of Paul D. Escott. He found that around one-fifth of all the ex-slaves interviewed had experienced at least a partial breakup of their families during slavery.[23] The difference between Escott's 20 percent and the South Carolina 26 percent appears to lie in the fact that during the period covered by the WPA respondents' reminiscences, South Carolina was a slave-exporting state.[24] South Carolina slaves were therefore more likely to be sold away than slaves residing in the American South as a whole, since slaves tended to be sold from the Upper South to the Lower South or westward.

A more specific summary of all family separations as related by WPA respondents yields significant outcomes on the nature of gifts of slaves and estate divisions between heirs. Of the eighty-seven ex-slaves who mentioned separations involving themselves or their family members, twenty described the giving away of slaves, compared with sixty-seven who referred to slave sales. Ten of the former testified that the gift of a slave (or slaves) was made to their master's daughter, and a further five said that such a gift had been presented to their owner's son. Five of these fifteen also specified that the gift had been made to mark the marriage of the owner's son or daughter, a trend that suggests that the giving of young slaves to their daughters when they entered matrimony was common. While gifts of slaves and estate divisions usually disrupted families arbitrarily, such networks could usually survive. Moreover, since most white families tended to reside relatively near to each other, the majority of gifts upon marriage were local in nature. This meant that the giving away of slaves need not have impinged upon the enslaved as much as long-distance sales, because their families' strength and resilience enabled them to maintain regular contact with each other and hence to cope with such upheaval.

Interesting gender-specific patterns among forced separations also become apparent upon further analysis. A total of forty-seven male ex-slaves (24.7 percent of all males) and forty female respondents (27.7 percent of all females) mentioned separations involving either themselves or other family members through sale or gift. Of these females, 12.5 percent had been sold alone, compared with 15 percent who had been given away. For the male ex-slaves, 17 percent of the sample had been sold alone, while 14.9 percent were given away. This pattern betrays the desirability of young house servants, whose ownership was passed to the sons or daughters of masters upon marriage.[25] Female ex-slaves were also more likely than males to have been parted from their families along with their mothers, with the percentages of the samples standing at 12.5 and 8.5 percent, respectively. A significant number of the women (25 percent, compared with 19.1 percent of the men) also mentioned being forcibly separated from their mother when she was either sold or given away.

It is noteworthy that many more of the male ex-slaves mentioned the sale of their fathers (19.1 percent, compared with 2.5 percent for fe-males). This does not mean that more fathers of slave boys and more mothers of slave girls were sold; instead it shows that these separations may have impacted on young slaves in somewhat different ways. Young boys may have attached more significance to being taken from their fa-thers, while young girls may have been more affected by being parted from their mothers. Family ties within slave communities may have op-erated, to some extent, along gender lines, with young girls being closer to their mothers, and young boys having stronger bonds with their fa-thers. Undoubtedly, though, forced separation affected whole families, and parents faced an agonizing experience in trying to explain sales to their children. Sometimes family stories or songs were used to help pre-pare them for what might lay ahead, an example of which reads:

> "Mammy, is ole Massa gwine sell us tomorrow?
> Yes, my chile.
> Whah he goin sell us?
> Way down South in Georgia."[26]

## Fear of Long-Distance Sales

The WPA respondent George Fleming, enslaved in Laurens County, vividly described the horror of the internal slave trade. He testified: "Some men, like old Joe Crews, was reg'lar nigger traders. Dey bought niggers, stole 'em frum Virginia and places and drove 'em through de country like a bunch of hogs. Dey come in great gangs. In town dey have big nigger sell-ings, and all de marsters frum all over de countryside be dar to bid on 'em. Dey put 'em up on de block and holler 'bout dis and dat dey could do and how strong dey was. 'Six hundred—Yip, yip, make it six-fifty.' I heard 'em call many times when I be dar wid marse. Some of dem throw a thousand dollars quick as dey would ten at a purty gal. Some traders stop a drove of niggers at de plantation and swap or sell some."[27]

Fear of these long-distance (rather than local) sales is apparent through-out slave source materials. Long-distance transactions often meant the ir-revocable separation of families, but this was not true of local sales. It will be shown that while the latter could severely disrupt families, their net-works, facilitated by the system of cross-plantation marriages, often meant that communities could cope with separations of this type. Within both the WPA and autobiographical narratives, frequent reference was made to the fear of long-distance sales, especially to Louisiana and Texas, where the treatment of slaves allegedly was worse. Jacob Stroyer, for example, had two sisters, Violet and Priscilla, who were married to men belonging to the brother of Stroyer's master. They all lived on one plantation. However, when their owner came into debt, he sold many of his slaves, including Stroyer's sisters, who were parted from their spouses. A trader named Mr. Manning bought Violet and Priscilla; he planned to take them to Louisiana where they would be sold. When the day of departure arrived, many slaves—Stroyer included—went to the depot to say goodbye. He recalled: "Louisiana was considered by the slaves as a place of slaughter, so those who were going did not expect to see their friends again. . . . As the cars moved away we heard weeping and wailing from the slaves as far as the human voice could be heard; and from that time to the present I have neither seen nor heard from my two sisters, nor any of those who left the Clarkson depot on that memorable day."[28] The ordeal faced by Stroyer's sisters illustrates the importance of wider familial—as well as spousal—ties. Violet and Priscilla were torn away from their brother as well as from their husbands.

The WPA respondent William Oliver, enslaved near Conway, also expressed his fears of being sold to the Southwest, where he believed slaves were treated more harshly: "The cruellest treatment I know of in the United States and all the other states was done in the Southwestern states. Take New Orleans. . . . Texas beat the country for cruelty. They tell me when your Master and Missus in this country want to make you do your task, they threaten to sell you to Texas. Had a regular 'Vander Range' in New Orleans. Place they keep the slaves and auction them off."[29] Other ex-slaves spoke more about the fear of familial separations created by long-distance sales. Sena Moore told her interviewer how her parents, who had resided in a cross-plantation marriage, were separated forever when her father's master decided to sell him away to Arkansas. She said: "My mammy weep 'bout dat but what could her do? Just nothin'."[30]

A fear of the separation of husbands and wives—along with a dread of the splitting up of parents and children—is evident in all slave testimony, which supports the claim that spousal relationships were vitally important to the enslaved. Tom Jones states in his autobiography that he married a slave named Lucilla who belonged to a Mrs. Moore. They resided in a cross-plantation marriage until Mrs. Moore moved away. Jones wrote: "I had a constant dread that Mrs. Moore, her mistress, would be in want of money and sell my dear wife. We constantly dreaded a final separation. . . . These fears were well-founded . . . [since] Mrs. Moore left Wilmington, and moved to Newburn. She carried away with her my beloved Lucilla, and my three children, Annie, four years old; Lizzie, two and a half years; and our sweet little babe Charlie. She remained there eighteen months. And, Oh, how lonely and dreary and desponding were those months of lonely life to my crushed heart! My dear wife and my precious children were seventy-four miles distant from me, carried away from me in utter scorn of my beseeching words."[31] Jones only saw his wife once more, when she passed through Wilmington on her way to Alabama with her mistress.[32]

Many of the WPA respondents also expressed a familiarity with the family separations that were created by long-distance sales. The Marion County ex-slave Sylvia Durant said to her interviewer: "Den dey'ud hab sale en sell some uv de colored peoples offen to annuder plantation hundred mile 'way some uv de time. 'Vide man en he wife. Dey sho' done it. I hear pa tell 'bout dat. Make em stand up on uh stump en bid em offen dere jes lak dey wuz hoss. Pa say de sell he brother Elic wife 'way wid de onlyest child dey hab. Ne'er didn't see dat wife en child no more."[33] Susan Hamlin said of her time as a slave in Charleston: "All time, night an' day, you could hear men an' women screamin' to de tip of dere voices as either ma, pa, sister, or brother wus take without any warnin' an' sell. Some time mother who had only one chile was separated fur life. People wus always dyin' frum a broken heart."[34] Hector Godbold testified: "Dey sho sell de colored peoples way plenty times cause I see dat done right here to Marion. Stand em up on a block en sell em to a speculator dere. I hear em bid off a 'oman en her baby dere en den dey bid off my auntie en uncle way down to de country."[35]

## The Importance of Cross-plantation Marriages

Abroad unions were vital in enabling families to cope with local separations. It has been argued in chapter 2 that these marriages accounted for some 34 percent of slave households and that, far from being weak and nominal relationships, they were vigorously maintained despite the circumstances. These partnerships (as well as extended family networks) often enabled slaves to cope with the hardships of local sales, and a reading of slave source materials supports this proposition. Charles Ball lived in a cross-plantation union; his wife was a chambermaid to Mrs. Symmes, while Ball belonged to Jack Cox, for whom he labored in the field. However, following a lawsuit to determine right of property, ownership of Ball was passed on to Levin Ballard. Ball wrote: "One day, whilst I was at work in the cornfield, Mr. Ballard came and told me I was his property. . . . I accordingly went with him, determining to serve him obediently and faithfully. I remained in his service almost three years, and *as he lived near the residence of my wife's master, my former mode of life was not materially changed by this change of home*" (italics added).[36] Undoubtedly, in an ideal world Charles Ball would have lived within a nuclear family, where he could eat and sleep in the same home as his wife and children. However, although he was denied this opportunity by the institution of bondage, he asserted his modicum of independence by choosing his own wife, and they lived as full a family life as was possible despite belonging to different masters. The fact that Ball changed owners did not inconvenience his marriage, since he still resided in the same area and was able to maintain his cross-plantation family ties.

Similarly, Mattie Jackson wrote in her autobiography that her parents lived in a cross-plantation union but still managed to maintain their relationship after her mother was sold twenty miles away. As she describes it, "My father, thereafter, visited my mother once a week, walking the distance every Saturday evening and returning on Sunday evening."[37] However, Jackson's familial situation was to change for the worse when her father was subjected to a long-distance sale: she never saw him again. While a local sale inconvenienced the marriage of Jackson's parents much more than that of Charles Ball, the strength of the spousal relationship meant that Jackson's parents strove to preserve their ties.

The WPA respondents described similar experiences with regard to local separations. Sylvia Cannon, eight years old in 1860, was sold locally when she was "a little small girl." Her experience illustrates well how familial relationships could be preserved despite disruption. Cannon testified: "Father en mother belong to old Bill Greggs en dat whe' Miss Earlie Hatchel buy me from. After dat, I didn' never live wid my parents any more, but I went back to see dem every two weeks. Got a note en go on a Sunday evenin' en come back to Miss Hatchel on Monday."[38] Cannon's arrangement with her new owner seems to have worked rather like a cross-plantation marriage, since she needed a pass to visit her parents. While she must have missed her parents a great deal in her new situation, she was at least able to maintain regular contact with them. In other cases, the sale of a parent meant that those who lived in nuclear households became cross-plantation families. Mack Taylor described how his family was all owned by the Clark family, who lived on the Wateree River in Winnsboro. Taylor's father was then sold to a new master in Columbia, but he managed to remain in regular contact with his family.[39] Similarly, Lucinda Miller and her mother were sold from their home in Spartanburg, leaving Lucinda's father behind. However, since the new owner was the brother of their former master and lived only "two or three plantations away," they maintained a family life with Lucinda's father.[40] Other respondents' parents successfully maintained cross-plantation marriages both before and after local sales. Lucretia Heyward was sold with her mother from their home in Beaufort to an overseer of her master, Joe Eddings. She stated: "Muh pa name Tony MacKnight and he b'long to Mr. Stephen Elliot. My ma name Venus MacKnight and she b'long to Mr. Joe Eddings. . . . De overseer been Edward Blunt. He been poor white trash, but he wuk haa'd and save he money and buy slave. He buy my ma." Lucretia and her mother maintained contact with Tony MacKnight, therefore surviving the perils associated with sale.[41]

Naturally, slaves did not fear local moves to the same extent as long-distance separations because there was a possibility that spousal (as well as broader familial) ties could be preserved when more manageable distances were involved. This was not the case with long-distance transactions, where family disruption was nearly always permanent. The fact that slaves desired to continue relationships with their spouses despite local sales also provides evidence of the strength of the bonds between them. Couples strove to stay together despite their being plunged into increased familial adversity by masters.

When slaveholders gave away those they held in bondage, undoubtedly some would have lost their ties to family members, especially if they were forced to move some distance. Others, however, would have been able to maintain their links, particularly when they resided within close proximity to their former owners. White familial ties therefore facilitated contact between slave family members who were owned within the same extended family. For example, the WPA informant Bill McNeil, enslaved in York County, was given (along with his mother and brother) to his master's daughter upon her marriage. McNeil's father, however, was able to get a pass so that he could visit his family.[42] As was the case with local sales, the giving away of slaves need not have impinged too severely upon family life. South Carolina slave testimony illustrates that the strength of the relationship between couples meant that even when they were forced into a cross-plantation marriage, or when those in abroad unions had their spouses move elsewhere after being given away, provided the distances involved were not insurmountable, spousal and broader familial links could be maintained.[43]

Other WPA respondents moved within their local area, having been bequeathed as gifts rather than sold. Often this only became apparent because they expressed familiarity with their surroundings. Adeline Jackson, for example, said: "When my younges' mistress, name Marion Rebecca, married her second cousin, marster Edward P. Mobely, I was give to her and went wid then to de June place. It was called dat because old Doctor June built it and sold it to Marster Ed."[44] It seems that the "June place" was relatively close to Jackson's previous residence. Others, but probably a minority of those who were given away, would have lost all contact with their family due to the distances involved. Henry Gladney stated: "Little Marse John's mother was another daughter of old Marster John. Her name was Dorcas. They live in Florida. I was took 'way down dere, cried pow'-ful to leave my mammy."[45]

Estate divisions also followed the interests of white, not black families, but those divided among heirs were often dispersed locally. Furthermore, as Tadman has noted, when an estate was sold or divided at the death of an owner, the lots in which slaves were divided tended to include slaves of all ages. As such, probate sales and nonsale divisions between heirs often enabled families to stay together.[46] Moses Roper, who was the son of his "young master," wrote that when the "old master" died all those he had held in bondage were divided among his children: "The way they divide their slaves is this: they write the names of different slaves on a small piece of paper, and put it into a box, and let them all draw. I think that Mr. Durham drew my mother, and Mr. Fowler drew me, so we were separated a considerable distance, I cannot say how far."[47] Roper illustrates the ties that bound the white slave-owning family together. However, these links were also important for slave communities, since they often facilitated the maintenance of their own familial relationships. Frequent contact between whites could increase the opportunities for contact between blacks. Unfortunately for Roper, he was eventually to lose touch with all of his family when he was sold to a trader headed further south.[48]

When assessing the impact of the forced separation of slaves, it is clear that the implications of removal would have varied depending on the geographical distance between the family members following sales or transfers. If newly separated slaves all resided within the same geographical district, the strength of the ties between spouses (and also communities at large) meant that family members were still able to see each other. The networks that existed across plantations, especially through marriage, enabled this contact. While all slaves must have feared being forcibly separated from their families, the relative lack of concern regarding local separations is significant. Cross-plantation family networks meant that local moves had a lesser impact upon family and community ties than did long-distance sales.

Overall, the anguish that slaves felt upon being forcibly separated from loved ones was undoubtedly immense. Larry E. Hudson Jr. has noted how "the level of affection in some slave families adds a special bite to one of the most cruel realities of slavery: the sale and separation of loved ones."[49] Charles Ball, having escaped from the South, arrived in Baltimore to find that his wife and children were not in their home; he later learned that a slave trader had taken them all. Ball writes: "This intelligence almost deprived me of life; it was the most dreadful of all the misfortunes that I had ever suffered. It was now clear that some slave-dealer had come in my absence and seized my wife and children as slaves, and sold them to such men as I had served in the South. They had now passed into hopeless bondage, and were gone forever beyond my reach. I myself was advertised as a fugitive slave, and was liable to be arrested at each moment, and dragged back to Georgia. I rushed out of my own house in despair, and returned to Pennsylvania with a broken heart."[50] However, despite the huge despair they must have caused, the positive accomplishments of slave communities in the face of enforced separations cannot be overlooked. In particular, marrying off their place of residence and sustaining their marriages despite sales, gifts, and estate divisions represents a significant achievement on the part of enslaved spouses. The threat of separation that loomed large for slaves also provided them with an incentive to mentally distance themselves from owners and to strive for their own, autonomous community life.

## Notes

1. See Johnson, *Soul By Soul*, 5–6.
2. Johnson has estimated that there were twice as many "local" sales as interstate sales in the antebellum South. He includes in his definition sales from neighbor to neighbor, state supervised probate and debt sales, and brokered sales within a single state (ibid., 6–7). This contrasts with my own definition of such sales, where "local" has been defined as "within visiting distance."
3. See chap. 2 for more on the distances involved in visiting loved ones.
4. Cody, "Sale and Separation," 120, and "Naming, Kinship, and Estate Dispersal." Brenda E. Stevenson has also shown how the life cycles of owners impacted upon their slaves in *Life in Black and White*, 215–16.
5. Censer, *North Carolina Planters and Their Children*, 138–39.
6. Slaves' comments also cast doubt on the validity of the claims made by Robert W. Fogel and Stanley L. Engerman on the nature of the interregional slave trade. Using data contained in sales records in New Orleans, they alleged that sales amounted to only 16 percent of the total interregional movement, with the rest being attributed to planter migration. This meant that only about 2 percent of the marriages of slaves were destroyed by long-distance separations. See *Time on the Cross*, 49. Fogel and Engerman's methodology has been extensively criticized by Michael Tadman, who has shown that the composition of the New Orleans trade (because of the demands of Louisiana's sugar crop) was unlike that of the rest of the trade. Fogel and Engerman took as their "indicators" of family separations cases where mothers and children were sold without fathers and cases where children were sold without parents. Tadman has shown, however, that the New Orleans trade (unlike the trade generally) specialized in adult male slaves and carried exceptionally low proportions of mother-and-child units and child-without-parents units. Unlike Fogel and Engerman, he also points out that many of the "single" adult males (sold without family) would also in fact have been separated from

wives and children. Tadman used the lists, letters, bills of sale, and accounts of slave traders to argue that the number of first marriages of slaves destroyed by forcible separations stood at around one in three and that one-fifth of slave children were separated from both parents by that trade. He also claims that the slave trade accounted for about 60 percent of interregional movements, compared with Fogel and Engerman's 16 percent. See *Speculators and Slaves*, 134, 170–71, 178. Also important is the work of Richard Sutch. He argues that male slaves were more likely to be exported from the upper South than female slaves because of the desire among slave-owners to retain "breeding" females. See "Breeding of Slaves for Sale."

7. Herbert G. Gutman has written of the "geometric" impact of spousal separations in *Black Family in Slavery and Freedom*, 145–48. For more on how slaves strove to reproduce communities fractured by the slave trade, see Johnson, *Soul by Soul*, 195–97.

8. For descriptions of the separations that afflicted the Manigault slaves, see Dusinberre, *Them Dark Days*, 110–11. He argues that sales, coupled with sickness and death, meant that family life for the enslaved was often fragile.

9. Ibid., 401–3.

10. See Gutman, *Black Family in Slavery and Freedom*. Gutman's study was written partly in reaction to the Moynihan report. Therefore, he was keen to emphasize the positive accomplishments of the slave community. Recently, however, there has been a tendency to suggest that Gutman was too optimistic about the resilience of slave families. See Kolchin, *American Slavery*, 137. This work argues, however, that it was the desire for autonomy on the part of slave communities, despite the constraints imposed by owners, that is of vital significance.

11. Dusinberre, *Them Dark Days*, viii.

12. Tadman, *Speculators and Slaves*, 112. Johnson estimates that there were twice as many intrastate sales as those that were interstate in nature. See *Soul by Soul*, 6–7.

13. Tadman, *Speculators and Slaves*, 120 n.18.

14. Ibid., 136.

15. Letter to Louis Manigault from Charles Manigault, 8 January 1857, in Clifton, ed., *Life and Labor on Argyle Island*, 239.

16. Letter to Louis Manigault from Charles Manigault, 13 January 1857, in Clifton, ed., *Life and Labor on Argyle Island*, 240.

17. Bill of sale for slaves sold to James Henry Hammond, 6 September 1843, Hammond-Bryan-Cumming Family Papers, SCL.

18. On the age structure of the interstate slave trade, see Tadman, *Speculators and Slaves*, 25–31.

19. See Russell, "Sale Day in Antebellum South Carolina"; "South Carolina's Largest Slave Auctioneering Firm"; and "'Articles Sell Best Singly.'"

20. See Russell, "'Articles Sell Best Singly,'" 1166–71, for a detailed description of the alleged composition of local sales.

21. Ibid., 1190–91.

22. Some of the respondents may have had an awareness of sales but might not have mentioned this to their interviewer. Moreover, many were very young during slavery times (and teenagers and young adults were far more at risk of being sold to traders).

23. Escott, *Slavery Remembered*, 46. Alternatively, Stephen Crawford estimates that approximately 23 percent of slave families were broken by sale. See "Quantified Memory," 163.

24. Tadman argues that by the 1820s, the state of South Carolina had become a net exporter of slaves in *Speculators and Slaves*, 12, 31–41.

25. Unfortunately, there was not enough testimony to undertake an investigation into the occupation of those respondents who mentioned slave sales.

26. Quoted in Schwartz, *Born in Bondage,* 167. See also King, *Stolen Childhood,* 103–4.

27. Rawick, *American Slave,* vol. 11, 133.

28. Stroyer, *My Life in the South,* 39–42.

29. Rawick, *American Slave,* vol. 3, pt. 3, 219.

30. Ibid., 209.

31. Jones, *Experience and Personal Narrative,* 24.

32. Ibid.

33. Rawick, *American Slave,* vol. 2, pt. 1, 339.

34. Augustus Ladson, who was black, conducted this interview. When Hamlin was interviewed by Jessie A. Butler, a white woman, she played down the significance of sales, talking of separations only in a general sense. She also testified that Mr. Fuller (her owner) "didn't sell none of us" (ibid., vol. 2, pt. 2, 231–32 and 235). See also Davidson and Lytle, *After the Fact,* 191–201.

35. Rawick, *American Slave,* vol. 2, pt. 2, 145.

36. Ball, *Fifty Years in Chains,* 25.

37. Jackson, *Story of Mattie J. Jackson,* 7.

38. Rawick, *American Slave,* vol. 2, pt. 1, 188.

39. Ibid., vol. 3, pt. 4, 158.

40. Ibid., vol. 3, pt. 3, 191

41. Ibid., vol. 2, pt. 2, 279–80.

42. Ibid., vol. 3, pt. 3, 1–2.

43. Richard S. Dunn presents a more negative picture of local sales in terms of their impact on slave families in his study of the large Mount Airy estate in Virginia. He writes that although the kinship network was pervasive, many families were widely dispersed among the nine family farms. Of thirty-five identifiable slave families, only five couples regularly lived together. This can be attributed to the distances involved in traveling to see spouses and families because the farms were spread over a distance of thirty miles. Hence, there was also a depressed fertility rate at Mount Airy. See "A Tale of Two Plantations," 50.

44. Rawick, *American Slave,* vol. 3, pt. 3, 164.

45. Ibid., vol. 2, pt. 2, 130.

46. See Tadman, *Speculators and Slaves,* 136.

47. Roper, *Narrative of the Adventures,* 2–3.

48. Ibid., 4.

49. Hudson, *To Have and to Hold,* 168.

50. Ball, *Fifty Years in Chains,* 430.

# Conclusion

The fight of slaves to find their missing family members and to legalize their marriages following the ending of the Civil War has been well documented.[1] It is likely that they sought to legally validate their partnerships in this way for various reasons, including the fact that it made their relationships acceptable to the law, their church, and to wider society as a whole. Some also hoped that being legally married would protect their children from being bound as apprentices by former owners who would define ex-slave children as "bastards" in order to indenture them.[2] Yet the behavior of the newly freed people also supports the notion that family relations and specifically the love between spouses were of primary importance to the enslaved. Reaffirming one's wedding vows before American law was the ultimate romantic gesture.

This book has shown that members of South Carolina slave communities desired a life that was independent of owners, striving to distance themselves as much as possible by creating a space between their respective lives. This illustrates that slaves were capable of trying to survive and to resist their oppression in various ways. Primarily, the strong and loving relationships between spouses created valuable cultural autonomy and systems of support in the face of adversity. The majority of slaves wished to meet, court, and marry a member of the opposite sex whom they chose despite their masters' imposition of rules and regulations in this realm of life.

While the majority of slaveholders saw themselves as benevolent and paternalistic, most slaves perceived them very differently. A gulf existed between the worldview of owners and their actual treatment of their slaves, a gulf that was vital in allowing slaves to psychologically distance themselves from those who held them in bondage. Masters' actions forced slaves into adopting an "underground" approach to many community activities: dancing and flirting on a Saturday night; mixing with those who lived on different quarters; celebrating the marriages of young couples in love; risking the wrath of masters and patrollers in visiting wives and children; and simply desiring to live within stable, loving, supportive partnerships. All slaves displayed subtle acts of resistance to their owners' attempts at control.

Slave testimony shows strong attachments to cross-plantation unions as a part of the wider desire of slaves to live according to their own cultural norms. The resilience and numerical importance of these partnerships shows that slaves were willing to fight in their quest to wed someone of their own choosing. They were also prepared to undergo great hardships in maintaining their marriages, a commitment that was particularly true for slave men. Chapter 2 has shown that it was men who were expected to do the visiting, and many undertook considerable risks in maintaining contact with their wives, children, and girlfriends. Using their wits to hide from owners and patrollers was widely admired among their peers, a factor that contradicts the notion that male slaves were emasculated by bondage without underestimating the hardships they were forced to endure.

Despite considerable gender differences, slave men and women went to great lengths in their desire to love, support, and protect their spouses, families, and communities. Gender differences were particularly pronounced in the realm of work, where owners would often segregate their slaves according to sex when assigning tasks. Slave source materials, however, suggest high levels of solidarity across communities, exemplified by the fact that an important minority of marriages brought field and house workers together. Furthermore, while slave women were subjected to a "triple burden" in having to work for their owners, carry out tasks for their families, and shoulder most of the child-rearing responsibilities, men also had their own familial duties and obligations. By virtue of the strong relationships between spouses, work for families was a shared responsibility. This was especially true when families were able to labor together, for example, in tending their garden plots. The gendered nature of work impacted upon the chances of slave women being awarded a high status, although some, especially elderly midwives, did play leading community roles. The work lives of slave men and women can best be characterized as different, but within a broad context of cooperation.

The lives of slave men and women were further differentiated by the impact of interracial sexual contact. Levels of abuse were high, especially of domestics by masters. However, the strength of spousal relationships meant that most couples could survive this form of exploitation, with men trying to protect the women in their lives from potential abusers and providing love and comfort in the face of adversity. Another form of exploitation that slaves were subjected to was forcible separation from loved ones through sale, gift, or estate division. As slave testimony reveals, these caused great anguish. Significantly, though, the system of cross-plantation marriages and familial networks coupled with the strength of the relationships between husbands and wives meant that in cases of local sales, gifts of slaves, and estate divisions (important areas that have not been sufficiently analyzed by historians) the consequences of these separations need not have been severe. While all slaves feared removal from those they cherished, spousal and familial ties meant that local separations generally had a lesser impact upon family and community ties than did long-distance sales. Slaves could often maintain contact with each other following local forced separations, albeit in an amended family form.

This book has emphasized resilience in the face of adversity. Despite the often horrendous exploitations inflicted by owners, slaves strove to live according to the norms of their own communities, and they resented the fact that their masters imposed a context of restraint on their lives. Falling in love and marrying before living in a loving, affectionate, and supportive relationship therefore created a mindset of cultural independence for the great majority of the enslaved. Furthermore, the survival of their marriages despite interference by owners represents an enormous achievement on the part of couples, especially those in cross-plantation unions, who faced additional hardships in their fight to live as man and wife. Love and affection despite exploitation characterizes slave community life in antebellum South Carolina.

## Notes

1. Herbert G. Gutman highlights the important role played by Union army clergymen and the Freedmen's Bureau in legitimizing slave and ex-slave marriages; he also emphasizes the length of their partnerships. See *Black Family in Slavery and Freedom*, esp. chaps. 1 and 9. More recently, Leslie A. Schwalm argues that many freedpeople resented the intrusion of the Freedmen's Bureau into their lives. They believed their marriages under slavery to be valid and regarded new ceremonies as superfluous or even insulting. See *A Hard Fight for We*, chap. 7. It is also true that the opportunities provided by emancipation enabled a minority of slaves to escape from antagonistic unions, as shown in chapter 2.

2. See Schwalm, *A Hard Fight for We*, 250–54, for more on apprenticeship in South Carolina. Barbara Jeanne Fields also considers the apprenticeship system in *Slavery and Freedom on the Middle Ground*, 35, 139–42, 152–55, as does Rebecca Scott in "The Battle over the Child."

# APPENDIX I

*Criteria Used in the Construction of a*
*Database Relating to the Comments of the*
*South Carolina WPA Respondents*

*Preliminary Points*

Respondent's name
Respondent's age
Date of interview
Age in 1865
Sex of respondent
Name of interviewer
Sex and race of interviewer
Location of respondent during slavery
Name of master
Name of mistress
Size of holding or number of slaves owned

*Family Background of Respondent*

Name and race of father
Name and race of mother
Residence of father
Comments on father visiting
Names and number of siblings
Deaths of siblings under slavery
Knowledge of grandparents
Stepparents
African relations
Blood ties to whites

*Work Patterns during Slavery*

Work of respondent as a child and adult during slavery
Age at which work began as a child and adult
Work of father and mother
Comments on hiring out

## Childbearing and Rearing

Treatment of pregnant women
Childbirth procedures or length of time off work
Childcare provision

## Family Structure and Family Life

Courtship rituals
Respondent married prewar or postwar
Length of marriage
Location of spouse during slavery
Number of marriages
Number of children
Work for family "after sundown" of respondent
Work for family "after sundown" of other slaves

## Realms of Exploitation and Relations with Owners

Relations with master
Relations with mistress
Sale/separation of family members
Sale/separation of other slaves
Comments on runaways
Physical punishments inflicted on respondent
Physical punishments inflicted on other slaves
Implementer of punishment
Reason for punishment
Comments on rape or sexual problems
General comments on the institution of slavery

## Community Life

Comments on female networks
Comments on friendship
Comments on free time—social life
Comments on free time—producing goods
Comments on witch doctors or conjurers
Comments on strong female characters
Attitudes toward religion

# APPENDIX 2

## Interracial Sexual Contact in the WPA Narratives

Rawick's collection of WPA slave narratives (including the supplementary volumes) was examined using Donald Jacobs's *Index to "The American Slave."* All index entries for "miscegenation" were consulted, and twenty-two cases were found in which respondents expressed a direct knowledge of sexual contact or abuse occurring between either their master or their overseer and enslaved women. These cases are detailed below (all references are to Rawick, *The American Slave: A Composite Autobiography*).

### Owners' Sexual Contact with House Slaves

Mary Reynolds had a sexual relationship with her master. Vol. 5, pt. 3: *Texas Narratives*, 242.

James Calheart was the son of his owner and a female house servant. Vol. 16, pt. 3: *Maryland Narratives*, 34.

Andrew Moss's master had a relationship with his grandmother, a house servant. Vol. 16, pt. 6: *Tennessee Narratives*, 50.

Anthony Christopher's sister had sexual contact with their owner. Supplement Series 2, vol. 3, pt. 2: *Texas Narratives*, 719.

Victor Duhon's mother was a house servant. He was his master's son. Supplement Series 2, vol. 4, pt. 3: *Texas Narratives*, 1238.

Adline Marshall's master kept a slave mistress in the Big House. Supplement Series 2, vol. 7, pt. 6: *Texas Narratives*, 2578.

### Owners' Sexual Contact with Field Slaves

Annie Osbourne was the daughter of her owner. Her mother worked in the field. Supplement Series 2, vol. 8, pt. 7: *Texas Narratives*, 2989.

### Other Sexual Contact between Owners and Slaves

Nannie Eaves was her master's daughter. Vol. 16, pt. 2: *Kentucky Narratives*, 61.

George Davis was his owner's son. Vol. 16, pt. 2: *Kentucky Narratives*, 70.

Candis Goodwin was her master's daughter. Vol. 16, pt. 5: *Virginia Narratives*, 19.

Ethel Daugherty said that her master sexually abused his female slaves. Supplement Series 1, vol. 5, pt. 1: *Indiana Narratives*, 61.

Albert Burks was the son of his owner. Supplement Series 2, vol. 1, pt. 10: *Nebraska Narratives*, 315.

Mrs. Thomas Johns said that her master had a relationship with one of his enslaved women. Supplement Series 2, vol. 6, pt. 5: *Texas Narratives*, 1973.

Mary Reynolds said that her master had a slave mistress. Supplement Series 2, vol. 8, pt. 7: *Texas Narratives*, 3292.

Robert Wilson was his owner's son. Supplement Series 2, vol. 10, pt. 9: *Texas Narratives*, 4207.

## White Overseers' Sexual Contact with Field Slaves

Minnie Fulks's mother was abused by a white overseer. Vol. 16, pt. 5: *Virginia Narratives*, 11.

## White Overseers' Sexual Contact with House Slaves

Scott Bond's father was the white plantation manager, and his mother was a house servant. Supplement Series 2, vol. 1, pt. 3: *Arizona Narratives*, 36–37.

Louise Neill was the daughter of a white overseer and a cook. Supplement Series 2, vol. 7, pt. 6: *Texas Narratives*, 2890–91.

## Other Sexual Contact between White Overseers and Slaves

Callie Grey was the daughter of an overseer. Supplement Series 1, vol. 8, pt. 3: *Mississippi Narratives*, 860.

Cora Gillam was the daughter of an overseer. Supplement Series 2, vol. 1, pt. 3: *Arizona Narratives*, 68.

Jacob Aldrich said that his overseer "fooled around" with slave women and had mulatto children. Supplement Series 2, vol. 2, pt. 1: *Texas Narratives*, 26.

Lu Lee said that her overseer "spoiled" a slave girl who bore his child. Supplement Series 2, vol. 6, pt. 5: *Texas Narratives*, 2298.

# BIBLIOGRAPHY

*Manuscript Collections*

William R. Perkins Library, Duke University, Durham, North Carolina
John C. Gorman Papers
Marshall Family Papers
McDonald-Furman Papers

South Carolina Department of Archives and History, Columbia
Antioch Baptist Church (Society Hill, S.C.), Minutes of Antioch Baptist Church, 1830–65
Barnwell Baptist Church (Barnwell, S.C.), Minutes of Barnwell Baptist Church, 1812–65
Bethany Baptist Church (Edgefield County, S.C.), Minutes and Other Records, 1810–65
Bethel Baptist Church (Edgefield County, S.C.), Minutes and Membership Lists of Bethel Baptist Church, 1853–65
Big Creek Baptist Church (Williston, S.C.), Minute Book of the Big Creek Baptist Church, 1801–65
Ebenezer Baptist Church (Florence County, S.C.), Minutes of Ebenezer Baptist Church, 1823–65
Elim Baptist Church (Effingham, S.C.), Minutes of Elim Baptist Church, 1847–65
First Baptist Church (Darlington, S.C.), Minutes of First Baptist Church, 1856–65
First Baptist Church (Edgefield, S.C.), Minutes of First Baptist Church, 1823–54
Hopewell Baptist Church (Chester County, S.C.), Minutes and Other Records of Hopewell Baptist Church, 1813–37
Lake Swamp Baptist Church (Timmonsville, S.C.), Minutes of Lake Swamp Baptist Church, 1832–65
Mountain Creek Baptist Church (Anderson County, S.C.), Minutes of Mountain Creek Baptist Church, 1798–1865
Mount Elon Baptist Church (Lydia, S.C.), Minutes of Mount Elon Baptist Church, 1831–65
New Providence Baptist Church (Hartsville, S.C.), Minutes of New Providence Baptist Church, 1808–65
Petitions to the South Carolina State Assembly 1800–65
Philadelphia Baptist Church (Pauline, S.C.), Minutes of Philadelphia Baptist Church, 1803–65
Sardis Baptist Church (Timmonsville, S.C.), Minutes of Sardis Baptist Church, 1863–65

Secona Baptist Church (Pickens, S.C.), Minutes of Secona Baptist Church, 1795–1865

Washington Baptist Church (Pelzer, S.C.), Minutes of Washington Baptist Church, 1821–65

South Caroliniana Library, University of South Carolina, Columbia
Lewis Malone Ayer Papers
Ada Bacot Diary, 1860–63
William Blanding Papers
Thomas Blewett Plantation Book, 1848–56
Conway-Black-Davis Family Papers
Anne Simons Deas, "Two Years of Plantation Life" (A fictionalized account of life on Cedar Grove Plantation)
Andrew Flinn Plantation Book, 1840
Glass Family Papers
Guignard Family Papers
Hammond-Bryan-Cumming Family Papers
Mary Esther Huger Reminiscences, 1890–92
Lawton Family Papers
Lide-Coker Family Papers
Charles Izard Manigault Papers
Manigault Family Papers
Noisette Family Papers
Benjamin Franklin Perry Papers
Emily Wharton Sinkler Letters
Townes Family Papers
Wallace-Rice-Duncan Family Papers

Southern Historical Collection, University of North Carolina at Chapel Hill
John Edwin Fripp Plantation Journal
David Gavin Diary, 1855–74
Samuel Cram Jackson Diary, 1832–33
Margaret Ann (Meta) Morris Diary, 1860–66
Ben Sparkman Plantation Journal, 1848, 1853–59
Springs Family Papers
William D. Valentine Diary, 1837–55

## Published Sources

Abrahams, Roger D. *Singing the Master: The Emergence of African-American Culture in the Plantation South.* New York: Penguin, 1992.

Aleckson, Sam. *Before the War and After the Union: An Autobiography.* Boston: Gold Mind Publishing, 1929.

Anderson, James D. "'Aunt Jemima in Dialectics': Genovese on Slave Culture." *Journal of Negro History* 61:1 (1976): 99–114.

Andrews, William L., ed. *Six Women's Slave Narratives.* New York: Oxford University Press, 1988.

Archer, Leonie J., ed. *Slavery and Other Forms of Unfree Labour.* London: Routledge, 1988.

Ball, Charles. *Fifty Years in Chains; or, The Life of an American Slave.* New York: Dover, 1970.

Bardaglio, Peter W. "Rape and the Law in the Old South: 'Calculated to Excite Indignation in Every Heart.'" *Journal of Southern History* 60:4 (1994): 749–72.

———. *Reconstructing the Household: Families, Sex, and the Law in the Nineteenth-Century South.* Chapel Hill: University of North Carolina Press, 1995.

Berlin, Ira. *Many Thousands Gone: The First Two Centuries of Slavery in North America.* Cambridge, Mass.: Belknap Press of Harvard University Press, 1998.

———. *Slaves without Masters: The Free Negro in the Antebellum South.* New York: Pantheon Books, 1974.

Berlin, Jean V., ed. *A Confederate Nurse: The Diary of Ada W. Bacot, 1860–1863.* Columbia: University of South Carolina Press, 1994.

Blassingame, John W. *The Slave Community: Plantation Life in the Antebellum South.* New York: Oxford University Press, 1979.

———. *Slave Testimony: Two Centuries of Letters, Speeches, Interviews, and Autobiographies.* Baton Rouge: Louisiana State University Press, 1977.

———. "Status and Social Structure in the Slave Community: Evidence from New Sources." In *Perspectives and Irony in American Slavery.* Ed. Harry P. Owens. 137–51. Jackson: University of Mississippi Press, 1976.

———. "Using the Testimony of Ex-Slaves: Approaches and Problems." In *The Slave's Narrative.* Ed. Charles T. Davis and Henry Louis Gates Jr. 78–98. New York: Oxford University Press, 1985.

Bleser, Carol, ed. *In Joy and Sorrow: Women, Family, and Marriage in the Victorian South.* New York: Oxford University Press, 1991.

———, ed. *Secret and Sacred: The Diaries of James Henry Hammond, a Southern Slaveholder.* New York: Oxford University Press, 1988.

Brown, Kathleen M. *Good Wives, Nasty Wenches, and Anxious Patriarchs: Gender, Race, and Power in Colonial Virginia.* Chapel Hill: University of North Carolina Press, 1996.

Brown, Steven E. "Sexuality and the Slave Community." *Phylon* 42 (1981): 1–10.

Brownmiller, Susan. *Against Our Will: Men, Women, and Rape.* Harmondsworth, U.K.: Penguin, 1975.

Bruce, Dickson D., Jr. *Archibald Grimke: Portrait of a Black Independent.* Baton Rouge: Louisiana State University Press, 1993.

Burton, Annie L. *Memories of Childhood's Slavery Days.* In *Six Women's Slave Narratives.* Ed. William L. Andrews. New York: Oxford University Press, 1988.

Burton, Orville Vernon. *In My Father's House Are Many Mansions: Family and Community in Edgefield, South Carolina.* Chapel Hill: University of North Carolina Press, 1985.

Burton, Orville Vernon, and R. C. McMath, eds. *Class, Conflict, and Consensus: Antebellum Southern Community Studies.* Westport, Conn.: Greenwood Press, 1982.

Bynum, Victoria E. *Unruly Women: The Politics of Social and Sexual Control in the Old South.* Chapel Hill: University of North Carolina Press, 1992.

Cade, John B. "Out of the Mouths of Ex-Slaves." *Journal of Negro History* 20:3 (1935): 294–337.

Carby, Hazel. *Reconstructing Womanhood: The Emergence of the Afro-American Woman Novelist.* New York: Oxford University Press, 1987.

Carney, Judith A. *Black Rice: The Origins of Rice Cultivation in the Americas.* Cambridge, Mass.: Harvard University Press, 2001.

Catterall, Helen Tunnicliff. *Judicial Cases Concerning American Slavery and the Negro.* Vol. 2: *Cases from the Courts of North Carolina, South Carolina, and Tennessee.* Washington, D.C.: Carnegie Institution of Washington, 1929.

Censer, Jane Turner. *North Carolina Planters and Their Children, 1800–1860.* Baton Rouge: Louisiana State University Press, 1984.

Cimbala, Paul A. "Fortunate Bondsmen: Black 'Musicianers' and Their Role as an Antebellum Southern Plantation Elite." *Southern Studies* 18 (1979): 291–303.

Clifton, James M., ed. *Life and Labor on Argyle Island: Letters and Documents of a Savannah River Rice Plantation.* Savannah, Ga.: Beehive Press, 1978.

Clinton, Catherine. "Caught in the Web of the Big House: Women and Slavery." In *The Web of Southern Social Relations: Women, Family, and Education.* Ed. Walter J. Fraser Jr., R. Frank Saunders Jr., and Jon L. Wakelyn. 19–34. Athens: University of Georgia Press, 1985.

———. *The Plantation Mistress: Woman's World in the Old South.* New York: Pantheon, 1982.

Cody, Cheryll Ann. "Naming, Kinship, and Estate Dispersal: Notes on Slave Family Life on a South Carolina Plantation, 1786–1833." *William and Mary Quarterly* 39 (1982): 192–211.

———. "Sale and Separation: Four Crises for Enslaved Women on the Ball Plantations, 1794–1854." In *Working toward Freedom: Slave Society and Domestic Economy in the American South.* Ed. Larry E. Hudson Jr. 119–42. New York: University of Rochester Press, 1994.

Collins, Bruce. *White Society in the Antebellum South.* London: Longman, 1985.

Cornelius, Janet Duitsman. "Slave Marriages in a Georgia Congregation." In *Class, Conflict, and Consensus: Antebellum Southern Community Studies.* Ed. Orville Vernon Burton and R. C. McMath. 128–45. Westport, Conn.: Greenwood Press, 1982.

———. *Slave Missions and the Black Church in the Antebellum South.* Columbia: University of South Carolina Press, 1999.

———. *"When Can I Read My Title Clear?": Literacy, Slavery, and Religion in the Antebellum South.* Columbia: University of South Carolina Press, 1991.

Crawford, Stephen. "Quantified Memory: A Study of the W.P.A. and Fisk University Slave Narrative Collections." Ph.D. dissertation, University of Chicago, 1980.

———. "The Slave Family: A View from the Slave Narratives." In *Strategic Factors in Nineteenth-Century American Economic History: Essays to Honor Robert W. Fogel.* Ed. Claudia Goldin and Hugh Rockoff. 331–50. Chicago: University of Chicago Press, 1992.

Creel, Margaret Washington. *"A Peculiar People": Slave Religion and Community Culture among the Gullahs.* New York: New York University Press, 1988.

David, Paul A., et al. *Reckoning with Slavery: A Critical Study in the Quantitative History of American Negro Slavery.* New York: Oxford University Press, 1977.

Davidson, James West, and Mark Hamilton Lytle. *After the Fact: The Art of Historical Detection.* New York: Knopf, 1986.

Davis, Angela. "Reflections on the Black Woman's Role in the Community of Slaves." *Black Scholar* 3:4 (1971): 2–15.

———. *Women, Race, and Class.* London: Women's Press, 1982.

Davis, Charles T., and Henry Louis Gates Jr., eds. *The Slave's Narrative.* New York: Oxford University Press, 1985.

Delany, Lucy A. *From the Darkness Cometh the Light; or, Struggles for Freedom.* In *Six Women's Slave Narratives.* Ed. William L. Andrews. New York: Oxford University Press, 1988.

D'Emilio, John, and Estelle B. Freedman. *Intimate Matters: A History of Sexuality in America.* Chicago: University of Chicago Press, 1997.

Diedrich, Maria. "'My Love Is Black as Yours Is Fair': Premarital Love and Sexuality in the Antebellum Slave Narrative." *Phylon* 47 (1986): 238–47.

Dill, Bonnie Thornton. "Fictive Kin, Paper Sons, and *Compadrazgo:* Women of Color and the Struggle for Family Survival." In *Women of Color in U.S. Society.* Ed. Maxine Baca Zinn and Bonnie Thornton Dill. 149–59. Philadephia: Temple University Press, 1994.

Drumgoold, Kate. *A Slave Girl's Story.* In *Six Women's Slave Narratives.* Ed. William L. Andrews. New York: Oxford University Press, 1988.

Dunn, Richard S. "A Tale of Two Plantations: Slave Life at Mesopotamia in Jamaica and Mount Airy in Virginia, 1799 to 1828." *William and Mary Quarterly* 34:1 (1977): 32–65.

Dusinberre, William. *Them Dark Days: Slavery in the American Rice Swamps.* New York: Oxford University Press, 1996.

Edgar, Walter. *South Carolina: A History.* Columbia: University of South Carolina Press, 1998.

Egerton, Douglas R. *He Shall Go Free: The Lives of Denmark Vesey.* Madison, Wis.: Madison House, 1999.

Engerman, Stanley L. "Concluding Reflections." In *Working toward Freedom: Slave Society and Domestic Economy in the American South.* Ed. Larry E. Hudson Jr. 233–41. Rochester, N.Y.: University of Rochester Press, 1994.

Engerman, Stanley L., and Eugene D. Genovese. *Race and Slavery in the Western Hemisphere.* Princeton, N.J.: Princeton University Press, 1975.

Equiano, Olaudah. *The Interesting Narrative and Other Writings.* Ed. Vincent Carretta. New York: Penguin, 1996.

Escott, Paul D. *Slavery Remembered: A Record of Twentieth-Century Slave Narratives.* Chapel Hill: University of North Carolina Press, 1979.

Faust, Drew Gilpin. *James Henry Hammond and the Old South: A Design for Mastery.* Baton Rouge: Louisiana State University Press, 1982.

Fields, Barbara Jeanne. *Slavery and Freedom on the Middle Ground: Maryland during the Nineteenth Century.* New Haven, Conn.: Yale University Press, 1985.

Finkelman, Paul, ed. *Women and the Family in a Slave Society.* New York: Garland, 1989.

Fleischner, Jennifer. *Mastering Slavery: Memory, Family, and Identity in Women's Slave Narratives.* New York: New York University Press, 1996.

Fogel, Robert W., and Stanley L. Engerman. *Time on the Cross: The Economics of American Negro Slavery.* New York: W. W. Norton, 1989.

Foreman, P. Gabrielle. "Manifest in Signs: The Politics of Sex and Representation in *Incidents in the Life of a Slave Girl.*" In *Harriet Jacobs and Incidents in the Life of a Slave Girl.* Ed. Deborah M. Garfield and Rafia Zafar. 76–99. Cambridge: Cambridge University Press, 1996.

Fox-Genovese, Elizabeth. "Strategies and Forms of Resistance: Focus on Slave Women in the United States." In *In Resistance: Studies in African, Caribbean, and Afro-American History*. Ed. Gary Y. Okihiro. 143–65. Amherst: University of Massachusetts Press, 1986.

———. *Within the Plantation Household: Black and White Women of the Old South*. Chapel Hill: University of North Carolina Press, 1988.

Franklin, John Hope, and Loren Schweninger. *Runaway Slaves: Rebels on the Plantation*. New York: Oxford University Press, 1999.

Fraser, Walter J., Jr., R. Frank Saunders Jr., and Jon L. Wakelyn, eds. *The Web of Southern Social Relations: Women, Family, and Education*. Athens: University of Georgia Press, 1985.

Frazier, E. Franklin. "The Negro Slave Family." *Journal of Negro History* 15:2 (1930): 198–259.

Fredrickson, George M. "The Skeleton in the Closet." *New York Review of Books*, 2 November 2000.

Frey, Sylvia R., and Betty Wood. *Come Shouting to Zion: African American Protestantism in the American South and British Caribbean to 1830*. Chapel Hill: University of North Carolina Press, 1998.

Garfield, Deborah M., and Rafia Zafar, eds. *Harriet Jacobs and Incidents in the Life of a Slave Girl*. Cambridge: Cambridge University Press, 1996.

Gaspar, David Barry, and Darlene Clark Hine, eds. *More Than Chattel: Black Women and Slavery in the Americas*. Bloomington: Indiana University Press, 1996.

Gebhard, Caroline. "Reconstructing Southern Manhood: Race, Sentimentality, and Camp in the Plantation Myth." In *Haunted Bodies: Gender and Southern Texts*. Ed. Anne Goodwyn Jones and Susan V. Donaldson. 132–55. Charlottesville: University Press of Virginia, 1997.

Genovese, Eugene. *Roll, Jordan, Roll: The World the Slaves Made*. New York: Vintage, 1974.

Golden, Claudia, and Hugh Rockoff, eds. *Strategic Factors in Nineteenth-Century American Economic History: Essays to Honor Robert W. Fogel*. Chicago: University of Chicago Press, 1992.

Goodson, Martia Graham. "The Slave Narrative Collection: A Tool for Reconstructing Afro-American Women's History." In *Black Women in American History: From Colonial Times through the Nineteenth Century*, vol. 2. Ed. Darlene Clark Hine. 485–97. New York: Carlson, 1990.

Gould, Lois Virginia Meacham. "In Full Enjoyment of Their Liberty: The Free Women of Color of the Gulf Ports of New Orleans, Mobile, and Pensacola, 1789–1860." Ph.D. dissertation, Emory University, 1991.

———. "Urban Slavery, Urban Freedom: The Manumission of Jacqueline Lemelle." In *More Than Chattel: Black Women and Slavery in the Americas*. Ed. David Barry Gaspar and Darlene Clark Hine. 298–314. Bloomington: Indiana University Press, 1996.

Greenberg, Kenneth. *Honor and Slavery*. Princeton, N.J.: Princeton University Press, 1996.

Gutman, Herbert G. *The Black Family in Slavery and Freedom, 1750–1925*. New York: Vintage, 1976.

———. *Slavery and the Numbers Game: A Critique of "Time on the Cross."* 1975. Reprint, Urbana: University of Illinois Press, 2003.

Gutman, Herbert G., and Richard Sutch. "Sambo Makes Good; or, Were Slaves Imbued with the Protestant Work Ethic?" In *Reckoning with Slavery: A Critical Study in the Quantitative History of American Negro Slavery.* Ed. Paul A. David et al. 55–93. New York: Oxford University Press, 1977.

———. "Victorians All? The Sexual Mores and Conduct of Slaves and Their Masters." In *Reckoning with Slavery: A Critical Study in the Quantitative History of American Negro Slavery.* Ed. Paul A. David et al. 134–62. New York: Oxford University Press, 1977.

Hadden, Sally E. *Slave Patrols: Law and Violence in Virginia and the Carolinas.* Cambridge, Mass.: Harvard University Press, 2001.

Harris, J. William. *Plain Folk and Gentry in a Slave Society: White Liberty and Black Slavery in Augusta's Hinterlands.* Middletown, Conn.: Wesleyan University Press, 1985.

Hawks, Joanne V., and Sheila L. Skemp, eds. *Sex, Race, and the Role of Women in the South.* Jackson: University Press of Mississippi, 1983.

Herskovits, Melville J. *The Myth of the Negro Past.* Boston: Beacon Press, 1964.

Higgins, W. Robert. "The Geographical Origins of Negro Slaves in Colonial South Carolina." *South Atlantic Quarterly* 70 (1971): 34–47.

Hine, Darlene Clark. "Rape and the Inner Lives of Black Women in the Middle West: Preliminary Thoughts on the Culture of Dissemblance." *Signs* 14 (1989): 912–20.

———, ed. *Black Women in American History: From Colonial Times through the Nineteenth Century.* 2 vols. New York: Carlson, 1990.

hooks, bell. *Ain't I a Woman? Black Women and Feminism.* Boston: South End Press, 1982.

———. "A Class Sister Act." *The Times Higher Education Supplement,* 13 October 1995, 20.

Hudson, Larry E., Jr., "'All That Cash': Work and Status in the Slave Quarters." In *Working toward Freedom: Slave Society and Domestic Economy in the American South.* Ed. Larry E. Hudson Jr. 77–94. Rochester, N.Y.: University of Rochester Press, 1994.

———. "'The Average Truth': The Slave Family in South Carolina, 1820–1860." Ph.D. dissertation, University of Keele, 1989.

———. *To Have and to Hold: Slave Work and Family Life in Antebellum South Carolina.* Athens: University of Georgia Press, 1997.

———, ed. *Working toward Freedom: Slave Society and Domestic Economy in the American South.* Rochester, N.Y.: University of Rochester Press, 1994.

Huggins, Nathan I. *Black Odyssey: The Afro-American Ordeal in Slavery.* London: George Allen and Unwin, 1979.

Hurmence, Belinda, ed. *Before Freedom, When I Just Can Remember.* Winston-Salem, N.C.: John F. Blair, 1989.

Iliffe, John. *Africans: The History of a Continent.* Cambridge: Cambridge University Press, 1995.

Jackson, Irene V. "Black Women and Music: A Survey from Africa to the New World." In *The Black Woman Cross-Culturally.* Ed. Filomina Chioma Steady. 383–401. Cambridge, Mass.: Schenkman Publishing, 1981.

Jackson, Mattie J. *The Story of Mattie J. Jackson.* In *Six Women's Slave Narratives.* Ed. William L. Andrews. New York: Oxford University Press, 1988.

Jacobs, Donald M., ed. *Index to "The American Slave."* Westport, Conn.: Greenwood Press, 1981.

Jacobs, Harriet. *Incidents in the Life of a Slave Girl.* Cambridge, Mass.: Harvard University Press, 1987.

Jennings, Thelma. "'Us Colored Women Had to Go through a Plenty': Sexual Exploitation of African-American Slave Women." *Journal of Women's History* 1 (1991): 45–74.

Johnson, Michael P. "Work Culture and the Slave Community: Slave Occupations in the Cotton Belt in 1860." *Labor History* 27:3 (1986): 325–55.

Johnson, Walter. *Soul by Soul: Life Inside the Antebellum Slave Market.* Cambridge, Mass.: Harvard University Press, 1999.

Johnston, James Hugo. *Race Relations in Virginia and Miscegenation in the South.* Amherst: University of Massachusetts Press, 1970.

Jones, Anne Goodwyn, and Susan V. Donaldson, eds. *Haunted Bodies: Gender and Southern Texts.* Charlottesville: University Press of Virginia, 1997.

Jones, Bobby Frank. "A Cultural Middle Passage: Slave Marriage and Family in the Antebellum South." Ph.D. dissertation, University of North Carolina at Chapel Hill, 1965.

Jones, Jacqueline. *Labor of Love, Labor of Sorrow: Black Women, Work, and the Family from Slavery to the Present.* New York: Basic Books, 1985.

Jones, Norrece T. *Born a Child of Freedom, yet a Slave: Mechanisms of Control and Strategies of Resistance in Antebellum South Carolina.* Hanover, N.H.: Wesleyan University Press, 1990.

Jones, Tom. *Experience and Personal Narrative of Uncle Tom Jones, Who Was for Forty Years a Slave; also the Surprising Adventures of Wild Tom, of the Island Retreat, a Fugitive Negro from South Carolina.* Boston: H. B. Skinner, 1855.

Joyner, Charles. *Down by the Riverside: A South Carolina Slave Community.* Urbana: University of Illinois Press, 1984.

———. *Shared Traditions: Southern History and Folk Culture.* Urbana: University of Illinois Press, 1999.

Kemble, Frances Anne. *Journal of a Residence on a Georgian Plantation in 1838–1839.* Athens: University of Georgia Press, 1984.

King, Wilma. "'Rais Your Children Up Rite': Parental Guidance and Child-Rearing Practices among Slaves in the Nineteenth-Century South." In *Working toward Freedom: Slave Society and Domestic Economy in the American South.* Ed. Larry E. Hudson Jr. 143–62. Rochester, N.Y.: University of Rochester Press, 1994.

———. *Stolen Childhood: Slave Youth in Nineteenth-Century America.* Bloomington: Indiana University Press, 1995.

Koger, Larry. *Black Slaveowners: Free Black Slave Masters in South Carolina, 1790–1860.* Columbia: University of South Carolina Press, 1995.

Kolchin, Peter. *American Slavery.* London: Penguin, 1993.

Kulikoff, Allan. "The Beginnings of the Afro-American Family in Maryland." In *Law, Society, and Politics in Early Maryland.* Ed. Aubrey C. Land, Lois Green Carr, and Edward C. Papenfuse. 171–96. Baltimore: Johns Hopkins University Press, 1977. Reprinted in *Women and the Family in a Slave Society.* Ed. Paul Finkelman. 251–76. New York: Garland, 1989.

———. *Tobacco and Slaves: The Development of Southern Cultures in the Chesapeake, 1680–1800.* Chapel Hill: University of North Carolina Press, 1986.

Land, Aubrey C., Lois Green Carr, and Edward C. Papenfuse, eds. *Law, Society, and Politics in Early Maryland.* Baltimore: Johns Hopkins University Press, 1977.

Levine, Lawrence W. *Black Culture and Black Consciousness: Afro-American Folk Thought from Slavery to Freedom.* New York: Oxford University Press, 1977.

Lowery, Rev. I. E. *Life on the Old Plantation in Ante-bellum Days; or, A Story Based on Facts.* Columbia, S.C.: The State Co., 1911.

Lystra, Karen. *Searching the Heart: Women, Men, and Romantic Love in Nineteenth-Century America.* New York: Oxford University Press, 1989.

Malone, Ann Patton. *Sweet Chariot: Slave Family and Household Structure in Nineteenth-Century Louisiana.* Chapel Hill: University of North Carolina Press, 1992.

McAdoo, H. Pipes, ed. *Black Families.* Newbury Park, Calif.: Sage Publications, 1988.

McClelland, Peter D., and Richard J. Zeckhauser. *Demographic Dimensions of the New Republic: American Interregional Migration, Vital Statistics, and Manumission, 1800–1860.* Cambridge: Cambridge University Press, 1982.

McLaurin, Melton A. *Celia, a Slave: A True Story.* New York: Avon Books, 1991.

Merritt, Carole E. "Slave Family and Household Arrangements in Piedmont, Georgia." Ph.D. dissertation, Emory University, 1986.

Miers, Suzanne, and Igor Kopytoff, eds. *Slavery in Africa: Historical and Anthropological Perspectives.* Madison: University of Wisconsin Press, 1977.

Miller, Randall M. *"Dear Master": Letters of a Slave Family.* Ithaca, N.Y.: Cornell University Press, 1978.

Moore, John Hammond, ed. *A Plantation Mistress on the Eve of the Civil War: The Diary of Keziah Goodwyn Hopkins Brevard, 1860–1861.* Columbia: University of South Carolina Press, 1993.

Morgan, Philip D. *Slave Counterpoint: Black Culture in the Eighteenth-Century Chesapeake and Lowcountry.* Chapel Hill: University of North Carolina Press, 1998.

Morton, Patricia. *Disfigured Images: The Historical Assault on Afro-American Women.* Westport, Conn.: Greenwood Press, 1991.

Moynihan, Daniel Patrick. *The Negro Family: The Case for National Action.* Washington D.C.: Office of Policy Planning and Research, U.S. Department of Labor, 1965.

Murray, Pauli. *Proud Shoes: The Story of an American Family.* New York: Harper and Row, 1978.

Norton, Mary Beth, and Ruth Alexander, eds. *Major Problems in American Women's History.* Lexington, Mass.: D. C. Heath, 1996.

Okihiro, Gary Y., ed. *In Resistance: Studies in African, Caribbean, and Afro-American History.* Amherst: University of Massachusetts Press, 1986.

Osofsky, Gilbert. "The Significance of Slave Narratives." In *Puttin' on Ole Massa: The Slave Narratives of Henry Bibb, William Wells Brown, and Solomon Northup.* Ed. Gilbert Osofsky. 9–44. New York: Harper and Row, 1969.

Owens, Harry P., ed. *Perspectives and Irony in American Slavery.* Jackson: University of Mississippi Press, 1976.

Parish, Peter. *Slavery: History and Historians.* New York: Harper and Row, 1989.

Patterson, Orlando. *Rituals of Blood: Consequences of Slavery in Two American Centuries.* New York: Basic Civitas, 1998.

Perdue, Charles L., Jr., Thomas E. Barden, and Robert K. Phillips, eds. *Weevils in the Wheat: Interviews with Virginia Ex-Slaves.* Charlottesville: University Press of Virginia, 1976.

Powers, Bernard E., Jr. *Black Charlestonians: A Social History, 1822–1885.* Fayetteville: University of Arkansas Press, 1994.

Radcliffe-Brown, A. R., and Daryll Forde, eds. *African Systems of Kinship and Marriage.* London: Oxford University Press, 1964.

Rainwater, Lee, and William L. Yancey. *The Moynihan Report and the Politics of Controversy.* Cambridge: Massachusetts Institute of Technology Press, 1967.

Rawick, George P. *The American Slave: A Composite Autobiography.* Vol. 2: *South Carolina Narratives.* Westport, Conn.: Greenwood Press, 1972.

———. *The American Slave: A Composite Autobiography.* Vol. 3: *South Carolina Narratives.* Westport, Conn.: Greenwood Press, 1972.

———. *The American Slave: A Composite Autobiography.* Vol. 7, pt. 2: *Mississippi Narratives.* Westport, Conn.: Greenwood Press, 1972.

———. *The American Slave: A Composite Autobiography.* Supplement Series 1, vol. 11: *North Carolina and South Carolina Narratives.* Westport, Conn.: Greenwood Press, 1977.

———. *The American Slave: A Composite Autobiography.* Supplement Series 2, vol. 5, pt. 4: *Texas Narratives.* Westport, Conn.: Greenwood Press, 1979.

———. *The American Slave: A Composite Autobiography.* Supplement Series 2, vol. 10, pt. 9: *Texas Narratives.* Westport, Conn.: Greenwood Press, 1979.

———. *From Sundown to Sunup: The Making of the Black Community.* Westport, Conn.: Greenwood Press, 1972.

Robertson, Claire. "Africa into the Americas? Slavery and Women, the Family, and the Gender Division of Labor." In *More Than Chattel: Black Women and Slavery in the Americas.* Ed. David Barry Gaspar and Darlene Clark Hine. 3–40. Bloomington: Indiana University Press, 1996.

Roper, Moses. *A Narrative of the Adventures and Escape of Moses Roper from American Slavery.* London: Harvey and Darton, 1840.

Rosengarten, Theodore. *Tombee: Portrait of a Cotton Planter with the Journal of Thomas B. Chaplin, 1822–1890.* New York: William Morrow, 1986.

Russell, Thomas. "'Articles Sell Best Singly': The Disruption of Slave Families at Court Sales." *Utah Law Review* 4 (1996): 1161–1209.

———. "Sale Day in Antebellum South Carolina: Slavery, Law, Economy, and Court-Supervised Sales." Ph.D. dissertation, Stanford University, 1993.

———. "South Carolina's Largest Slave Auctioneering Firm." *Chicago Kent Law Review* 68:3 (1993): 1241–82.

Saville, Julie. *The Work of Reconstruction: From Slave to Wage Laborer in South Carolina, 1860–1870.* Cambridge: Cambridge University Press, 1994.

Schafer, Judith K. "'Open and Notorious Concubinage': The Emancipation of Slave Mistresses by Will and the Supreme Court in Antebellum Louisiana." *Louisiana History* 28 (1987): 165–82.

Schwalm, Leslie A. *A Hard Fight for We: Women's Transition from Slavery to Freedom in South Carolina.* Urbana: University of Illinois Press, 1997.

Schwartz, Marie Jenkins. *Born in Bondage: Growing Up Enslaved in the Antebellum South.* Cambridge, Mass.: Harvard University Press, 2000.

Scott, Anne Firor. "Historians Construct the Southern Woman." In *Sex, Race, and the Role of Women in the South.* Ed. Joanne V. Hawks and Sheila L. Skemp. 95–110. Jackson: University Press of Mississippi, 1983.

———. *The Southern Lady: From Pedestal to Politics, 1830–1930.* Charlottesville: University Press of Virginia, 1995.

Scott, Rebecca. "The Battle Over the Child: Child Apprenticeship and the Freedmen's Bureau in North Carolina." *Prologue: The Journal of the National Archives* 10 (1978): 101–13.

Seidman, Steven. *Romantic Longings: Love in America, 1830–1980.* New York: Routledge, 1991.

Shepherd, Gloria. "The Rape of Black Women during Slavery." Ph.D. dissertation, State University of New York at Albany, 1988.

Sides, Sudie Duncan. "Slave Weddings and Religion: Plantation Life in the Southern States before the American Civil War." *History Today* 24 (1974): 77–87.

Smith, Mark M. *Debating Slavery: Economy and Society in the Antebellum American South.* Cambridge: Cambridge University Press, 1998.

Sommerville, Diane Miller. "The Rape Myth in the Old South Reconsidered." *Journal of Southern History* 61:3 (1995): 481–518.

Spindel, Donna J. "Assessing Memory: Twentieth-Century Slave Narratives Reconsidered." *Journal of Interdisciplinary History* 27 (1996): 247–61.

Stampp, Kenneth M. *The Peculiar Institution: Slavery in the Antebellum South.* New York: Knopf, 1975.

Stauffer, Michael E. *The Formation of Counties in South Carolina.* Columbia: South Carolina Department of Archives and History, 1994.

Steady, Filomina Chioma, ed. *The Black Woman Cross-Culturally.* Cambridge, Mass.: Schenkman Publishing, 1981.

Steckel, Richard H. *The Economics of U.S. Slave and Southern White Fertility.* New York: Garland, 1985.

———. "Slave Marriage and the Family." *Journal of Family History* 5:4 (1980): 406–21.

Sterling, Dorothy, ed. *We Are Your Sisters: Black Women in the Nineteenth Century.* New York: W. W. Norton, 1984.

Stevenson, Brenda E. "Distress and Discord in Virginia Slave Families, 1830–1860." In *In Joy and Sorrow: Women, Family, and Marriage in the Victorian South.* Ed. Carol Bleser. 103–24. New York: Oxford University Press, 1991.

———. *Life in Black and White: Family and Community in the Slave South.* New York: Oxford University Press, 1996.

Steward, Austin. *Twenty-two Years a Slave and Forty Years a Freeman.* Reading, Mass.: Addison-Wesley, 1969.

Stroyer, Jacob. *My Life in the South.* Salem, Mass.: Newcombe and Gauss, 1898.

Stuckey, Sterling. *Slave Culture: Nationalist Theory and the Foundations of Black America.* New York: Oxford University Press, 1987.

Sudarkasa, Niara. "Interpreting the African Heritage in Afro-American Family Organization." In *Black Families.* Ed. H. Pipes McAdoo. 27–43. Newbury Park, Calif.: Sage Publications, 1988.

Sutch, Richard. "The Breeding of Slaves for Sale and the Westward Expansion of Slavery, 1850–1860." In *Race and Slavery in the Western Hemisphere: Quantitative Studies.* Ed. Stanley Engerman and Eugene Genovese. 173–210. Princeton, N.J.: Princeton University Press, 1975.

Tadman, Michael. "The Persistent Myth of Paternalism." *Sage Race Relations Abstracts* 23:1 (1998): 7–23.

———. "Slave Trading and the Mentalities of Masters and Slaves." In *Slavery and Other Forms of Unfree Labour.* Ed. Leonie J. Archer. 188–205. London: Routledge, 1988.

———. *Speculators and Slaves: Masters, Traders, and Slaves in the Old South.* Madison: University of Wisconsin Press, 1996.

Taylor, Orville W. " 'Jumping the Broomstick': Slave Marriage and Morality in Arkansas." *Arkansas Historical Quarterly* 17 (1958): 217–31. Reprinted in *Women and the Family in a Slave Society.* Ed. Paul Finkelman. 373–87. New York: Garland, 1989.

Thornton, John. *Africa and Africans in the Making of the Atlantic World, 1400–1680.* Cambridge: Cambridge University Press, 1992.

Van Deburg, William L. "Slave Drivers and Slave Narratives: A New Look at the 'Dehumanized Elite.' " *The Historian* 39 (1977): 717–32.

Weiner, Marli F. *Mistresses and Slaves: Plantation Women in South Carolina, 1830–1880.* Urbana: University of Illinois Press, 1998.

Welter, Barbara. "The Cult of True Womanhood, 1820–1860." In *Major Problems in American Women's History.* Ed. Mary Beth Norton and Ruth Alexander. 115–22. Lexington, Mass.: D. C. Heath, 1996.

West, Emily. "The Debate on the Strength of Slave Families: South Carolina and the Importance of Cross-Plantation Marriages." *Journal of American Studies* 33:2 (1999): 221–41.

———. "Masters and Marriages, Profits and Paternalism: Slave Owners' Perspectives on Cross-Plantation Unions in Antebellum South Carolina." *Slavery and Abolition* 21:1 (2000): 56–72.

———. "Surviving Separation: Cross-Plantation Marriages and the Slave Trade in Antebellum South Carolina." *Journal of Family History* 24:2 (1999): 212–31.

White, Deborah G. *Ar'n't I a Woman? Female Slaves in the Plantation South.* New York: W. W. Norton, 1985.

———. "Female Slaves: Sex Roles and Status in the Antebellum Plantation South." *Journal of Family History* 8:3 (1983): 248–61.

White, Shane, and Graham White. "Slave Clothing and African-American Culture in the Eighteenth and Nineteenth Centuries." *Past and Present* 148 (1995): 149–86.

———. "Slave Hair and African American Culture in the Eighteenth and Nineteenth Centuries." *Journal of Southern History* 61:1 (1995): 45–76.

———. *Stylin': African American Expressive Culture from Its Beginnings to the Zoot Suit.* Ithaca, N.Y.: Cornell University Press, 1998.

Wood, Betty. "Some Aspects of Female Resistance to Chattel Slavery in Low County Georgia, 1763–1815." *The Historical Journal* 30 (1987): 603–22.

———. *Women's Work, Men's Work: The Informal Slave Economies of Lowcountry Georgia.* Athens: University of Georgia Press, 1995.

Wood, Peter. *Black Majority: Negroes in Colonial South Carolina from 1670 through the Stono Rebellion.* New York: W. W. Norton, 1974.

Woodward, C. Vann. "History from Slave Sources." In *The Slave's Narrative.* Ed. Charles T. Davis and Henry Louis Gates Jr. 48–59. New York: Oxford University Press, 1985.

Wyatt-Brown, Bertram. "The Mask of Obedience: Male Slave Psychology in the Old South." *American Historical Review* 93:5 (1988): 1228–52.

———. *Southern Honor: Ethics and Behavior in the Old South.* New York: Oxford University Press, 1982.

Yellin, Jean Fagan. "Texts and Contexts of Harriet Jacobs' Incidents in the Life of a Slave Girl: Written by Herself." In *The Slave's Narrative.* Ed. Charles T. Davis and Henry Louis Gates Jr. 262–82. New York: Oxford University Press, 1985.

Young, Jeffrey R. "Ideology and Death on a Savannah River Rice Plantation, 1833–1867: Paternalism amidst 'A Good Supply of Disease and Pain.'" *Journal of Southern History* 59:4 (1993): 673–706.

Zinn, Maxine Baca, and Bonnie Thornton Dill, eds. *Women of Color in U.S. Society.* Philadelphia: Temple University Press, 1994.

# INDEX

Locations given in **bold** indicate a definition or explanation (for example: key/favored slaves, **10**).

EMILY WEST is a lecturer in American history at the University of Reading, United Kingdom.

*The University of Illinois Press*
*is a founding member of the*
*Association of American University Presses.*

---

*Composed in 9.5/12.5 Trump Medieval*
*by Type One, LLC*
*for the University of Illinois Press*
*Manufactured by Thomson-Shore, Inc.*

*University of Illinois Press*
*1325 South Oak Street*
*Champaign, IL 61820-6903*
*www.press.uillinois.edu*

**EMILY WEST** is a lecturer in American history at the University of Reading (UK).